Mastering Software Variability
with FeatureIDE

Jens Meinicke • Thomas Thüm •
Reimar Schröter • Fabian Benduhn •
Thomas Leich • Gunter Saake

Mastering Software Variability with FeatureIDE

 Springer

Jens Meinicke
Carnegie Mellon University
Pittsburgh, PA, USA

Thomas Thüm
TU Braunschweig
Braunschweig, Germany

Reimar Schröter
Otto-von-Guericke Universität Magdeburg
Magdeburg, Germany

Fabian Benduhn
Otto-von-Guericke Universität Magdeburg
Magdeburg, Germany

Thomas Leich
Hochschule Harz
Wernigerode, Germany

Gunter Saake
Otto-von-Guericke Universität Magdeburg
Magdeburg, Germany

ISBN 978-3-319-87080-9   ISBN 978-3-319-61443-4   (eBook)
DOI 10.1007/978-3-319-61443-4

Printed on acid-free paper

This Springer imprint is published by Springer Nature
The registered company is Springer International Publishing AG
The registered company address is: Gewerbestrasse 11, 6330 Cham, Switzerland

Foreword by Don Batory

Jay Misra once told me "The quality of a research area is measured by the quality of its teaching materials" (Misra 2004). A corollary is "and by the quality of its tools."

Although the term software product lines (SPLs) is about 20 years old, the concept of SPLs goes back 50 years, known back then as SYStem GENeration (SYSGEN) for the custom creation of operating systems (Wikipedia 2017). It was given a more visionary form by McIlroy in 1968, when he conceptualized software variability by the composition of components (McIlroy 1968). In the intervening 30 years grew the recognition that the custom production of software, not just operating systems, is a core activity of software engineering; the study of SPLs, unto themselves, was a worthy area of scientific and engineering research.

In the beginning, tools for SPL development were primitive—the use of C preprocessor dominated. Analyses that were specific to SPLs and their amenities were lacking. That was good enough for many in the trenches; the status quo was unacceptable to scientists. There should be Engineering (with a capital "E"), not hacking, behind SPLs. This embodied the thrust of SPL scientific/engineering research for the last 20 years. Scientific progress lagged far behind industrial tools prior to 2005. Now the situation has reversed—industrial tools for SPLs are far behind scientific advances. This is the normal state of scientifically-driven research areas.

FeatureIDE is an Eclipse plug-in that showcases many of the core conceptual advances in the last 10 years of SPL research. *FeatureIDE* presents the best tooling (in my opinion) of classical feature models—models that are devoid of numeric attributes, feature replication, and feature modularization,[1] a widely-accepted set of feature model analyses (tests for void models, dead features, false-optional features, generalizing/specializing feature models via edits), and amenities—such as visual prompts for feature-expression completion, next-generation tooling to distinguish the source code of different features with different colors, runtime-variability support, and *Javadoc* support for SPLs. Orthogonal to these analyses is the choice among several distinct ways to encode variability in source code (different preprocessors) and different ways to modularize features (*FeatureHouse*, *AHEAD*).

---

[1] Researchers—Take a hint at what to focus on next!

FeatureIDE is a much needed and necessary step forward. It presents the analyses and amenities that one might/should see in next-generation SPL tooling. I have used *FeatureIDE* for many years and am very pleased to see SPL research ideas come to life. So will you. I thank the *FeatureIDE* team for their tireless work and contribution to the SPL field.

University of Texas at Austin   Don Batory
Austin, TX, USA

Preface

In the era of mobile devices and the Internet of things, software systems are ubiquitous. A multitude of hardware specifics, fast development of applications, and the need of personalization foster the requirements for software reuse even more than in the past. Mastering *variability* is one of the key concerns of modern software engineering.

To master variability in industry-scale software development, tool support is absolutely essential. More than 10 years ago, we started the development of *FeatureIDE* as an Eclipse plug-in to address these needs. This software went through several severe redesigns over the years but is now a stable tool for feature-based implementation of variable software systems used in a large number of university courses as well as in industrial projects. *FeatureIDE* is the only open-source IDE for managing software variability with this stability and with support of several implementation techniques for mastering variability. Because of this central role of *FeatureIDE* for teaching and development, the core implementation team decided to write this book.

This book is a self-contained practical introduction to the use of *FeatureIDE* to implement variable systems. Each presented technique can directly be tried out in a *FeatureIDE* installation on your own computer. All code examples are added to the standard distribution and can immediately be used for own modifications. The book contains three major thematic parts: modeling variability using features, implementing variability with conditional compilation, and implementing variability with feature-oriented programming.

The book is suited both for students using a tool for deepening the theoretical foundations of variability modeling and implementation, as well as a reference for practitioners needing a stable and scalable tool for industrial application. *FeatureIDE* is used in industrial settings with several thousand features for analyzing variability models and generating products.

More than a decade of developing an open-source project involved more students and developers than one can mention in a preface. During the production of the book, however, several persons were involved. We want to mention them explicitly: Sebastian Krieter, Christopher Sontag, Joshua Sprey, Marcus Pinnecke, Andy Kenner, Christopher Kruczek, Jacob Krüger, and Wolfram Fenske. Furthermore, we gratefully acknowledge fruitful discussions and contributions to the open-source project by Christian Kästner, Sven Apel, Ina Schaefer, Stefan Krüger, Mustafa Al-Hajjaji, Juliana Alves Pereira, Sofia Ananieva, Timo Günther, Matthias Kowal, Alexander Knüppel, Klaus Birken, Hendrik Speidel, Frederik Kramer, Roman Popp, Roland Beckert, Jörg Liebig, Sandro Schulze, Janet Siegmund, and Norbert Siegmund.

The work on FeatureIDE was supported by several fundings, among them grants by German Federal Ministry of Education and Research (BMBF: 01IS14017A, 01IS14017B) and by German Research Foundation (DFG: SA 465/34-2, SA 465/49-1, LE 3382/2-1, SCHA 1635/4-2, and LO 2198/2-1). Last, but not least, we are grateful to our families and friends for their support, which was essential for the success of this endeavor.

Pittsburgh, PA, USA   Jens Meinicke
Braunschweig, Germany   Thomas Thüm
Magdeburg, Germany   Reimar Schröter
Magdeburg, Germany   Fabian Benduhn
Wernigerode, Germany   Thomas Leich
Magdeburg, Germany   Gunter Saake
May 2017

Contents

Part I
Introduction

Software Variability

1

Variability of products is part of our daily life. We do not want to buy just a car—we want a car in our favorite color, with five doors, a cooling system, and a navigation system. Classical engineering copes well with this kind of variant-rich production.

Variability of software products differs in several aspects from classical production. One of the main specifics is the role of the product finalization costs—the cost of making copies of software stored in files is close to zero. As a result, it may be cheaper to deliver a software product with the majority of functionality being unused by the customer instead of customizing it for the specific needs. How many people do you know who have ever tried more than 20% of the menu buttons of their word processing system?

Another difference to classical engineering is that it is apparently easy and cheap to deliver a variant of a software system. One can copy software sources at almost zero cost and change functionality slightly by modifying the code. This method is an established technique in practical software construction and is known as *clone-and-own* (Dubinsky et al. 2013; Rubin et al. 2013; Rubin and Chechik 2013; Antkiewicz et al. 2014). At first glance, clone-and-own is an appealing approach; however, it may lead to maintenance nightmare if the same steps have to be consistently performed on a plenitude of slightly modified code clones. Still, there are reasons for customizing software, like for a tailored car specialized to the customer's requirements.

In order to ease the customization of software, this book presents a tool-driven approach for software variability management based on feature-oriented software development (Apel et al. 2013a). We present our tool FeatureIDE, an open-source plug-in for *Eclipse*, that allows to quickly conduct projects in the context of software product lines. Before we start, we briefly discuss software variability in general and how it is handled without dedicated tool support.

© Springer International Publishing AG 2017   3
J. Meinicke et al., *Mastering Software Variability with FeatureIDE*,
DOI 10.1007/978-3-319-61443-4_1

1.1   What Is Software Variability?

Software comes in different shapes. Early software construction was a process not much different from the creation of *handcrafted* goods—a few experts produce a specific functionality for a specific hardware and sell it in small numbers. This style of software construction does neither scale for a large number of customers and complex software nor allows for a cheap derivation of variants for slightly changing customer requirements.

Similar to mass production for physical goods, one can agree on standard platforms allowing to produce the same software, such as operating systems, for millions of users. Such *standard software* is a perfect choice for market segments, where the functionality is well defined and stable for several years. However, standard software leads to one-size-fits-all solutions. The software has to satisfy the needs of almost all possible users, even if most of the users will only use a small percentage of the implemented functions. This approach may lead to software that is slow, complex to use, and error prone.

Assume we have developed a software product that we start selling to a small number of customers. As our product starts to become successful, new customers are attracted. However, each customer is different and has some unique requirements and ideas on how the software should be improved to fulfill these requirements. At some point, we decide to incorporate new functionality into the standard software to satisfy the new customers. The problem with such incremental extensions is that we have to be careful about which functions we should actually include because not only the relevant customers but all customers will have to live with the result. Therefore, it is preferable to have a production process enabling to produce software which fits the requirements of a specific customer (like in handcrafted systems) and at the same time supports the desired properties of mass production. The concept of software product lines targets this combination (Apel et al. 2013a).

The sources of software variability are diverse. On the one hand, variability can manifest in different functional enhancements which are desired by a user. On the other hand, even the same set of functional properties may be realized by different algorithms or realized on a different hardware or software platforms. Both functional and non-functional variations can be described by features.

A *feature* is a characteristic or user-visible behavior of a software system (Apel et al. 2013a). The commonalities and differences of different products can be described in terms of their features. A *software product line* consists of single products, where a specific *product* corresponds to a selection of features. In general, features may have dependencies that restrict their possible combinations. For example, a car with an electric engine cannot have a catalyst. Such dependencies can be modeled using *feature models*. The idea of *software product-line engineering* is that we invest some initial work to provide a code basis that later allows us to generate a large number of customized products with relatively low effort. This view on variable software leads to the design principles known as *domain engineering* and *product derivation* used in software product-line engineering.

Figure 1.1 gives an overview of the constituents of software product-line engineering [adopted from Apel et al. (2013a)]. The design principle for domain

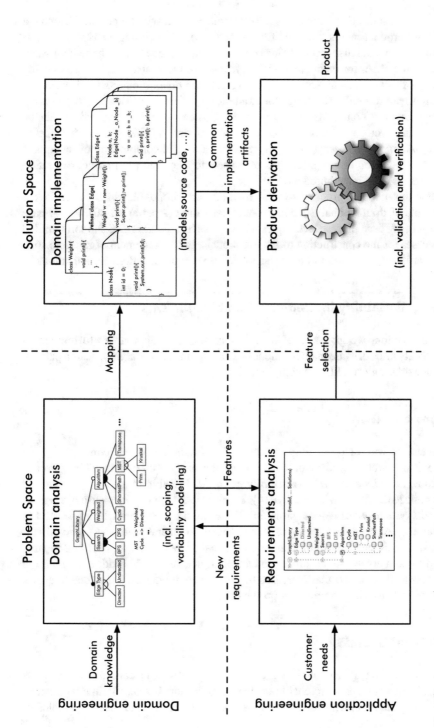

Fig. 1.1 An overview on software product-line engineering

engineering states that software is not constructed for a specific product. Instead, a software product line is designed for a specific domain defining a space of similar systems such that reusing code from a common, shared code basis is beneficial. Such a domain can be, for example, control systems for elevators. Domain engineering consists of two tasks as visualized in Fig. 1.1: the *domain analysis* constructs an explicit feature model resulting, for example, in a feature model, and the *domain implementation* constructs software artifacts, such as code parts, which can be reused in several products. The construction of one specific product is done in the *application engineering* process, where first a valid combination of features is selected based on the requirements of a specific user, and the product derivation delivers the customized product.

For this general process, several methods are proposed which differ in the concepts of domain analysis and product derivation (Apel et al. 2013a). To ease handling of these diverse techniques and approaches, *FeatureIDE* supports unified processes for the construction of feature models, the management of reusable software artifacts, the configuration process, and several product derivation methods.

1.2   Variability Implementation Mechanisms

In this section, we give a brief overview on common approaches to implement variability into software, namely, clone-and-own, runtime variability, design pattern, frameworks, and conditional compilation.

Clone-and-Own

The easiest way of producing a variant of a certain software product is to copy an existing product and modify it to adopt the new requirements. This approach is known as *clone-and-own* (Dubinsky et al. 2013; Rubin et al. 2013; Rubin and Chechik 2013; Antkiewicz et al. 2014). To support the approach, the use of *version-control systems* gives it some structure. For example, a new branch can be used to develop a new product. Cloning of software leads to several problems, especially for software maintenance. Modifications in the main product, such as for bug repairs, need to be merged into all other products and vice versa. This additional merging process leads to effort that increases for every new product. Thus, clone-and-own cannot scale to a large number of products.

Runtime Variability

Another way to realize variability is to code it explicitly using conditional code parts (e.g., if-else branches). To enable or disable conditional code, runtime parameters (i.e., program arguments) or global constants can be used. Thus, code is enabled or modified depending on the given parameters, and the program behaves differently. Providing programs with command-line parameters is a common way to provide customizable software. However, such programs usually contain the whole code, which, for example, causes a high footprint.

Conditional Compilation

One of the most widely used techniques for implementing variable software is *conditional compilation* using preprocessors. *Preprocessors*, such as the well-known C preprocessor *CPP*, use annotations in the form of user directives to mark code fragments as to be included (or excluded) in the compilation. CPP is used in the majority of C and C++ projects, and is applied for coding variability in large software product lines like operating systems, such as Linux.

Large software systems with intensive use of preprocessor directives tend to become hard to maintain. One of the weak points is the often missing explicit feature model together with arbitrary nesting of directives. Some authors even coined the phrase of *#ifdef hell* for the problems arising possibly there (Spencer and Collyer 1992; Lohmann et al. 2006; Feigenspan et al. 2013).

Besides the fact that the use of preprocessors to implement variability has received severe criticism, they in turn show some clear benefits. Most software developers are familiar with the easy-to-use concept of conditional compilation using preprocessor directives. Moreover, preprocessors allow for fine-grained variability without involving architectural overhead.

Even if preprocessors belong to the criticized conventional approaches, their benefits make them one of the most interesting variability implementation techniques, where most disadvantages can be cured with proper tool support and explicit variability modeling (Meinicke et al. 2016a).

Frameworks, Components, and Services

Frameworks, *components*, and *services* are architectural approaches to implement variability. A framework is an incomplete set of collaborating classes to be extended for specific use cases, such as plug-ins for browsers. Components and services are units of composition with well-defined interfaces which can be composed to build a specific product. Frameworks, components, and services are well suited to realize variation in software products. If feature functionality can be modularized properly, they realize an appropriate separation of variable code from other code. However, all these approaches require a certain know-how and discipline of the software developers, do not work for fine-grained variability, and may require additional overhead at runtime.

Feature-Oriented Programming

The goal of frameworks, components, and services is to achieve separation of concerns (i.e., features are implemented separately). However, these approaches rely on the provided interfaces which they use to interact with each other which makes these approaches inflexible if the interfaces cannot be adapted. *Feature-oriented programming* is a more flexible approach to extend an existing program (Batory 2006; Apel et al. 2013b). Instead of implementing given interfaces, feature-oriented composition is able to refine existing code, for example, by overriding a method or by introducing new classes.

Aspect-Oriented Programming

Aspect-oriented programming has a similar goal as feature-oriented programming (Kiczales et al. 1997). Instead of relying on interfaces, an aspect can directly change existing code to realize variability. In contrast to feature-oriented programming, an aspect can implement *crosscutting concerns* efficiently. A crosscutting concern is a functionality that affects multiple parts of a program. For example, when adding the option to log all constructor calls, all constructors need to be changed. However, such a function can be realized efficiently in only few lines of code with a single aspect.

1.3   Mastering Variability with FeatureIDE

Development of variable software comes with several challenges as the brief discussion of conventional approaches showed. Independent of the specific approach, tool support is needed that helps to implement software product lines. With *FeatureIDE*, we provide an extensive support for feature-oriented development of a software product line that is largely independent of a particular technique, such as preprocessors or feature-oriented programming. That is, features are central elements used to specify intended, implemented, and selected implemented variability of a software product line. In particular, *FeatureIDE* provides support for:

- *Domain analysis* using feature models specifying valid combinations of features
- *Requirements analysis* with configuration support in concert with the feature model
- *Domain implementation* for diverse implementation languages and tools
- *Product derivation* for several generation tools without IDE support or support for features
- *Feature traceability* to trace features in feature model, configurations, and code
- *Quality assurance* for building reliable software product lines

1.4   Structure of the Book

In this book, we present *FeatureIDE* as a tool that helps developers manage the variability of software. *FeatureIDE* is based on *Eclipse* and extends the integrated development environment (*IDE*) with support for all phases of the development process for feature-oriented software product lines. As many readers are likely to read only a subset of all chapters, Fig. 1.2 provides an overview on the dependencies between chapters. That is, once a reader has identified relevant chapters using the description below, the overview can be used to identify further chapters that are necessary for understanding. For reading, we recommend to use the order of chapters in the book, whereas certain chapters can be skipped.

In Part I, we share some preliminaries that are needed for subsequent parts. As most chapters contain instructions for hands-on experience with *FeatureIDE*, Chap. 2 gives some assistance to download and install *FeatureIDE*, which can be skipped if you already have a recent version of *FeatureIDE* running. In Chap. 3, we briefly introduce essential functionalities of *FeatureIDE*, which is especially useful for those readers that have not worked with *FeatureIDE* before. Finally, we explain a running example of an elevator in Chap. 4 instead of repeating these explanations in each of the subsequent chapters.

In Part II, we provide details on product-line development independent of an implementation technique. As features are central to development, we start by describing how to specify features and their valid combinations with feature models in Chap. 5. These feature models can then be employed to derive valid

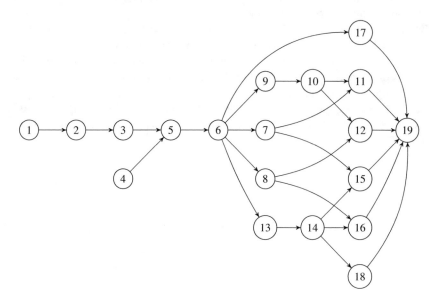

Fig. 1.2 Dependencies of book chapters for selective reading (transitive dependencies excluded for brevity)

configurations as illustrated in Chap. 6. In our terminology from above, these chapters are devoted to domain analysis and requirements analysis. The knowledge of those two chapters is fundamental to all following chapters, and there are different options to continue reading from there.

Parts III and IV each focus on a particular implementation technique, namely, conditional compilation and feature-oriented programming, and share the overall structure. In Chaps. 9 and 13, we first explain how to implement product lines with conditional compilation and feature-oriented programming, in general, and with dedicated command-line tools, in particular. Based on this introduction, we explain how our running example of Chap. 4 can be migrated to a product line with conditional compilation and feature-oriented programming in Chaps. 10 and 14, respectively. For those two techniques, we focus on domain implementation and product derivation.

Parts II–IV also contain dedicated chapters for feature traceability and quality assurance. In large product lines, it is essential to find all artifacts relevant for a certain feature. In Chap. 7, we explain how colors can be used to easily trace relevant features in large feature models or numerous configurations. Similarly, feature traceability is achieved by means of colors in conditional compilation and feature-oriented programming, as discussed in Chaps. 11 and 15, respectively.

Variability is essential for product lines but also easily leads to defects and inconsistencies. We present *FeatureIDE*'s tool support to find inconsistencies in feature models and configurations in Chap. 8. Even if those are free of problems, there can be further problems within the mapping to source code. In Chaps. 12 and 16, we illustrate dedicated testing and verification techniques in *FeatureIDE* for conditional compilation and feature-oriented programming, respectively. All three chapters together are devoted to quality assurance in software product lines.

In Part V, we give an overview on topics not being addressed in prior parts. In Chap. 17, we illustrate some other implementation techniques in *FeatureIDE*, such as runtime variability, black-box frameworks, and aspect-oriented programming. Largely orthogonal to implementation techniques is that all require typical maintenance tasks, such as refactorings or source-code documentation, as discussed in Chap. 18. Finally, we give a brief overview on *FeatureIDE*'s functionality in Chap. 19.

Getting Started

2

FeatureIDE is an *Eclipse* plug-in that supports the development of feature-oriented software product lines. To use the tool, we first need to set up *Eclipse* and install all the plug-ins required for the content of this book.

In this chapter, we provide step-by-step instructions on how to set up the system to use *FeatureIDE*. First, we explain how to install and configure *Eclipse*. We then introduce the general procedure of how to install *Eclipse* plug-ins. Finally, we show which *FeatureIDE* plug-ins need to be installed for different purposes. Developers who are already familiar with *Eclipse* and its installation mechanisms for plug-ins can skip this chapter. As an alternative to set up *FeatureIDE* manually, we provide a packaged version on our website that can be used without any further setup.

In particular, in Sect. 2.1, we explain how to install Java on your machine as it is required to run *Eclipse*. In Sect. 2.2, we show how *FeatureIDE* can be set up using a preinstalled *Eclipse*. Alternatively, we explain how to download *Eclipse* and how to install *FeatureIDE* in Sect. 2.3.

2.1 Download and Installation of Java

Java is required to run *Eclipse* and *FeatureIDE*. You may skip this section if Java is already installed on your system. However, we recommend that the current version of Java is installed, as *Eclipse* might not work with older versions. We recommend to use a Java 8 version. Which Java versions are required is specified on the *Eclipse* documentation website.[1] How to install Java on your system is explained in Instruction 2.1.

---

[1] https://wiki.eclipse.org/Eclipse/Installation.

© Springer International Publishing AG 2017
J. Meinicke et al., *Mastering Software Variability with FeatureIDE*,
DOI 10.1007/978-3-319-61443-4_2

Instruction 2.1 (Download and Installation of Java)

1. Download the latest Java version from https://www.java.com/download/
2. Complete the installer and restart your machine

2.2   Download of FeatureIDE

To ease the usage of *FeatureIDE*, we provide prepackaged versions of *Eclipse* with *FeatureIDE* already installed. On our website we provide two different versions. One version only contains the parts for *feature modeling*. The other version contains all *FeatureIDE* extensions and the required external plug-ins. Depending on how *FeatureIDE* will be used, the feature modeling version might be sufficient as it also requires less memory. The prepackaged versions are essentially zip files that only need to be extracted on your system. How to download and set up the prepackaged versions is explained in Instruction 2.2. If there is no current version of *FeatureIDE* available for your system, follow the description in Sect. 2.3.

Instruction 2.2 (Download Prepackaged *FeatureIDE*)

1. Download the latest prepackaged *FeatureIDE* version from
   http://wwwiti.cs.uni-magdeburg.de/iti_db/research/featureide/
2. Unzip *FeatureIDE* into a folder with full permissions
3. Start *Eclipse* and create a new workspace

2.3   Installation of FeatureIDE

In this section, we describe how to install *FeatureIDE*. We explain in detail how to download and set up *Eclipse*. Then we explain the general procedure of how to install plug-ins in *Eclipse*. Finally, we give an overview of which *FeatureIDE* plug-ins need to be installed for different purposes.

Download and Setup of Eclipse

The *Eclipse* IDE is available on their website and just needs to be downloaded and unzipped. How to install and configure *Eclipse* on your system is explained in Instruction 2.3. We recommend to use the most recent version of *Eclipse* available to ensure that the functionalities of *FeatureIDE* are working properly.

Instruction 2.3 (Setup *Eclipse*)

1. Download "Eclipse IDE for Java Developers" from
   https://eclipse.org/downloads/
2. Unzip *Eclipse* into a folder with full permissions
3. Configure *Eclipse* to avoid out-of-memory errors
   (a) Find and open the file "eclipse.ini" in the *Eclipse* folder (might be hidden)
   (b) After "-vmargs" set the argument "-Xmx" to "-Xmx1024m"
4. Start *Eclipse* and create a new workspace

Installation of Eclipse Plug-Ins

After the initial configuration of *Eclipse*, we can start to install *FeatureIDE* including all dependent plug-ins. Since the installation of all plug-ins is similar, we start with a general description of a plug-in installation procedure. Afterward, we present details of the *FeatureIDE* installation.

Eclipse offers two ways to install plug-ins using the (a) the menu entry *Install New Software* and (b) *Eclipse Marketplace* (see Fig. 2.1 on the following page). We give a short introduction to both possible ways. For an installation based on *Install New Software*, we can use the following menu entry to open the wizard: *Help → Install New Software*. In this wizard, you can define a specific location you want to use for a search of the desired plug-ins. Several locations already exist, such as the default repository of the specific *Eclipse* version (e.g., for *Eclipse* Neon, a default plug-in location is http://download.eclipse.org/releases/neon). After the definition of the search location, we provide an overview of all available plug-ins as a result.[2] Now, we select all desired plug-ins and continue the installation using the button *Next*. Please follow the wizard instruction to complete the installation. Typically, the wizard asks to agree to the license agreement before the plug-in can be installed. Finally, restart *Eclipse* to finish the plug-in installation. After *Eclipse* is restarted, the newly installed plug-ins will be available.

The *Eclipse Marketplace* is the second way to install new plug-ins. Therefore, the user needs to select the following menu entry: *Help → Eclipse Marketplace*. A wizard opens with an extensive search mechanism to satisfy our needs. If the desired plug-ins are found, we select the install button and confirm the installation. The next

---

[2]On the bottom of the wizard exist several check boxes that can be used to filter the results. Sometimes it is helpful to select or deselect one of them to get the correct overview of the desired plug-in. For instance, the check box *Group items by category* often hinders a correct plug-in representation.

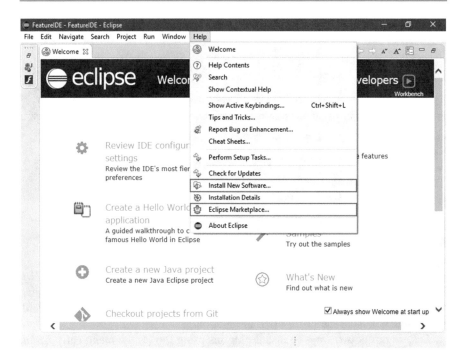

Fig. 2.1 Install New plug-ins using *Install New Software* or *Eclipse Marketplace*

steps are equal to the previous installation procedure, in which we have to agree to the license and restart *Eclipse*. We summarize the plug-in installation procedure in Instruction 2.4.

Instruction 2.4 (Installation of *Eclipse* Plug-Ins)

1. Open the *Help* menu and select *Install New Software* or *Eclipse Market-place*
2. Specify the desired repository by any of the following options:
   - For *Install New Software*: type in the update site
   - For *Eclipse Marketplace*: search for the tool name
3. Select the desired plug-ins
4. Press *Next*
5. Agree to the license agreement
6. Press *Finish* and restart *Eclipse*

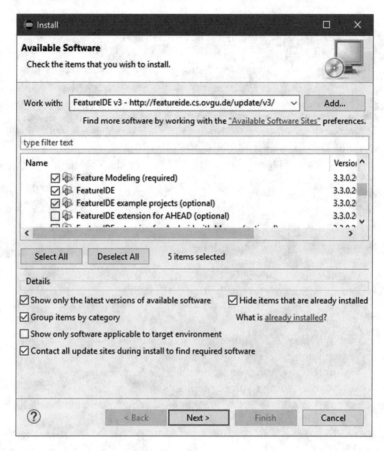

Fig. 2.2 Selecting the desired *FeatureIDE* plug-ins

Installation of FeatureIDE Plug-Ins

We clarified the general plug-in installation procedure and are ready to start with the *FeatureIDE* installation. *FeatureIDE* can be installed in two ways. Either use the *FeatureIDE* update site[3] or use the *Eclipse* Marketplace and search for *FeatureIDE* (see Fig. 2.2).

With *FeatureIDE* we provide support for several different types of feature-oriented software development. Thus, depending on how *FeatureIDE* will be used, only certain plug-ins need to be installed. An overview on the plug-ins needed for the preceding of the book is given in Instruction 2.5.

---

[3]http://featureide.cs.ovgu.de/update/v3/.

Instruction 2.5 (Installation of *FeatureIDE* Plug-Ins)

1. Some *FeatureIDE* extensions require to install further external plug-ins.
   For instance, if we want to create a product line based on C/C++ or
   AspectJ, we have to install the specific plug-ins first. A compatibility list
   for various *Eclipse* versions can be found under
   http://wwwiti.cs.uni-magdeburg.de/iti_db/research/featureide/#
   download
   - *C/C++ Development Tooling* (CDT) (only required for working C or
     C++ in Sect. 13.4 on Page 150)
   - *AspectJ Development Tools* (AJDT) (only required for working with
     AspectJ in Sect. 17.3 on Page 207)
2. Install *FeatureIDE* via *Eclipse* marketplace or with our update site[3] and
   select some or all of the following plug-ins:
   - FeatureIDE
   - ⇒ Contains all core and UI functionality
   - *Feature Modeling*
   - ⇒ Contains feature modeling functionalities, such as the *Feature Model
     Editor*
   - FeatureIDE *example projects* (used in Parts I–V)
   - ⇒ Contains several example product lines
   - FeatureIDE *extension for Munge* (used in Sect. 9.2 on Page 99)
   - ⇒ Extension for the Munge preprocessor
   - FeatureIDE *extension for Antenna* (used in Sect. 9.3 on Page 101)
   - ⇒ Extension for the Antenna preprocessor
   - FeatureIDE *extension for FeatureHouse* (used in Sect. 13.2 on
     Page 146)
   - ⇒ Extension for the FeatureHouse composer
   - FeatureIDE *extension for AHEAD* (used in Sect. 13.3 on Page 148)
   - ⇒ Extension for the AHEAD composer
   - FeatureIDE *extension for FeatureC++* (used in Sect. 13.4 on
     Page 150)
   - ⇒ Extension for the FeatureC++ composer
   - FeatureIDE *extension for AspectJ* (used in Sect. 17.3 on Page 207)
   - ⇒ Extension for the AspectJ composer
   - FeatureIDE *extension for Android with Munge*
   - ⇒ Extension for Android projects with the Munge preprocessor

2.4 Summary

In this chapter, we discussed how to set up *Eclipse* and *FeatureIDE*. Thus, we can now use *FeatureIDE* to develop a software product line. In Chap. 3, we give a brief overview on the functionalities of *FeatureIDE* and how it can be used to develop variable software. In the rest of the book, we will delve deeper into specialized functionalities.

FeatureIDE in a Nutshell

3

FeatureIDE implements a general support to implement feature-oriented software product lines. In this chapter, we give a general overview on the functionalities of *FeatureIDE*. To get a first impression of *FeatureIDE*, we use a small "Hello World" application. As *FeatureIDE* supports all phases of the feature-oriented software development process, we introduce how all these phases are realized.

First, we explain how to configure *Eclipse* to display the *FeatureIDE* perspective in Sect. 3.1. In Sect. 3.2, we show how to load an example product line which we will use in this chapter for illustration purposes. Based on this example, we explain the general structure of *FeatureIDE* projects in Sect. 3.3. The support for domain engineering in the form of feature models is introduced in Sect. 3.4. In Sect. 3.5, we show how to implement variability using feature-oriented programming. After implementing software variability, the program can be configured by selecting the required features. How product configuration is supported is explained in Sect. 3.6. Finally, we show in Sect. 3.7 how the configured program can be generated and executed.

3.1 Opening the FeatureIDE Perspective

For an optimal functional support, *Eclipse* offers several specialized perspectives. A perspective predefines views, editors, and menu entries that provide dedicated support for specific tasks (e.g., debugging) or programming languages (e.g., Java).

FeatureIDE provides a perspective to support product-line development. The standard representation consists of several views, such as *FeatureIDE Outline*, *Collaboration Diagram*, *Feature Model Edits*, and *FeatureIDE Statistics*, which are discussed in detail later in the book. Furthermore, besides others, the perspective also consists of the editor and the package explorer that is also used by other plug-ins. To select the *FeatureIDE* perspective, follow Instruction 3.1. After the *FeatureIDE* perspective is selected, it appears in the top-right corner of *Eclipse* (Fig. 3.1).

© Springer International Publishing AG 2017
J. Meinicke et al., *Mastering Software Variability with FeatureIDE*,
DOI 10.1007/978-3-319-61443-4_3

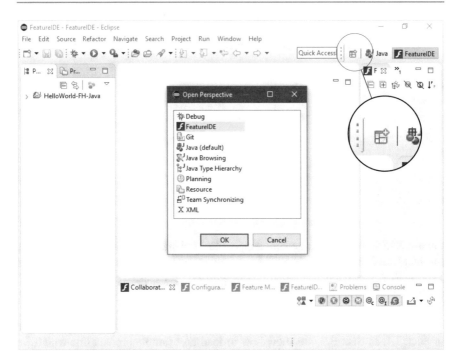

Fig. 3.1 Open the perspective selection dialog via the button (*right*). Select the *FeatureIDE* entry (*left*) *FeatureIDE*

Instruction 3.1 (Open the *FeatureIDE* Perspective)

1. Open the perspective selection dialog by any of the following options:
   - Press the button with the tooltip *Open Perspective* in the upper-right menu toolbar of *Eclipse*
   - Press *Window* → *Perspective* → *Open Perspective* → *Other...* in the menu bar of *Eclipse*
2. Select the entry for *FeatureIDE*.

3.2   Loading FeatureIDE Examples

To introduce to the *FeatureIDE*, we use a simple hello world product line. To ease the comprehension and to get an optimal overview, we use an existing example that can be installed via *FeatureIDE*'s example wizard. It is required that the plug-in *FeatureIDE example project* is installed.

In Fig. 3.2, we present an overview of the example wizard which provides all example projects of *FeatureIDE*. Using the pages (e.g., *Composer* or *Book*

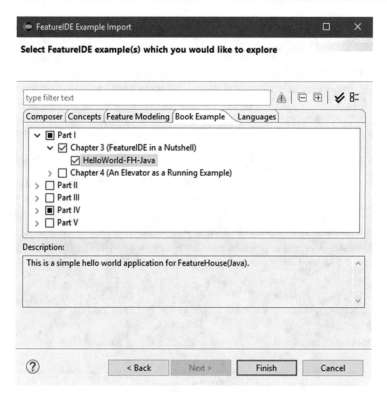

Fig. 3.2 Overview of existing projects in the *Example Wizard* of *FeatureIDE*

Example), we cluster the example into categories. In this book, we always refer to the examples in the page *Book Example*. In this chapter, we use a *HelloWorld* project created with the composition tool *FeatureHouse* (Apel et al. 2013b). It is possible to directly select the project in the project overview, or to filter the overview by the filter text box. If the user identified a specific project of interest, the project must be checked and confirmed using the *Finish* button. The *Example Wizard* always presents all *FeatureIDE* example projects regardless of the installed *FeatureIDE* plug-ins.

The projects of the Example Wizard can be in different states: *normal* (black), *warning* (yellow), and *error* (red). In detail, projects have an error state if they would result in an error after or during the installation step. It is not allowed for a developer to install projects with an error state (i.e., the *Finish* button is not selectable). For instance, if a project is already installed in the current workspace, it is not possible to install this project without an error. By contrast to projects with an error state, the warning state does not block an installation of the specific project. However, it is also likely that the project will not correctly work with the given *Eclipse* setting. The warning gives some suggestions to solve the project's problem. For instance, the warning state can be the result of a missing plug-in that has to be installed before we can use the project.

In the remainder of this chapter, we use the project *HelloWorld-FH-Java*. How to check out the project using the example wizard is explained in Instruction 3.2. Using this example, we will explain the main parts of *FeatureIDE* to understand its general process to develop product lines, namely, the project structure, feature modeling, implementation, configuration, product generation, and execution.

Instruction 3.2 (Import the HelloWorld-FH-Java Example)

1. Open the example wizard by any of the following options:
   - Press *New* → *Example* in the context menu of the Project/Package Explorer
   - Press *New* → *Examples* → *FeatureIDE* → *FeatureIDE Examples* in the upper-left menu toolbar of *Eclipse*
   - Press *File* → *New* → *Example* in the menu bar of *Eclipse*
2. Select *FeatureIDE Examples*
3. Press *Next*
4. Select *Book Example* tab
5. Select the project *Part I* → Chapter 3 → *HelloWorld-FH-Java*
6. Press *Finish*

3.3   Structure of FeatureIDE Projects

With *FeatureIDE*, we aim to support all phases of feature-oriented software development. Independent of the generation mechanisms, we need (a) a *feature model* to define features and their interdependencies, (b) *configurations* to define specific features representative of a certain product, (c) files that implement the feature's functionalities, and (d) generated source files that represent the product for the selected configuration. In the following, we give an overview on how *FeatureIDE* supports all these phases using the HelloWorld project.

After loading the HelloWorld project using the Example Wizard, we take a first look into the *FeatureIDE* project structure. In the following, we assume that the *FeatureIDE* perspective is active as some buttons may not be available in other perspectives. In this perspective, the loaded project is shown in the package explorer (cf. Fig. 3.3a). In the structure, we can see all main parts of a *FeatureIDE* project: (1) the `model.xml` for the domain modeling, (2) the directory `features` for the feature implementations, (3) the directory `configs` that consists of product configurations, and (4) the folder `src` that contains the generated product. The *current configuration*, marked with a green pencil (cf. the file `BeautifulWorld.config`), is used to generate the product using the feature implementation. Depending on the generation tool, the directory for feature implementations can be the same as for the generated product (e.g., for Antenna and AspectJ).

(a)   (b)

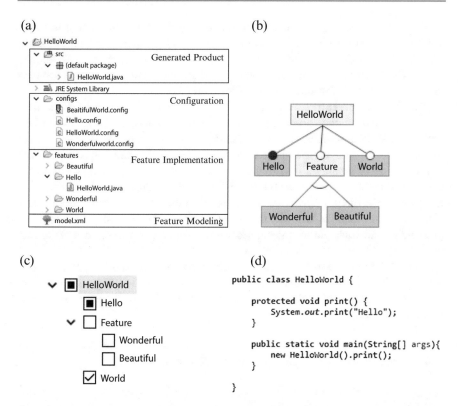

(c)   (d)

Fig. 3.3 Default project structure of a *FeatureIDE* project based on feature-oriented programming and Java, including feature modeling, configuration feature implementation, and generation of products. (**a**) General structure of FeatureIDE projects. (**b**) Feature modeling. (**c**) Configuration. (**d**) Feature implementation

The model.xml represents the domain model of a software product line using a feature model. Feature models are used to describe the common and variable parts of a software product line. *FeatureIDE* can use these information for other parts of the development cycle (e.g., domain implementation, product generation). By default, the model.xml is connected to the *Feature Model Editor* (cf. Fig. 3.3b). Using this editor, we can edit the feature model in a graphical manner. In Sect. 3.4, we present a brief overview of the facilities using the *Feature Model Editor*. In addition, we present a closer look in Chap. 5 on Page 43.

Let us consider the directory configs that is used for a product configuration. This directory contains a set of files with the extension *config*. Each of them is one specific product configuration in compliance to the feature model that is described in the model.xml. In addition, one of the existing files is marked with a pencil symbol (in Fig. 3.3 the file BeautifulWorld.config), which indicates that this product is selected for product generation and execution (see Sect. 3.7). *FeatureIDE* offers a specialized editor (i.e., the *Configuration Editor*) which allows a developer to configure specific products and to prevent mistakes during the configuration process (cf. Fig. 3.3c). The *Configuration Editor* is the default editor of the configuration files (i.e., automatically opened using double-click). We present a brief overview on the configuration and execution of products in Sect. 3.6. More details are given in Chap. 6 on Page 63.

The directory `features` represents the domain implementation of *FeatureIDE* projects based on *feature-oriented programming* (FOP; see Chap. 13 on Page 143 for more details). FOP separates the implementation of each feature that we introduced in the `model.xml` in a dedicated subdirectory of the directory `features`. The directory is separated into folders for each feature, which each contains the corresponding program artifacts (cf. Fig. 3.3d which implements the feature `Hello`). Each file in the directory *features* is connected to the default *Eclipse* editor. Thus, if we double-click on a Java file, the *Java Editor* will be opened. Afterward, it is possible to edit each file in a straightforward manner as given in an *Eclipse* Java project.

Finally, the selected features from the current configuration are generated into the source folder `src`. This folder is then compiled by the underlying compiler (e.g., the Java compiler for Java projects). Thus, the generated product can be executed as usual in *Eclipse*.

3.4   Modeling Variability with Feature Models

Instruction 3.3 (Opening the Feature Model Editor)
Open the feature model editor by:

• Double-click on the model.xml in the Project/Package Explorer

As described in the last section, the feature model of a product line is stored in the file *model.xml* of each *FeatureIDE* project. In this section, we describe the default editor for the *model.xml*, the *Feature Model Editor*. To open the *model.xml* using the *Feature Model Editor*, follow Instruction 3.3.

In Fig. 3.4, we depict the *FeatureIDE Feature Model Editor* using our example project *HelloWorld-FH-Java*. This editor offers three tabs that can be used for

Fig. 3.4 The *Feature Model Editor* allows product-line developers to edit feature models, such as the *Hello World* feature diagram of the example *HelloWorld-FH-Java*

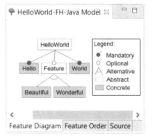

Fig. 3.5 The *Constraint Dialog* supports the product-line developers during the creation of cross-tree constraints

editing. First, the editor offers a tab for graphical editing of feature diagrams. The second tab allows a developer to define the feature order, which may be needed to ensure a correct product generation of a *FeatureIDE* project (more details are given in Chap. 5 on Page 43). Third, the *Feature Model Editor* also offers a tab that allows a developer to directly edit the textual representation as **.xml* file.

Let us take a closer look into the graphical editor. In Fig. 3.4 on the next page, we depict the feature model of the project *HelloWorld-FH-Java* with the page *Feature Diagram*. With the editor, a developer is able to add, remove, and change features and their dependencies. For instance, it is possible to rename the feature Feature to Specification or to add the feature Perfect as a child feature to the existing Alternative-group. Furthermore, we can change dependencies so that, for instance, the feature Feature is a mandatory feature. In particular, it is also possible to add *cross-tree constraints* to the feature model. The developer can describe an arbitrary propositional formula based on the set of existing features. Therefore, *FeatureIDE* offers an additional dialog that ensures the syntactical correctness of described cross-tree constraints (see Fig. 3.5 on the following page). The dialog can be opened using the context menu or a double-click on an existing cross-tree constraint. Using the *Constraint Dialog*, the developer immediately gets feedback about the correctness of the constraint to prevent the creation of incorrect constraints.

3.5 Implementation of Software Variability

The implementation of a product line and the respective implementation procedure differs according to the used programming language (e.g., Java, C++) and generation mechanism (e.g., preprocessors). In this chapter, we only focus on an introduction based on the programming language Java and the generation mechanism *feature-oriented programming* (FOP) using the *FeatureIDE* project

HelloWorld-FH-Java. In Chap. 17 on Page 199, we give some further insights into the support of other languages and paradigms.

As presented in Sect. 3.3 on Page 22, a *FeatureIDE* project based on FOP consists of two source folders: the folder *src* for generated source files and the folder *features* for implementation artifacts. Thus, the editable implementation artifacts of a product line based on FOP are located in the folder *features*. In contrast, the folder *src* is only the output folder for the generator and the content changes by each product generation (i.e., build process). Therefore, it is not intended to manually change the files of folder `src`. Nevertheless, the folder `src` can be helpful if program failures occur and more details are needed to find the error. To avoid accidentally changing the generated code, the files are marked as derived and the user gets a warning when trying to modify them.

Let us take a look into the folder *features*. The folder consists of a set of subfolders that represents the feature modules of the specific FOP project. In detail, each concrete feature of the feature model described in the *model.xml* is represented by one subfolder in which implementation artifacts and respective program files can be described. For instance, the example project *HelloWorld-FH-Java* (see Fig. 3.4 on the previous page) consists of four concrete features (`Hello`, `World`, `Beautiful`, and `Wonderful`) that are represented as subfolders in the source folder *features* (see Fig. 3.3 on Page 23). Each of the feature modules contains implementation artifacts, Java files, which we can edit to change the behavior of the product line's products. To open a source file, follow Instruction 3.4.

Instruction 3.4 (Open a Source File for a Specific Feature in Feature-House)
Open a feature implementation by:

- Double-click on *features* → *<feature>* → *<class>.java* in the Project/ Package Explorer

---

3.6   Creating Configurations

Instruction 3.5 (Opening the Configuration Editor)
Open the configuration editor by:

- Double-click on a *.config file in the config folder of the Project/Package Explorer

---

Before we are able to run a specific product of the *Hello World* product line, we need to select all features that should be included. Therefore, *FeatureIDE* provides configuration files, in which the selection is stored. As described above, all existing configurations of a project are stored in the directory `config` and the

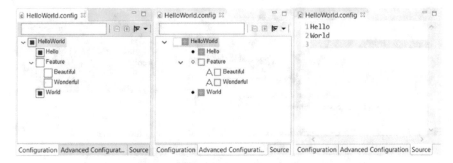

Fig. 3.6 The *Configuration Editor* with *Configuration*, *Advanced Configuration*, and *Source* tab to support the config file editing

active configuration (i.e., the product that is used for the build process) is marked by a *green pencil*. Typically only the active configuration is built automatically on each change. To open a configuration with the *Configuration Editor*, follow Instruction 3.5.

A developer can use *FeatureIDE*'s *Configuration Editor* to have a look into the selected features of a **.config* file and to change the selection. Therefore, the Configuration Editor provides three pages, (a) a *Configuration Page*, (b) an *Advanced Configuration Page*, and (c) a *Source* tab for the textual representation of the file. Whereas the Source tab presents all selected features in a textual manner, the Configuration and Advanced Configuration tabs support the configuration process and ensure that the selection does not lead to invalid configurations. In Fig. 3.6, we depict the Configuration and Advanced Configuration tabs using our *Hello World* example. In Chap. 6 on Page 63, we present a more detailed description of the configuration process.

3.7   Product Generation and Execution

Instruction 3.6 (Executing the Current Configuration)
Run the Current Configuration by any of the following options:

* Press *Run As. . .* → *Java Application* in the upper menu toolbar of *Eclipse*
* Press *Run As* → *Java Application* in the context menu of the Project/Package Explorer
* Press *Run* → *Run (Ctrl + F11)* in the menu bar of *Eclipse*

Once the feature modeling, feature implementation, and product selection is done, we can start to build and run a specific *Hello World* product. Therefore, *FeatureIDE* reuses all well-known procedures that *Eclipse* provides for a project build and launch. Thus, *FeatureIDE* allows a developer to use all ways to create and run an *Eclipse Run Configuration* for *FeatureIDE* projects.

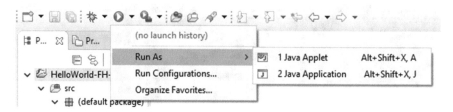

Fig. 3.7 Create a *Run Configuration* for *FeatureIDE* projects using the toolbar

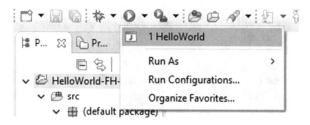

Fig. 3.8 Rerun the *Run Configuration*

Even if the concept of *Run Configurations* is well known by developers who use *Eclipse* as an integrated development environment, we give a short overview on how to create and use it. As mentioned above, *Eclipse* provides multiple ways to create a *Run Configuration* as described in Instruction 3.6 (cf. Fig. 3.7). Depending on the programming language, the submenu varies slightly. In this example, the *FeatureIDE* project is based on a Java project. Thus, the submenu allows us to create and launch a *Run Configuration* for Java. Afterward, we can reuse the created *Run Configuration* to relaunch the project's configuration (see Fig. 3.8).

Due to false settings, such as possible start parameters, the created *Run Configuration* may not launch the project correctly. In this case, we have to set up the created *Run Configuration*. Therefore, we use the menu entry *Run Configurations...* (cf. Fig. 3.7). Using this menu entry, we can open the default dialog for *Eclipse* configurations (cf. Fig. 3.9) that allows us to edit or create all kinds of configurations. Depending on the type of the *Run Configuration*, we can define all needed start information, such as the starting class or start parameters.

3.8   Summary and Further Reading

In this chapter, we gave a general overview on the basic functionalities of *FeatureIDE*. We introduced to the support of *FeatureIDE* for the main phases of feature-oriented software development. We showed how *FeatureIDE* supports domain engineering with support to create and edit feature models. We explained the general process of implementing variability in software. Then, we introduced

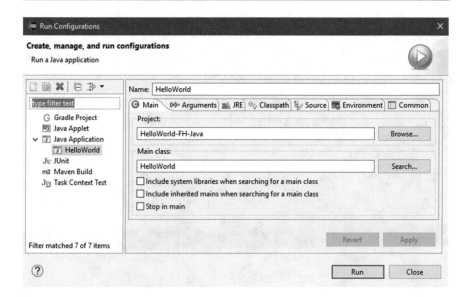

Fig. 3.9 Setup of *Run Configurations*

how *FeatureIDE* provides support to configure products. And finally, we showed how these products can be generated and executed.

As this chapter's purpose is only to give a general overview on the functionalities of *FeatureIDE*, we give detailed descriptions and more specialized support in the rest of this book. Support for feature modeling and product configuration will be discussed in Part II. How *FeatureIDE* supports implementation with conditional compilation (aka preprocessors) is explained in Part III. The support of feature-oriented programming as used in this chapter is explained in Part IV. In Part V, we shortly describe support for further generation mechanisms, namely, runtime variability, black-box frameworks, and aspect-oriented programming. We also give an overview on the purpose of all *FeatureIDE* views and editors in the last part.

An Elevator as a Running Example

4

For the description of *FeatureIDE*'s functionality, we use the running example of an elevator. Elevator systems can appear in multiple variations, such as different scheduling algorithms, or security properties. In this chapter, we explain a simple elevator system with the scheduling algorithm sabbath (i.e., the elevator automatically moves from the bottom floor to the top and back, while it stops at each floor). The system is used as a basis in the later chapters to implement an elevator product line. This chapter has two goals. First, it should familiarize with the default functionalities of Java in *Eclipse*. And second, we introduce the initial elevator implementation that will be used and extended in the proceeding of this book.

As the basis elevator has no variability, we create a default Java project to depict the functionality. We create the classes `Elevator` and `ControlUnit` to represent the main functionality and the class `SimulationUnit` for simulation purposes. In the following, we show stepwise how to create the initial version of our running example and how to execute it. These details are required to completely comprehend the example and to extend it in the remaining chapters. However, for the following chapters, we recommend to initialize the elevator project using the *FeatureIDE*'s *Example Wizard* as described in Instruction 4.1.

4.1   Creating the Elevator

First of all, we start to create a new elevator project as described in Instruction 4.2. Afterward, we need to create the necessary classes. The class `Elevator` (see Listing 4.1) represents a container class, in which we store all information and states of the elevator. The class provides information about the number of floors and the current floor, the direction, and the current state of the elevator. As the elevator can be in different states, we create the enumeration `ElevatorState` (see Listing 4.2) which represents all possible states. In the initial version of the elevator, we create three possible states named MOVING_UP, MOVING_DOWN, and FLOORING. Thus, the

© Springer International Publishing AG 2017
J. Meinicke et al., *Mastering Software Variability with FeatureIDE*,
DOI 10.1007/978-3-319-61443-4_4

current state of the elevator is represented by one of these states and is used as base information to control the elevator.

Instruction 4.1 (Import the Elevator Example)

1. Open the example wizard by any of the following options:
   - Press *New → Example* in the context menu of the Project/Package Explorer
   - Press *New → Examples → FeatureIDE → FeatureIDE Examples* in the upper-left menu toolbar of *Eclipse*
   - Press *File → New → Example* in the menu bar of *Eclipse*
2. Select *FeatureIDE Examples*
3. Press *Next*
4. Select *Book Example* tab
5. Select the project *Part I →* Chapter 4 *→ Elevator*
6. Press *Finish*

Instruction 4.2 (Creating a New Elevator Project)

1. Open the Java perspective if not active (cf. Instruction 3.1)
2. Open the Java project wizard by any of the following options:
   - Press *New → Java Project* in the context menu of the Project/Package Explorer
   - Press *New → Java → Java Project* in the upper-left menu toolbar of *Eclipse*
   - Press *File → New → Java Project* in the menu bar of *Eclipse*
3. Enter a project name (e.g., MyElevator)
4. Press *Finish*

Listing 4.1 Class `Elevator` of our reference example

```
1 public class Elevator {
2   private final int maxFloor;
3   private final int minFloor = 0;
4
5   private ElevatorState direction =
        ElevatorState.MOVING_UP;
6
7   private int currentFloor = 0;
8   private ElevatorState currentState =
        ElevatorState.FLOORING;
9
```

```
10    public Elevator(int maxFloor) { this.maxFloor =
         maxFloor; }
11
12    public int getMaxFloor() { return maxFloor; }
13    public int getMinFloor() { return minFloor; }
14
15    public ElevatorState getDirection() { return direction;
         }
16    public void setDirection(ElevatorState direction) {
17       this.direction = direction; }
18
19    public void setCurrentFloor(int currentFloor) {
20       this.currentFloor = currentFloor; }
21    public int getCurrentFloor() { return currentFloor; }
22
23    public ElevatorState getCurrentState() { return
         currentState; }
24    public void setCurrentState(ElevatorState state) {
25       currentState = state; }
26 }
```

Listing 4.2 Enum ElevatorState of our reference example

```
1 public enum ElevatorState { MOVING_UP, MOVING_DOWN,
     FLOORING }
```

The second class ControlUnit, shown in Listing 4.3, controls the elevator and contains the main functionality of the project. In detail, the class holds one instance of the elevator (Line 2) and uses two main methods (run and calculateNextState) to manage the control flow of this elevator instance. Whereas the method calculateNextState (Line 30–47) calculates the next state that the elevator needs to achieve, the method run (Line 5–21) executes this step.

In the case of our initial elevator, the ControlUnit needs to implement the sabbath mode. Therefore, the method calculateNextState calculates the state of the elevator that we want to achieve based on the current state in which the elevator currently exists. A switch-case statement is used for this purpose (see Line 32–46). If the elevator is in one of the moving states, the next state have to be FLOORING (default case, Line 44–45). In the case that the elevator is currently in the state FLOORING, we need to decide whether the next state have to be the state MOVING_DOWN or MOVING_UP. For this decision, we use the direction information that is stored in the elevator instance (Line 34).

Listing 4.3 Class ControlUnit of our reference example

```
 1 public class ControlUnit implements Runnable {
 2   private Elevator elevator;
 3   public ControlUnit(Elevator elevator) {
 4     this.elevator = elevator; }
 5   public void run() {
 6     while (true) {
 7       final ElevatorState state;
 8       state = calculateNextState();
 9       elevator.setCurrentState(state);
10       switch (state) {
11       case MOVING_UP:
12         elevator.setDirection(ElevatorState.MOVING_UP);
13         elevator.setCurrentFloor(elevator.getCurrentFloor()
              + 1);
14         break;
15       case MOVING_DOWN:
16         elevator.setDirection(ElevatorState.MOVING_DOWN);
17         elevator.setCurrentFloor(elevator.getCurrentFloor()
              - 1);
18         break;
19       case FLOORING:
20         this.triggerOnTick(); break;
21       }
22       try { Thread.sleep(700); } catch
              (InterruptedException e) {
23         e.printStackTrace(); }
24       switch (state) {
25       case MOVING_UP: this.triggerOnTick(); break;
26       case MOVING_DOWN: this.triggerOnTick(); break;
27       }
28     }
29   }
30   private ElevatorState calculateNextState() {
31     final int currentFloor = elevator.getCurrentFloor();
32     switch (elevator.getCurrentState()) {
33     case FLOORING:
34       switch (elevator.getDirection()) {
35       case MOVING_DOWN:
36         return (currentFloor <= elevator.getMinFloor()) ?
37           ElevatorState.MOVING_UP :
                ElevatorState.MOVING_DOWN;
38       case MOVING_UP:
39         return (currentFloor >= elevator.getMaxFloor()) ?
40           ElevatorState.MOVING_DOWN :
                ElevatorState.MOVING_UP;
41       default:
42         return ElevatorState.MOVING_UP;
43       }
44     default:
45       return ElevatorState.FLOORING;
46   }
47 }
```

```
48    private List<ITickListener> tickListener = new
          ArrayList<>();
49    public void addTickListener(ITickListener ticker) {
50      this.tickListener.add(ticker); }
51    private void triggerOnTick() {
52      for (ITickListener listener : this.tickListener) {
53        listener.onTick(elevator); }
54    }
55 }
```

Listing 4.4 Interface ITickListener of our reference example

```
1 public interface ITickListener {
2   void onTick(Elevator elevator); }
```

After the calculation of the next elevator state, the method run executes the step. We change the current elevator state (Line 9). Then, if the state that we want to achieve is MOVING_UP, we increase the current floor (Line 11–14). If the state is MOVING_DOWN, the floor will be decreased (Line 15–18).

The statements of the method run to sleep the thread are used for simulation purposes and can be ignored for now (Line 23). The method call triggerOnTick (Lines 20, 25–26) is used to inform some listener that the control unit executed one step. For this purpose, the control unit allows the system to register several listeners that are able to react on this information (Line 48–54). To provide this mechanism, we also create the interface ITickListener (see Listing 4.4) that forces an implementation of the method onTick that is called for each listener during each step of the control unit.

The last main component of our initial elevator project is represented by the class SimulationUnit (see Listing 4.5) that simulates the elevator mechanism. This class is also the starting point for the simulation and includes the main method for our elevator project (Line 4–8). Here, we instantiate the SimulationUnit and a graphical component for the purpose of visualization (class MainWindow, not discussed in this book) and start the execution of the simulation with the call to the method start. The method start implements the simulation and creates one elevator instance (Line 11) and one instance of the ControlUnit (Line 12). As the ControlUnit implements the interface Runnable, we create a specific thread that handles the execution. Before the thread is started (Line 27), we register two ITickListener: one nested class that represents an ITickListener to present the information of the current elevator state in the Java console (Line 15–23) and a second ITickListener that is represented by the graphical component (Line 24).

If applicable, create the classes and interfaces, as explained in Instruction 4.3 (not necessary if the elevator is imported using the example wizard).

Listing 4.5 Class SimulationUnit of our reference example

```
 1 public class SimulationUnit {
 2   private static MainWindow simulationWindow;
 3
 4   public static void main(String[] args) {
 5     SimulationUnit sim = new SimulationUnit();
 6     simulationWindow = new MainWindow();
 7     sim.start(5);
 8   }
 9
10   public void start(int maxFloor) {
11     Elevator elevator = new Elevator(maxFloor);
12     ControlUnit controller = new ControlUnit(elevator);
13
14     Thread controllerThread = new Thread(controller);
15     controller.addTickListener(new ITickListener() {
16       public void onTick(Elevator elevator) {
17         System.out.printf(String.format(
18           "%s - %s -- Current Floor %d \n",
19           new SimpleDateFormat("HH:mm:ss").format(new
             Date()),
20           elevator.getCurrentState(),
21           elevator.getCurrentFloor())));
22       }
23     });
24      controller.addTickListener(simulationWindow);
25
26     simulationWindow.initialize(elevator.getMaxFloor());
27     controllerThread.start();
28   }
29 }
```

Instruction 4.3 (Creating an Elevator)

1. Create the packages *core* and *sim*:
   (a) Open the Java package wizard by any of the following options:
       • Press *New* → *Package* in the context menu of the Project/Package Explorer, while selecting the project where the package should be created
       • Press *New* → *Java* → *Package* in the upper-left menu toolbar of *Eclipse*
       • Press *File* → *New* → *Package* in the menu bar of *Eclipse*
   (b) Enter the package name
   (c) Press *Finish*

(continued)

Instruction 4.3 (continued)
2. Add the classes `ControlUnit`, `ITickListener`, `Elevator`, and `ElevatorState` to the package *core* and add the class `SimulationUnit` to the package *sim*:
   (a) Open the Java class/interface wizard by any of the following options:
      • Press *New* → *Class/Interface* in the context menu of the Project/ Package Explorer
      • Press *New* → *Java* → *Class/Interface* in the upper-left menu toolbar of *Eclipse*
      • Press *File* → *New* → *Class/Interface* in the menu bar of *Eclipse*
   (b) Enter the name for the class or interface
   (c) Press *Finish*
   (d) Add the code to the file

4.2 Execution of the Running Example

In the previous section, we present all main components of our initial elevator project. By contrast, we do not show any details of the graphical component `MainWindow`. However, the graphical representation of the elevator using the instance of `MainWindow` (cf. Line 2 of Listing 4.5) is not necessary for the core functionality of the elevator, and thus, it is possible to remove all lines with references on this instance. Thus, the presented classes, the interface, and the enum can be used to start the simulation.

To execute the initial elevator, follow Instruction 4.4. The simulation unit runs the elevator and creates an output as depicted in Fig. 4.1. However, the initial elevator product that is available in our example wizard holds this graphical representation of class `MainWindow`. Therefore, additionally to this output given in the Java console, a frame will be created and a graphical representation of the elevator is visible. We depict the corresponding frame in Fig. 4.2. On the left side, we can see the elevator with six floors and on the right side the elevator cabin.

Instruction 4.4 (Executing the Elevator)
Run the Elevator by any of the following options:

• Press *Run As...* → *Java Application* in the upper menu toolbar of *Eclipse*
• Press *Run As* → *Java Application* in the context menu of the Project/ Package Explorer
• Press *Run* → *Run (Ctrl + F11)* in the menu bar of *Eclipse*

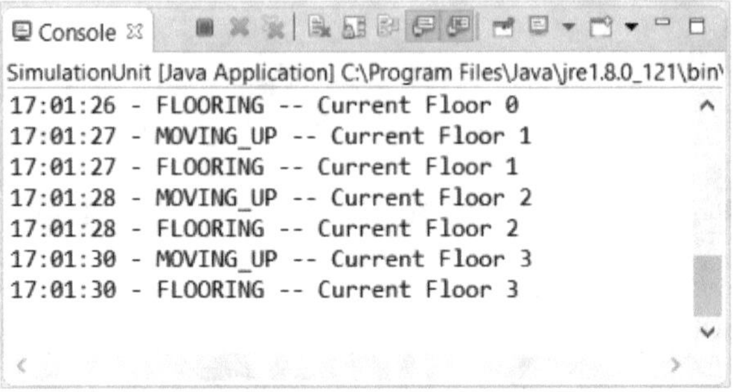

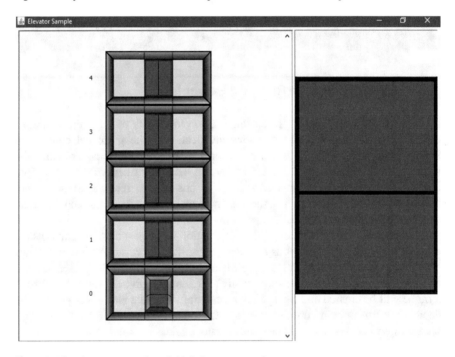

Fig. 4.1 Output of our initial elevator example in the Java console of Eclipse

Fig. 4.2 Visual component of our initial elevator example

4.3   Summary and Further Reading

To present the facilities of *FeatureIDE*'s functionalities, it is necessary to have a unique example for all parts of this book. For this purpose, we use an elevator that can switch the floors on different modes, such as the sabbath mode. Based on a small example that focuses on the core functionality of the elevator, we will instantiate a small product line for different kinds of paradigms. In Chap. 10 on

Page 105, we show how to initialize an elevator product line based on preprocessor annotations. By contrast, in Chap. 14 on Page 155, the product line is instantiated using the concept of feature-oriented programming. Afterward, we use this initial elevator product line to show how it is possible to extend the set of features for each paradigm using *FeatureIDE*.

Part II

**Tool Support for Feature Modeling
and Configuration**

Feature Modeling

5

A feature model is the central part of a software product line. Feature models are used to describe how features can be combined to form the different products of a software product line. Thus, feature models are also the central part of projects in *FeatureIDE*. All parts of the development process with *FeatureIDE* depend on the feature model, from modeling the domain and implementing the source code to deriving and analyzing products.

In this chapter, we introduce the concept of a *feature diagram*, which is a tree structure that represents the variability of the product line (i.e., the feature model). We exemplify the use of *FeatureIDE* to create feature diagrams based on the *Feature Model Editor*. Therefore, we introduce a new product line for an elevator that we will use in the remaining chapters of the book.

In detail, we explain how to create feature models with *FeatureIDE* in Sect. 5.1. In Sect. 5.2, we show how to create the tree structure of the feature model. Additionally, we explain how to edit cross-tree constants of the feature model in Sect. 5.3. In Sect. 5.4, we show how to handle and visualize larger feature models in the *Feature Model Editor*. As feature models are often used to communicate variability, we explain in Sect. 5.5 how to import and export feature models. Finally, we explain further pages of the *Feature Model Editor* in Sect. 5.6.

5.1 Creation of Feature Models

Before we can actually model the features and their dependencies, we first need to create a new feature model. As a first step, we create a new *FeatureIDE* project that is specialized for feature modeling only (cf. Instruction 5.1). Such *FeatureIDE*

© Springer International Publishing AG 2017
J. Meinicke et al., *Mastering Software Variability with FeatureIDE*,
DOI 10.1007/978-3-319-61443-4_5

Fig. 5.1 After creating a new project, *FeatureIDE* creates an initial model with a root feature named after the project and a feature called Base

projects are used only for feature modeling and configuration without actual source code. As we are designing the domain of an elevator, we name the project *Elevator*.

Instruction 5.1 (Creating a New FeatureIDE Project)

1. Open the *FeatureIDE* perspective if not active (cf. Instruction 3.1)
2. Open the feature project wizard by any of the following options:
   • Press *New → FeatureIDE Project* in the context menu of the Project/Package Explorer
   • Press *New → FeatureIDE → FeatureIDE Project* in the upper-left menu toolbar of *Eclipse*
   • Press *File → New → FeatureIDE Project* in the menu bar of *Eclipse*
3. Select *Feature Modeling* as composer
4. Press *Next*
5. Enter a project name (e.g., MyElevator-FeatureModeling)
6. Press *Finish*

As a result, *FeatureIDE* will create and open an initial *feature model* with two features, depicted as rectangles. The shown *feature diagram* is designed as tree. The *root feature* (i.e., the feature on top) with the name of the project (i.e., feature `Elevator` in our example) is always included in any configuration. Each feature may also have children below. The parent-child relation means that if the child is selected, the parent has to be selected, too (i.e., the child feature implies the parent feature).[1] In the example, a feature named `Base` is initially created, too (cf. Fig. 5.1). Alternatively, it is also possible to create a single feature model in other projects (e.g., simple Java projects). How to create a new feature model without a *FeatureIDE* project is explained in Instruction 5.2.

---

[1]Further relations among features will be discussed in the next section.

Instruction 5.2 (Creating a Feature Model Independent of a *FeatureIDE* Project)

1. Open the feature model wizard by any of the following options:
   - Press *New* → *Feature Model* in the context menu of the Project/Package Explorer
   - Press *New* → *FeatureIDE* → *Feature Model* in the upper-left menu toolbar of *Eclipse*
   - Press *File* → *New* → *Feature Model* in the menu bar of *Eclipse*
2. Enter a path where the model should be created
3. Press *Finish*

Adding Features to Feature Models

To design the initial feature model, we first define the features of the product line. A central part of our *Elevator* product line are the modes that control the behavior of the elevator. A simple mode is the so-called *Sabbath* mode in which the elevator constantly moves from the bottom to the top floor and back, while stopping at each floor on its way. Thus, the users do not need to use any buttons to interact with the elevator (a property that is sometimes used for religious reasons, hence the name). To define the feature, we rename the feature Base and give it the new name Sabbath (see Instruction 5.3). The result of this step is depicted in Fig. 5.2.

Instruction 5.3 (Renaming a Feature in the Feature Diagram)

1. Select a feature in the feature diagram
2. Open an editing field by any of the following options:
   - Click on the feature again
   - Press *Rename (F2)* in the context menu of the selected feature
   - Press *F2*
3. Enter the new desired name of the feature
4. Press *Enter*

Beyond the sabbath mode, the elevator can have more complex modes. As a first step, we use the operation *Create Feature Above* to add a feature called Modes above the feature Sabbath. This feature helps to structure the model (see Instruction 5.4), as seen in Fig. 5.3.

Fig. 5.2 Feature Base has been renamed to Sabbath

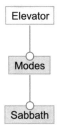

Fig. 5.3 Added the feature Modes to structure the feature model

---

Instruction 5.4 (Adding a Feature)

1. Select a feature in the feature diagram
2. Create a new feature by any of the following options:
   - Press *Create Feature Above* in the context menu of the selected feature
   - Press *Create Feature Below (Ins)* in the context menu of the selected feature
3. Replace the default feature name (e.g., NewFeature1) with the new desired name
4. Press *Enter*

To complete the initial model, we add two more features below the feature Modes. ShortestPath represents a strategy in which the elevator considers the distance between the levels of incoming calls to find the shortest order, and the feature FIFO which realizes a first come, first serve strategy. Furthermore, the modes rely on the availability of certain buttons that are used to call the elevator from a specific level of the building. Thus, we add a feature called CallButtons below the root feature. We further add two features below the feature CallButtons: feature DirectedCall and feature UndirectedCall. The complete model contains some more features as depicted in Fig. 5.4. As an *exercise*, add the missing features to your feature model.

As a result, the feature model consists of 13 features. Most of the features are currently defined as *concrete*, and only the root feature is *abstract*. These two types of features are used to distinguish between features that represent actual artifacts (i.e., concrete features) and features that are only used to structure the diagram (i.e., abstract features). How to change the type of a feature is described in Instruction 5.5.

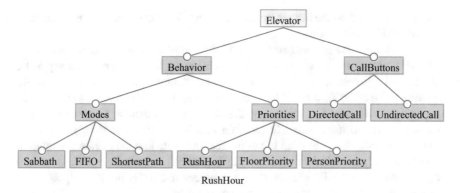

Fig. 5.4 The initial feature model containing all features of the feature model

As the features Behavior, Modes, Priorities, and CallButtons are used to structure the tree, we set them to be abstract.

Instruction 5.5 (Marking a Feature as Abstract or Concrete)

1. Select a feature in the feature diagram
2. Mark the selected feature as *Abstract* by:
   - Check *Abstract* in the context menu of the selected feature to make it abstract
3. Mark the selected feature as *Concrete* by:
   - Uncheck *Abstract* in the context menu of the selected feature

---

The result of changing the features to abstract is a feature model with eight concrete features and five features to group them. Beyond this parent-child relation, we did not define any further dependencies among features. In the next section, we explain how to define these dependencies, for example, that only one of the scheduling modes can be selected at the same time.

5.2   Modeling Tree Constraints

One way to specify constraints in feature diagrams is using its hierarchy. These kinds of constraints are also called *tree constraints* as they are expressed using the tree structure. We have already introduced the basic tree constraints that are implicit to the structure of the feature model. In detail, the *root feature* must be included in all products. In addition, the selection of a feature implies the selection of its parent features. This constraint is also referred to as *parent-child relationship*. In this section, we introduce further structural feature dependencies, such as mandatory features and feature groups.

At this point, all features (except the root feature) are marked as *optional* with a white circle on top of the feature. However, some features are necessary to be selected if its parent feature is selected, too. For example, the elevator necessarily requires a behavior. To include this constraint, we define the feature `Behavior` as mandatory as described in Instruction 5.6. The result is that the feature `Behavior` is always selected if its parent feature is also selected. The *mandatory* relation is expressed with a black circle on top of the feature. Note that the mandatory relation of a feature only models the dependency to its parent (i.e., even if a feature is marked as mandatory, it may be unselected if the parent feature is unselected, too). We further change the feature `Modes` to be mandatory, too.

Instruction 5.6 (Marking a Feature as Optional or Mandatory)

- Mark a feature as *mandatory* by any of the following options:
  - Double-click on the circle on top of the feature (circle is black now)
  - Check *Mandatory* in the context menu of a selected feature
- Mark a feature as *optional* by any of the following options:
  - Double-click on the circle on top of the feature (circle is white now)
  - Uncheck *Mandatory* in the context menu of a selected feature

---

A further way to define additional dependencies between features is based on *group types*. For instance, either each elevator can have only one button on each floor that is used to call the elevator or each floor has two buttons that are used to indicate the direction in which the passenger wishes to move. If we want to express such alternative features, we can use an *Alternative-group*. We change the group type of the feature `CallButton` to an Alternative-group as explained in Instruction 5.7 until there is an unfilled arc below the parent feature. The Alternative-group specifies that if the parent feature is selected, then exactly one of its child features has to be selected, too. We further also change the group type of the feature `Modes` to be alternative as the elevator should only implement one mode.

Instruction 5.7 (Changing the Group Type of a Feature)

- Mark a group type as *and* by any of the following options:
  - Double-click on the line connecting the feature with its child features
  - Check *And* in the context menu of a selected group
- Mark a feature as *or* by any of the following options:

(continued)

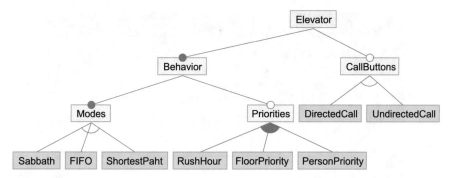

Fig. 5.5 The feature model with tree constraints to express feature dependencies

Instruction 5.7 (continued)
 – Double-click on the line connecting the feature with its child features
 – Check *Or* in the context menu of a selected group
• Mark a feature as *alternative* by any of the following options:
 – Double-click on the line connecting the feature with its child features
 – Check *Alternative* in the context menu of a selected group

Regarding the priorities, we want to allow products to include any combination of priorities from which the customer can choose during runtime. However, each elevator must include at least one priority mode for the elevator system to be able to operate. Such a relationship can be expressed with an *Or-Group*. This group expresses that at least one of the child features must be selected if the parent feature is selected. We change the group type of the feature Priorities to an Or-group. The resulting feature model is shown in Fig. 5.5.

The expressiveness of tree constraints is sufficient for most dependencies among features. Furthermore, it is easier to comprehend as their corresponding propositional formulas. However, there may be constraints among features that cannot be expressed with tree constraint, such as constraints among features across the tree.

5.3   Modeling Cross-Tree Constraints

Some dependencies cannot directly be expressed by the structure of the feature model. In this case, it is possible to add arbitrary propositional formulas among features to define their relations. Such formulas are called *cross-tree constraints*.

Fig. 5.6 The *Constraint Dialog* is used to create and edit cross-tree constraints that define additional dependencies between features

The feature `DirectedCall` only supports the mode `ShortestPath`. To define this dependency, we create a constraint expressing this relationship in terms of the following formula: *DirectedCall* $\implies$ *ShortestPath* (cf. Instruction 5.8).

The *Constraint Dialog* assists the user by checking the constraint on the fly. If the constraint contains syntactical errors, the button *Create Constraint* is not available. Furthermore, the user is warned if the constraint leads to logical inconsistencies in the feature model (cf. Chap. 8 on Page 81). *FeatureIDE* also supports to edit existing constraints as explained in Instruction 5.9.

Using cross-tree constraints, arbitrary relations among features can be expressed. However, they are harder to comprehend than simple tree constraints. Thus, relations among features should be rather expressed using the tree structure if possible.

Instruction 5.8 (Create a Cross-Tree Constraint)

1. Open the constraint editor (see Fig. 5.6) by any of the following options:
   - Press *Create Constraint* in the context menu of the feature model editor (no element selected)
   - Press *Create Constraint* in the context menu of a selected constraint
   - Press *Create Constraint starting with "<feature>"* in the context menu of a selected feature
2. Enter a constraint by any of the following options:
   - Double-click features and using the buttons for operations
   - Enter the constraint directly with the help of the content assist
3. Press *Create Constraint*

Instruction 5.9 (Edit an Existing Cross-Tree Constraint)

1. Select a constraint in the feature diagram
2. Open the constraint editor by any of the following options:
   - Double-click on the constraint in the feature diagram
   - Press *Edit Constraint* in the context menu of the selected constraint
3. Modify the constraint by any of the following options:
   - Double-click features and using the buttons for operations
   - Enter the constraint directly with the help of the content assist
4. Press *Update Constraint*

Final Feature Model

To complete the model, we add the two missing cross-tree constraints as depicted in Fig. 5.7. Alternatively, we provide the final feature model as project within our example wizard. To check out the final feature model, follow Instruction 5.10.

Instruction 5.10 (Import the Elevator-FeatureModeling Example)

1. Open the example wizard by any of the following options:
   - Press *New* → *Example* in the context menu of the Project/Package Explorer

(continued)

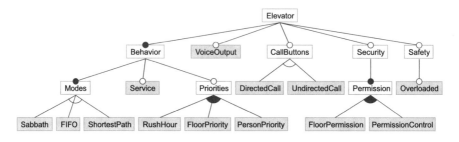

Fig. 5.7 The complete feature model of the elevator product line

---

Instruction 5.10 (continued)
- Press *New → Examples → FeatureIDE → FeatureIDE Examples* in the upper-left menu toolbar of *Eclipse*
- Press *File → New → Example* in the menu bar of *Eclipse*
2. Select *FeatureIDE Examples*
3. Press *Next*
4. Select *Book Example* tab
5. Select the project *Part II →* Chapter 5 *→ Elevator-FeatureModeling*
6. Press *Finish*

5.4   Visualizing Large Feature Models

We have introduced the most important concepts that are used in *FeatureIDE* to model features and their dependencies. Thus, we can complete the feature model, resulting in the model depicted in Fig. 5.7. As the complete model illustrates, the size of the model can easily get large. To help comprehending larger feature models, *FeatureIDE* provides three mechanisms, namely, collapsing subtrees, layouting the tree structure, and an outline view.

Collapsing of Subtrees

Even though feature models may get large, it is usually not necessary to see all features at once. Thus, we support to collapse the children of features. This will hide the complete subtree of a feature, while showing the number of hidden features. How to collapse the subtree is explained in Instruction 5.11. How the displayed

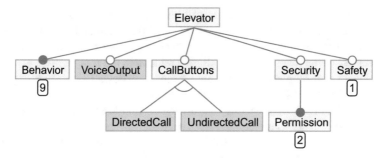

Fig. 5.8 Collapsing of subtrees in the feature model editor

diagram looks after collapsing the features Behavior, Permission, and Safety is depicted in Fig. 5.8. For example, the nine below the feature Behavior indicates that nine child features are collapsed.

Instruction 5.11 (Collapsing and Uncollapsing Subtrees)

1. Optionally import the complete Elevator example (cf. Instruction 4.1)
2. Select a feature in the feature diagram
3. Collapse subtree below the selected feature (if uncollapsed) by any of the following options:
   - Double-click on the selected feature
   - Press *Collapse (Ctrl + C)* in the context menu of the selected feature
   - Press *Ctrl + C*
4. Uncollapse subtree below the selected feature (if collapsed) by any of the following options:
   - Double-click on the selected feature
   - Press *Collapse (Ctrl + C)* in the context menu of the selected feature
   - Press *Ctrl + C*

Layouting Feature Models

To further improve the readability of feature models, the Feature Model Editor supports several layouting strategies. Layout strategies define how and in which order the feature of the model are displayed. The default layout, which we used so far, is called top-down ordered layout. In many situations, this layout is a suitable option. However, sometimes it is useful to change the layout of the model. *FeatureIDE* supports the following layout strategies:

- Top Down (ordered). This is the default layout. Features are arranged top down below the root feature. Child features are aligned relative to their parent feature.
- Top Down (centered). Features are arranged top down below the root feature. Each level of the feature model is aligned relative to the root feature.
- Top Down (left-aligned). Features are arranged top down below the root feature. Each level of the feature model is aligned to the left.
- Left To Right (ordered). Features are arranged from left to right next to the root feature. Child features are aligned relative to their parent feature.
- Manual Layout: Features can be arranged individually by using drag and drop. The option auto-layout constraints is used to arrange constraints automatically, while features use the manual layout.

How the feature model looks like after applying the individual layout mechanism is shown in Fig. 5.9. To change the layout in *FeatureIDE*, follow Instruction 5.12.

Instruction 5.12 (Change the Layout of the Feature Diagram)

1. Optionally import the complete Elevator example (cf. Instruction 4.1)
2. Open the layout submenu of the feature diagram by:
   - Press *Set Layout* in the context menu of any feature diagram element except the constraints and legend
3. Select the desired layout

Feature Model Outline

Both mechanisms, collapsing of features and layouting of feature models, help to improve the readability of the model. To further help comprehending the model, we provide an additional outline view that displays the model as a simple tree structure. In Fig. 5.10, you can see the *FeatureIDE Outline* which extends the default outline view of *Eclipse* to display the feature model. The model shown in the outline view is always in sync with the model in the editor. For example, changing the mandatory type of a feature in the editor will also change the type of the feature in the outline. Also, collapsing features in the outline will automatically collapse features in the editor. The *FeatureIDE Outline View* is part of the *FeatureIDE* perspective and should already be open in *Eclipse*. If the view is not open in the current perspective, follow Instruction 5.13 to open the view.

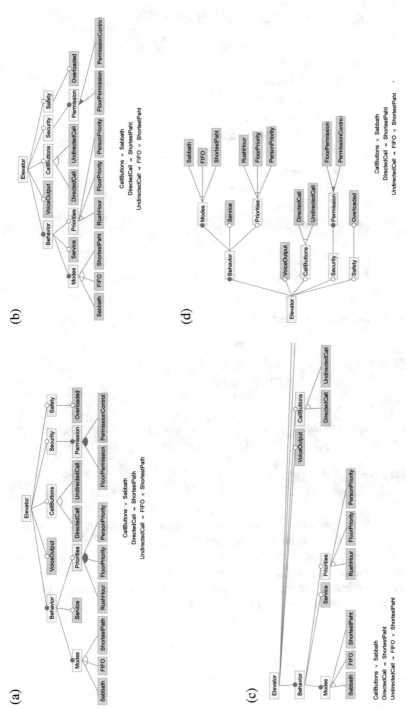

Fig. 5.9 Different layout mechanisms supported by the feature model editor. (a) Top Down (ordered). (b) Top Down (centered). (c) Top Down (left-aligned). (d) Left To Right (ordered)

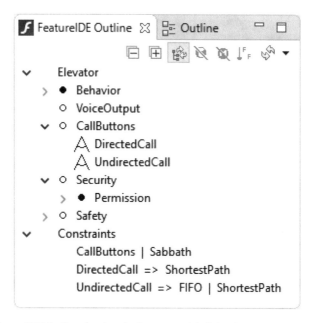

Fig. 5.10 *FeatureIDE* Outline showing the feature model of the elevator product line

---

Instruction 5.13 (Open the *FeatureIDE* Outline)
Open the feature model outline by any of the following options:

- Press *FeatureIDE Outline* in the right part of *Eclipse* next to the *Eclipse* outline
- Press *Window* → *Show View* → *FeatureIDE Outline* in the menu bar of *Eclipse*

The outline view supports the same editing functionalities as the feature model editor via the context menu (i.e., right-click on a feature). Furthermore, the representation of the shown model is usually more compact than in the feature model editor. However, with the shown format, it is harder to comprehend the actual relations among features in the tree structure. Thus, the actual advantage of feature diagrams gets lost when only using the outline view.

5.5   Importing and Exporting Feature Models

The goal of feature models is mainly to define the domain of the software product line. However, they are also meant to *communicate* the variability of the software. In this section, we show how feature models can be printed and how feature models can be imported and exported with different file formats.

Printing a Feature Model

Printing a feature model is useful to easily communicate a model. In the *Feature Model Editor*, we provide support to print the model to several picture formats, such as *Portable Network Graphic (*.png)*, *JPEG (*.jpg)*, and *Bitmap (*.bmp)*. Printing helps to avoid using a screen capture which might be of bad quality. How to print a feature model as picture is explained in Instruction 5.14.

Instruction 5.14 (Printing a Feature Model as Picture)

1. Open the feature model (cf. Instruction 3.3)
2. Open the export wizard by:
    • Press *Export As* in the context menu of the feature model editor
3. Select the picture format
4. Enter the name and the path of the picture
5. Press *Save*

The pictures might be pixelated if the zoom level is too high. To generate higher-quality pictures, we suggest to print the feature model as *PDF*. As the generated picture will be in *vector graphic*, the quality will always be high independent of the zoom level. To do so, a PDF-Printer is required on the system. How to print a feature model as PDF is explained in Instruction 5.15.

Instruction 5.15 (Printing a Feature Model as Vector Graphic)

1. Open the feature model (cf. Instruction 3.3)
2. Open the printing dialog by:
    • Press *File → Print…* in the menu bar of *Eclipse*
3. Follow the dialog and select a PDF-Printer to print the feature model

With these two ways, feature models can easily be communicated as pictures. Note that, when printing, the model will appear as seen in the editor. If there are highlightings with colors, they will be printed in these colors, too. Also the legend will only be printed if it is not hidden.

Handling Diverse File Formats with the Feature Model Editor

Beyond the informal communication of the feature models, the models may also be communication between different tools. However, often tools have their own file format to save feature models. In *FeatureIDE*, we support *importing* as well as *exporting* of several feature model formats, namely, *GUIDSL*, *SXFM* (S.P.L.O.T.), *Velvet*, and *DIMACS*. For the formats of *FaMa* and *SPL Conquerer*, we only support exporting of models. Furthermore, the feature model can be exported as its *conjunctive normal form* (CNF). When exporting a model, the model will be saved into a new file. However, when importing a model, the current file will be overwritten with the model of the imported file. How to import and export a feature model is described in Instruction 5.16.

Instruction 5.16 (Importing and Exporting Feature Models)

1. Select a feature model in the Package/Project Explorer
2. Import a feature model (i.e., the current file will be overwritten) by:
   (a) Open the importing dialog by:
       • Press *FeatureIDE → Import model from <format> format* in the context menu of the Package/Project Explorer
   (b) Select the model to import
   (c) Press *Open*
3. Export a feature model by:
   (a) Open the exporting dialog by:
       • Press *FeatureIDE → Export model to <format> format* in the context menu of the Package/Project Explorer
   (b) Enter the name and the path
   (c) Press *Save*

An alternative way to use models with file formats different from the *FeatureIDE*-xml is to simply open the file with the *Feature Model Editor*. For example, if you have a file in DIMACS format in any eclipse project, the file can be displayed and edited using the *Feature Model Editor*. Therefore, it is not even necessary to have the model in a *FeatureIDE* project. When opening the model, *FeatureIDE* reconstructs a feature model from the file (i.e., there might be no information on the tree structure of the model). Editing and saving the model is done as usual. How to open a feature model file is explained in Instruction 5.17. After opening the model once with the *Feature Model Editor*, the file will be opened that way in the future using *double-click*. To always associate a specific file with the *Feature Model Editor*, follow Instruction 5.18.

Instruction 5.17 (Using the Feature Model Editor on Diverse File Formats)

1. Select a feature model with a different file format
2. Open the choose editor dialog by:
   • Press *Open With → Other...* in the context menu of the Package/Project Explorer
3. In the dialog, search and select the *Feature Model Editor* in the list of internal editors
4. Press *OK*

Instruction 5.18 (Associate File Extensions with the Feature Model Editor)

1. Open the file association page in the preferences by:
   • Press *Window → Preferences → General → Editors → File Associations* in the menu bar of *Eclipse*
2. Add an entry for the file type (e.g., "*.dimacs") using *Add...* in the top part of the page
3. Select the newly created entry
4. In the part for *Associated editors*, add the *Feature Model Editor* using the *Add...* button
5. Optionally if there are other editors already associated with the format, select the entry for the *Feature Model Editor* and press the button *Default*

The *Feature Model Editor* allows several ways to communicate feature models. The models can be exported as pictures, printed to PDF files. Furthermore, the editor is capable of handling file formats of external tools using import and export mechanisms, as well as directly editing these files.

5.6   Further Pages of the Feature Model Editor

The feature model editor consists of several pages. Next to the default page showing the feature diagram, the feature model editor has two further pages for the feature order and the file content. On the bottom of the editor, the different pages can be selected.

(a)   (b)

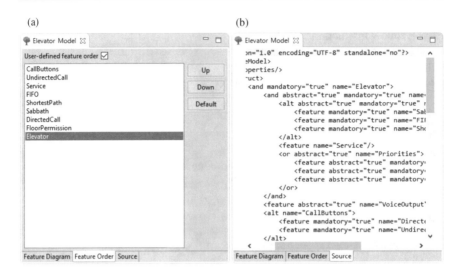

Fig. 5.11 Further pages of the feature model editor. (**a**) Feature order page. (**b**) Source page

Feature Order

The *feature order* defines in which sequence the features will appear in the generated configurations. By default, the features are ordered in *pre-order*. Meaning that first the parent feature is added, then the left subtree is traversed, and afterward the right subtree is traversed. However, for some reasons, the order in which the features are required differs from the pre-order defined in the feature model. For example, in feature-oriented programming, the order matters in which features are composed as we will show in Part III.

To define the feature order, the feature model editor provides a page to specify a custom order. How to change the feature order is explained in Instruction 5.19. The adjusted feature order tab for the elevator feature model is shown in Fig. 5.11a. As shown, the feature `Elevator` which is by default the first feature is now the last.

Instruction 5.19 (Change the Feature Order)

1. Open the *Feature Order* page by:
   • Press *Feature Order* in the bottom bar of the feature model editor
2. Check *User-defined feature order*
3. Select one or more features (hold either *Ctrl* or *Shift* to select multiple features)
4. Move features by any of the following options:

(continued)

Instruction 5.19 (continued)
- Press *Up* to move the selected features up by one position
- Press *Down* to move the selected feature down by one position
5. Save the feature model by any of the following options:
   - Press *Ctrl + S*
   - Press *Save (Ctrl + S)* in the upper-left menu toolbar of *Eclipse*
   - Press *File → Save (Ctrl + S)* in the menu bar of *Eclipse*

Source Page

The last page of the feature model editor is the source page. This page simply shows the sources of the xml file. In general, this page should not be used to edit the feature model as it does not have any assist for editing. However, if you just want to copy-paste a model from somewhere else, then the source page may be used. When going back to the default page of the editor after changing the content on the source page, the displayed feature model will already represent the new content. The source page of the elevator feature model is shown in Fig. 5.11b.

5.7   Summary and Further Reading

In this chapter, we introduced the concept of feature models. We explained how feature models can be created using the feature model editor. We further showed how dependencies among features can be expressed using the hierarchy in the feature diagram (i.e., tree constraints) and arbitrary propositional formulas (i.e., cross-tree constraints). With this concept of feature models, the variability of the product line can be expressed in a comprehensible form. Finally, we showed how *FeatureIDE* helps to manage larger feature model using different layouting mechanisms, collapsing of subtrees, and the outline view.

In the upcoming chapter, we show further support for feature models in *FeatureIDE*. First of all, feature models are used to express the variability of the product line and then define the configuration space. Thus, we explain the support for product configuration in Chap. 6 on Page 63. When feature models get large, it may be difficult to find certain features or groups thereof. The support feature traceability in *FeatureIDE* is discussed in Chap. 7 on Page 73. Third, constraints among features may be difficult to define. Thus, it can happen that constraints cause failures in the feature model (e.g., a feature might be no longer selectable because it is excluded in all configurations). In Chap. 8 on Page 81, we illustrate the support analysis of feature models.

Feature models have been proposed in 1990 to document the result of a feature-oriented domain analysis (Kang et al. 1990). Since then, those feature models have been extended, resulting in numerous feature modeling languages with differing expressiveness (Schobbens et al. 2007; Benavides et al. 2010; Berger et al. 2013). The feature modeling language used in *FeatureIDE* is closest to that of GUIDSL (Batory 2005). A unique feature of both languages is that features are explicitly marked as abstract or concrete (Thüm et al. 2011); however, *FeatureIDE* relaxes GUIDSL's restriction that features are abstract if and only if they have children. The restriction turned out to be counterintuitive to our students. The flexible distinction between abstract and concrete features in *FeatureIDE* results in a better overview which features do influence the implementation (i.e., which are not yet implemented or only used to group other features).

Product Configuration

6

Product configuration is the process to select the features that should be contained in the final product. In Chap. 5, we showed how feature models define the domain. Feature models define the features and their relationships, meaning which features are required and how features need to be selected together. We showed how *FeatureIDE* helps to design feature models using the *Feature Model Editor*.

In this chapter, we introduce how to configure products with *FeatureIDE*. In general, text files are used to store the selected features. We show how to create configurations and how configurations can be specified with the *FeatureIDE*'s *Configuration Editor*. As feature models can get complex, it also becomes difficult to define correct configurations. To help configure the program, the *Configuration Editor* is always in sync with the feature model and ensures that the configuration is valid.

We explain in detail how to create configuration in Sect. 6.1. Then, we show how *FeatureIDE* helps to edit configuration with the *Configuration Editor* in Sect. 6.2. Finally, in Sect. 6.2, we show how the deselection of features helps to define the configuration.

Instruction 6.1 (Import the Elevator-FeatureModeling-Configuration Example)

1. Open the example wizard by any of the following options:
   - Press *New* → *Example* in the context menu of the Project/Package Explorer

---

(continued)

© Springer International Publishing AG 2017
J. Meinicke et al., *Mastering Software Variability with FeatureIDE*,
DOI 10.1007/978-3-319-61443-4_6

Instruction 6.1 (continued)
  • Press *New → Examples → FeatureIDE → FeatureIDE Examples* in the
    upper-left menu toolbar of *Eclipse*
  • Press *File → New → Example* in the menu bar of *Eclipse*
2. Select *FeatureIDE Examples*
3. Press *Next*
4. Select *Book Example* tab
5. Select the project *Part II* → Chapter 6 → *Elevator-FeatureModeling-Configuration*
6. Press *Finish*

The descriptions in this chapter will be based on the elevator example. To check out the example, follow Instruction 6.1.

6.1   Creating Configurations

FeatureIDE provides mechanisms to generate a product based on a valid feature selection (cf. Chap. 3 on Page 19). This selection is handled in a configuration file (`*.config`). Thus, we first need to create a new empty configuration that we can use as a starting point. To create a new configuration, follow Instruction 6.2. The *Configuration Wizard* opens in which the name of the configuration can be defined (cf. Fig. 6.1). In the figure, the name of the corresponding project of the new configuration is already entered and the name of the configuration can directly be specified (e.g., "CustomElevator"). After finishing the *Configuration Wizard*, a new configuration file is created in the folder `config`, and the configuration is shown in the *Configuration Editor*.

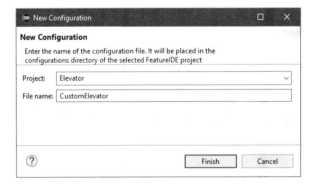

Fig. 6.1 Configuration wizard

Instruction 6.2 (Creating a New Configuration)

1. Open the *FeatureIDE* perspective if not active (cf. Instruction 3.1)
2. Open the configuration file wizard by any of the following options:
   - Press *New → Configuration File* in the context menu of the Project/ Package Explorer
   - Press *New → FeatureIDE → Configuration File* in the upper-left menu toolbar of *Eclipse*
   - Press *File → New → Configuration File* in the menu bar of *Eclipse*
3. Enter a configuration file name (e.g., CustomElevator)
4. Press *Finish*

Set Current Configuration

Instruction 6.3 (Set Current Configuration)
Set the current configuration by:

- Press *FeatureIDE → Set Configuration* in the Package/Project Explorer on the configuration that should be set as *Current Configuration*

When developing software product lines in *FeatureIDE*, a major part is to generate a product from the source code. As *FeatureIDE* is extending the existing *Eclipse* projects (e.g., Java projects), there can only be one configuration that is built at a time. This is because *FeatureIDE* reuses the existing source location to build and compile the project. However, we allow a project to contain multiple user-defined configurations. The configuration that should be used to build the project can then be defined by the user. How to select the configuration and mark it as *current configuration* is explained in Fig. 6.2. As shown in Instruction 6.3, after setting a configuration as current, a marker on the file appears (i.e., a *green pencil* indicates the current configuration).

6.2   Editing Configurations

All project-related configuration files (i.e., files with the extension `*.config`) of *FeatureIDE* are located in the directory `configs` (cf. Fig. 3.3 on Page 23). Since the default editor of a configuration file is the *Configuration Editor*, it is possible to double-click on a configuration file to open this editor.

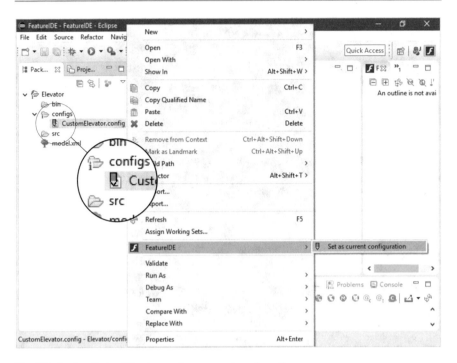

Fig. 6.2 Setting CustomElevator.config as current configuration

The *Configuration Editor* consists of three pages. At the bottom of the editor, the specific page can be selected. The first page, called *Configuration*, is the default page to select features. The second page, called *Advanced Configuration*, allows to additionally deselect features. In the last page, called *Source*, the files content is displayed. We recommend not to use this page to edit configurations as the validity of the configuration is no longer guaranteed. The *Configuration* and the *Advanced Configuration* page use a tree structure to represent the configuration. The tree is structured similar to the feature model, that is, child features of the feature model are also children in the tree representation.

At the header of the *Configuration Editor* exists a toolbar (cf. Fig. 6.3). At the left-hand side of the toolbar, the status of the current configuration is shown. The status is either *invalid* (cf. Fig. 6.3a) or *valid* (cf. Fig. 6.3b). Note that with the configuration editor, it is not possible to select invalid feature combinations (e.g., two features that exclude each other cannot be selected together). The status also shows how many configurations are possible using the current selections. However, the number might just be an estimation for larger feature models. The text field in the middle of the toolbar is a *search bar*. By typing a substring of the name, the editor scrolls to the features starting with that substring by pressing enter. With the *plus* and *minus* buttons, the tree can be expanded and collapsed, respectively. The other three buttons will be explained in detail in Sect. 7.2 on Page 77.

(a)

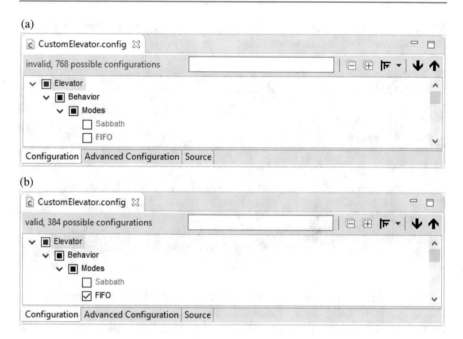

(b)

Fig. 6.3 Toolbar of the configuration editor indicating the validity of the editor and showing additional functionalities for search collapsing and resolution. (**a**) Status bar indicating an invalid configuration. (**b**) Status bar indicating a valid configuration

Table 6.1 Selection states for features in the default configuration editor page for various operating systems

	Windows 7	Windows 8	Windows 10	MacOS	Ubuntu	*FeatureIDE*
Automatically selected	■	■	■	⊖	⊖	▨
Manually selected	✓	✓	✓	✓	✓	⊞
Undefined	☐	☐	☐	☐	☐	☐
Manually deselected	n.a.	n.a.	n.a.	n.a.	n.a.	⊟
Automatically deselected	☐	☐	☐	☐	☐	▬

Five-valued selection states of the advanced configuration editor page in the most right column

Features in configurations can have different states, three for the *Configuration* page and five for the *Advanced configuration* page. The symbols for the states are shown in Table 6.1. The state *undefined* means that the feature selection is not decided yet. It can be selected or deselected. The undefined state is seen as unselected from outside (e.g., for product generation). For selection and deselection, there is a difference between *manually (de)selected* and *automatically (de)selected*. If the state is manual, the assignment can be changed by the user. However, if the state is automatic, then the state is implied by other feature selection and the feature selection state cannot be changed directly. The symbol for the automatically deselected state for the *Configuration* page is the same as for the undefined state.

However, this state is displayed with a gray font color. How to select and deselect features is described in Instruction 6.4.

Instruction 6.4 (Editing Configurations)

1. In the *Configuration* page:
   - Check an undefined box to manually select a feature
   - Uncheck a manually selected box to make the feature undefined
2. In the *Advanced Configuration* page:
   - Check an undefined or deselected feature to manually select it
   - Uncheck a manually selected feature to make it undefined
   - Right-click on an undefined or selected feature to manually deselect it
   - Right-click on a manually deselected feature to make it undefined
   - Press *Space* to switch through the three states

The *Configuration Editor* aims to prevent users from invalid feature selections and to guide to valid configurations. In Fig. 6.4a, we exemplary show a new configuration in which some features are already defined, such as Elevator, Behavior, and Modes. This is due to the fact that these features are core features (i.e., they have to be selected in all configurations).

In the next step, we select the feature ShortestPath by clicking on the corresponding check box. As a result, the features FIFO and Sabbath are grayed (i.e., these features cannot be selected anymore). Furthermore, the feature CallButtons is automatically selected as it is implied by the constraints of the feature model. The selection of the feature ShortestPath also leads to the green highlighted features DirectedCall and UndirectedCall. This green color indicates that the selection of these features leads to a valid configuration (i.e., either one of the features has to be selected). If we select one of the green highlighted features (e.g., DirectedCall), the configuration gets valid according to the feature model. As a result, the configuration is valid as indicated in the header of the editor (cf. Fig. 6.3). Finally, we can save the configuration. Afterward, the configuration is stored permanently, and we can see the result in the textual representation of *Source*.

Feature Deselection

Defining a valid configuration can be a difficult process as it may be unknown which features are required. To ease this process, an option to *deselect features* can be helpful as it might be known which features are not needed or too expensive. Thus, *FeatureIDE* also provides support for the deselection of features based on the *Advanced Configuration Page* (see Fig. 6.5a) that is available at the bottom of the editor. Instead of check boxes, the selection of features is represented by different icons (see Table 6.1). The green plus indicates a selected feature and the red minus a

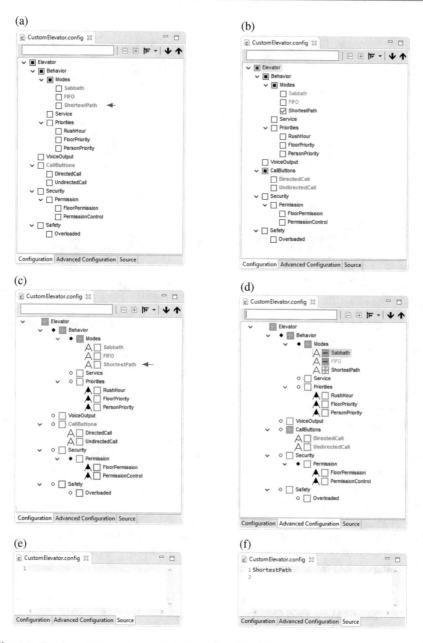

Fig. 6.4 The three pages of the configuration editor. The *left parts* represent an initial state of the configuration file. The *right parts* show the automatically updated states after selecting the ShortesPath. (**a**) Initial selection of core features in the configuration editor. (**b**) Automated selection of features and recommendation of required features. (**c**) Initial selection of core features in the advanced configuration editor. (**d**) Automated selection of features and recommendation of required features. (**e**) Initially no concrete features are contained in the sources of the configuration file. (**f**) Adding concrete features to the sources of the configuration file

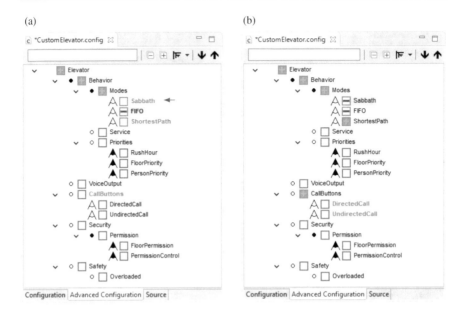

(a)   (b)

Fig. 6.5 Extended functionality of the Advanced Configuration page in the Configuration Editor. (**a**) Deselection of features with the Advanced Configuration editor page. (**b**) Automatic selections after deselection of the feature Sabbath

deselected feature. How to select and deselect feature in the *Advanced Configuration* page is explained in Instruction 6.4.

To ease the selection and to comprehend the automated selections in the *Advanced Configuration* page, the editor also shows the connection type of the features. The symbol before the selection state of the feature shows its tree constraint. Mandatory features have a filled circle, optional features have an empty circle, features in an Alternative-group have an empty arc, and features in an Or-group have a filled arc (cf. Fig. 5.7 on Page 52).

All pages of the configuration editor are synchronized. Thus, they always represent the same configuration. However, as the *Advanced Configuration* page can represent the state for manual deselection, this information might get lost when switching back to the first page of the editor.

6.3   Summary and Further Reading

In this chapter, we showed how *FeatureIDE* helps to create configurations efficiently using the *Configuration Editor*. We showed how to create new configurations and how to edit existing configurations. As the configuration editor is always in sync with the feature model of the project, the *Configuration Editor* ensures that the edited configurations are valid according to the constraints defined in the model.

In Chap. 5 on Page 43, we showed how *FeatureIDE* helps to create feature models using the *Feature Model Editor*. Both the configuration and the feature model play an essential role when developing software product lines, as we will show in Part III for conditional compilation and in Part IV for conditional compilation. The feature model defines the domain, and the configuration uses the feature model to define the actual products. In Chap. 7, we show how to trace features in larger feature models and configurations. In Chap. 8 on Page 81, we then show how *FeatureIDE* helps to further ensure the validity of configurations and how to automatically generate configurations for the quality assurance of the product line.

For a general overview on product configuration for software product lines, we refer to the book of Apel et al. (2013a) and related literature (Czarnecki et al. 2005; Mendonca and Cowan 2010; Krueger 2002; White et al. 2008).

Feature Traceability in Feature Models and Configurations

7

Feature traceability is the ability to find features. We already discussed how the *Feature Model Editor* helps to create and handle larger feature models (cf. Chap. 5 on Page 43). In Chap. 6 on Page 63, we also discussed how the *Configuration Editor* helps to efficiently configure products. However, when working with large feature models, it can be hard to identify certain features across the project, in the feature model, in configuration files, and source artifacts.

In *FeatureIDE*, we provide several mechanisms that ease tracing features. In this chapter, we discuss how feature traceability is supported during feature modeling and configuration. This support is used as a basis for feature traceability in the product-line implementations that we discuss in the subsequent chapters.

We show in detail how to trace features in the feature model in Sect. 7.1. How to trace these features also in configurations is shown in Sect. 7.2. Both sections rely on highlighting features with colors to make it easier to identify them.

7.1 Tracing Features in the Feature Model

To find a certain feature in a feature model can be hard as a feature model can become very large. To support finding a certain feature, *FeatureIDE* allows a user to simply tap the name (or any prefix thereof) and, as known from other editors, the corresponding editor scrolls to the feature and automatically selects it.

When focusing on a certain feature, the question arises as to which features are affected by the current feature. To this end, the feature model editor highlights all cross-tree constraints where the current feature is involved. For instance, in Fig. 7.1, we focus on the feature DirectedCall of our elevator example, and the constraint DirectedCall $\Rightarrow$ ShortestPath is highlighted. Vice versa it is helpful to know the impact of a *cross-tree constraint*. Thus, we similarly highlight all features that

© Springer International Publishing AG 2017
J. Meinicke et al., *Mastering Software Variability with FeatureIDE*,
DOI 10.1007/978-3-319-61443-4_7

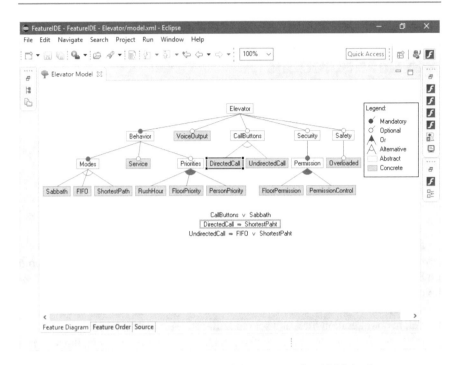

Fig. 7.1 Focused feature `DirectedCall` and the corresponding highlighted cross-tree constraint

are included in the selected constraint. For instance, if we focus on the constraint `DirectedCall` $\Rightarrow$ `ShortestPath`, the features `DirectedCall` and `ShortestPath` are highlighted with a thick borderline.

Colors are shown to be helpful to understand and identify features [e.g., to identify preprocessor code (Feigenspan et al. 2013; Kästner and Apel 2009)]. To identify features in the feature model, we allow to mark certain features with colors. However, the idea in *FeatureIDE* is to color *all* occurrences of the feature. Thus, the colors are also applied to further views, editors, and the source code. Initially, a new *color scheme* has to be created. *FeatureIDE* allows to create multiple schemes, so the current scheme can be switched to focus on different features as we show in the preceding chapters. To create and enable a new color scheme, we can use the context menu of a *FeatureIDE*'s project (cf. Fig. 7.2). Using Instruction 7.1, a color scheme will be created and automatically activated. To deactivate the color scheme later, deselect the scheme using same menu of Fig. 7.2.

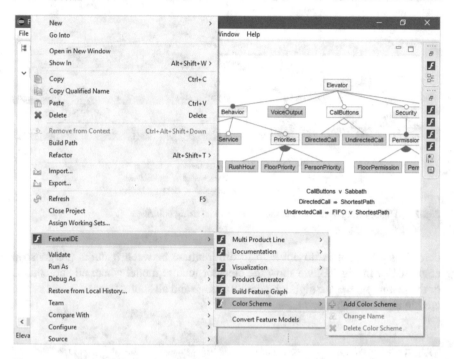

Fig. 7.2 Color scheme menu for a specific *FeatureIDE* project

Instruction 7.1 (Create a New Color Scheme)

1. Open the new color scheme dialog by:
   • Press *FeatureIDE* → *Color Cheme* → *Add Color Scheme* in the context menu of the Project/Package Explorer
2. Enter a color scheme name
3. Press *Finish*

After the color scheme is activated, colors can be assigned to features using the *Feature Model Editor*. To assign a color, follow Instruction 7.2.[1] The dialog allows to specify a strategy in which multiple features can be highlighted at once. For example, it is possible to choose a strategy that selects also all children of the selected feature. To specify the feature color, we allow only ten, but distinctive

---

[1]Note that the colors from analyses will override assigned colors (cf. Chap. 8 on Page 81).

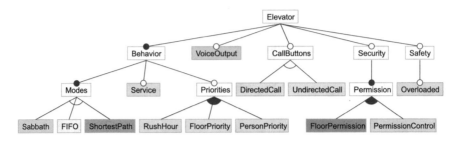

CallButtons ∨ Sabbath
DirectedCall ⇒ ShortestPaht
UndirectedCall ⇒ FIFO ∨ ShortestPaht

Fig. 7.3 Highlighting of features in the feature model using colors

colors, as more colors do not help to differentiate between features (Feigenspan et al. 2013). In Fig. 7.3, we show the elevator feature model where all subfeatures of the feature `Modes` are highlighted with orange and all subfeatures of `Permission` are highlighted with red.

Instruction 7.2 (Set a New Feature Color)

1. Select a feature in the feature diagram
2. Open the set feature color dialog by:
   • Press *Feature Color* in the context menu of the selected feature
3. If there is no color scheme selected, create or select a color scheme in the dialog and press *Finish*
4. Choose whether subfeatures should be colored
5. Select a desired color
6. Press *Finish*

As an alternative view on the feature model, we provide a *Feature Model Outline*. The outline shows the feature model as a simple tree view as shown in Fig. 7.4. The outline view provides the same functionalities as the *Feature Model Editor* using the context menu by right-clicking on an entry. For example, group types can be changed or features can be added. Additionally, subtrees can be hidden so that only parts of the tree are visible at once. For instance, besides the feature `Behavior`, we collapsed all features from the second level of the tree. Furthermore, as shown in Fig. 7.4, the colors are applied to the outline view as well.

Fig. 7.4 Outline view of the
feature model

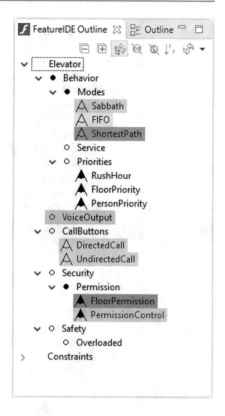

7.2   Tracing Features in Configurations

Configuring a product is often hard as it can be a challenge to find the desired
features. Therefore, *FeatureIDE* provides basic support to search a feature in
the configuration editor. Furthermore, we also present advanced techniques of
FeatureIDE to find a desired feature to achieve a valid product.

To support the traceability of features, the configurations represented in the
Configuration Editor are also arranged according to the tree structure of the feature
model. In addition, *FeatureIDE* allows the user to search for features using the
search bar, which is especially important for huge feature models. In Fig. 7.5,
we illustrate the application of the *search bar* that is depicted on the top of the
editor. When typing a substring of the feature's name, the editor jumps to the
features containing the entry. Therefore, it doesn't matter whether the feature is
currently visible to the user as the tree will be automatically expanded. For instance,
when typing "Saf" in the search bar, the feature Safety is selected (cf. Fig. 7.5).
Furthermore, it is also possible to benefit from the assignment of colors in the feature
model editor. In detail, the assigned colors are also applied to the configuration
editor and help the user to find the features of interest easier (cf. Fig. 7.5).

Fig. 7.5 Support for feature traceability in the configuration editor

Besides the basic support for feature traceability, *FeatureIDE* also provides techniques to trace open decisions for feature selections. With the knowledge about open decisions, we can focus on the features that need to be selected or deselected to achieve a valid configuration that fulfills all dependencies of the feature model. For instance, we assume that the feature CallButtons is selected (cf. Fig. 7.6). Using Instruction 7.3, we can search for an open configuration decision. As a result, we can see that the feature CallButtons is highlighted with a blue foreground whereas the features DirectedCall and UndirectedCall are highlighted with green. To close the decision, we can select one of the green or deselect the blue feature. Here, we decide to select the green feature UndirectedCall. The result of this decision is depicted on the left side of Fig. 7.7. As the configuration is still invalid, we search for the next open decision using Instruction 7.3. The configuration editor will highlight the features FIFO and ShortestPath with green (cf. right side of Fig. 7.7). If we select one of these features, we achieve a valid product configuration.

Fig. 7.6 Trace open decisions in a configuration. Deselect *blue* features or select a *green* feature to close the decision

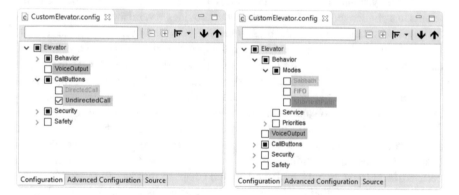

Fig. 7.7 Further open decisions to achieve a valid configuration

---

Instruction 7.3 (Trace and Close *Open Configuration Decisions*)

1. Switch to the next open decision by any of the following options:
   - Press ↑ in the upper-right menu toolbar of the configuration editor
   - Press ↓ in the upper-right menu toolbar of the configuration editor
2. Close the decision by any of the following options:
   - Select a green highlighted feature
   - Deselect a blue highlighted feature

To ease the finding of open decisions, it is also possible to set up the configuration editor so that the next open clause is automatically presented after the current decision is closed. In detail, the configuration editor expands only a path of a tree if there is a specific subfeature for which we need a decision. Therefore, *FeatureIDE* provides an automatic expansion mechanism. To select the expansion mechanism *Show Next Open Clause*, we use the description of Instruction 7.4.

Instruction 7.4 (Select an Automatic Expansion Mechanism)

1. Open the mechanism options menu by:
   • Press ⊩ in the upper-right menu toolbar of the configuration editor
2. Select the desired mechanism.

7.3   Summary and Further Reading

As variable systems can consist of thousands of features, finding the desired features results in a challenge. Therefore, *FeatureIDE* provides several mechanisms to trace a feature in an efficient way. In detail, *FeatureIDE* provides mechanisms to efficiently search, focus, or highlight features in the feature model editor, *FeatureIDE* views, and in the configuration editor. One of these powerful options is the assignment of colors to features that can be used to recognize the feature in all parts of *FeatureIDE*.

Similar to the mechanisms to colorize the *FeatureIDE*'s modeling and configuration, *FeatureIDE* also supports colors in other parts of the development cycle. In detail, Part III presents how to use conditional compilation with *FeatureIDE* and Part IV introduces feature-oriented programming. In these parts, we also present a chapter about feature traceability that also reuses the color mechanism to highlight code artifacts (see Chap. 11 on Page 123 and Chap. 15 on Page 173). However, the chapters introduce further mechanisms such as content assist and further outlines.

Feature traceability is an important topic of variable systems. In particular, the usage of colors to trace features is well studied. For instance, Feigenspan et al. as well as Kästner and Apel have shown that background colors can help the developer to identify features (Feigenspan et al. 2013; Kästner and Apel 2009). However, it is also known that the concept of colors does not scale for more than ten colors as it is not possible to distinguish them (Feigenspan et al. 2013). Furthermore, we presented a tool demo, in which we describe how to trace open decisions of product configurations (Pereira et al. 2016). Besides these mechanisms, we describe further techniques to scale the product configuration in *FeatureIDE*.

Quality Assurance for Feature Models and Configurations

8

Feature modeling and product configuration are central parts of software product-line development. They define the domain and which features are contained in the final products. With the feature model editor, *FeatureIDE* supports creating and editing feature models and the dependencies among features (cf. Chap. 5 on Page 43). The configuration editor helps to select the features as desired (cf. Chap. 6 on Page 63). Finally, *FeatureIDE* also helps to trace features in the feature model and in configurations (cf. Chap. 7 on Page 73).

Feature modeling and product configuration, however, are manual and thus error-prone tasks. Thus, the design of a feature model comes with several pitfalls for validity. It is necessary to support the user during the creation as much as possible. A qualitative feature model is even important as it affects all other parts, such as product configuration and generation. Therefore, this chapter gives an overview on *FeatureIDE*'s support to assure the quality of feature models and configurations.

We show in detail how to detect errors using the feature model editor in Sect. 8.1. In Sect. 8.2, we show how to get statistics on the feature model using *FeatureIDE*'s statistics view. Furthermore, we give some insights into the quality assurance of configurations in Sect. 8.3 and the fundamentals to also assure the quality of resulting products in Sect. 8.4. To exercise the content of this chapter, we recommend to check out the example project as explained in Instruction 8.1.

8.1 Quality Assurance for Feature Models Using the Editor

The hierarchical structure of feature models and the available graphical notations are the main reasons for the wide adoption of feature models. However, the tree-like structure is often not enough to express all meaningful dependencies between features. In the previous chapter, we discussed the notion of *cross-tree constraints* which increase the expressive power of feature models to that of propositional logic. The downside of allowing cross-tree constraints is inherited from propositional logic; feature models with cross-tree constraints can easily contain inconsistencies.

© Springer International Publishing AG 2017
J. Meinicke et al., *Mastering Software Variability with FeatureIDE*,
DOI 10.1007/978-3-319-61443-4_8

Instruction 8.1 (Import the Elevator-Antenna-v1.0 Example)

1. Open the example wizard by any of the following options:
   - Press *New → Example* in the context menu of the Project/Package Explorer
   - Press *New → Examples → FeatureIDE → FeatureIDE Examples* in the upper-left menu toolbar of *Eclipse*
   - Press *File → New → Example* in the menu bar of *Eclipse*
2. Select *FeatureIDE Examples*
3. Press *Next*
4. Select *Book Example* tab
5. Select the project *Part II → Chapter 8 → Elevator-Antenna-v1.0*
6. Press *Finish*

A prominent example of an inconsistency is a contradicting cross-tree constraint, which has the result that the feature model does not allow a single valid feature combination [i.e., the feature model is called *void* (Kang et al. 1990)].

We give an overview on the most important analyses to uncover *inconsistencies* in feature models using *FeatureIDE*. Tool support for inconsistency detection is inevitable, as feature models for industrial applications do often contain hundreds or even thousands of features. Our experience with feature modeling shows that debugging such feature models is tedious and error prone. Each of the following analyses is supposed to detect inconsistencies or at least smells in feature models. We show how to apply the analyses to feature models in *FeatureIDE* and how a user can get attention of these inconsistencies and smells.

Detecting Void Feature Models

In Fig. 8.1, we slightly changed the previous feature model of the elevator to demonstrate a particular inconsistency. The reader may want to exercise the manual detection of the inconsistency by means of visual acuity. Even in this tiny feature model with 21 features and only five constraints, it may take some time to find the cause of the inconsistency. Even worse, it is typically not known whether there are inconsistencies or not. Hence, a human typically faces a problem when the modeling is finished and the configuration does not allow to create a desired feature combination.

The good news is that the inconsistency that we introduced into the feature model can easily be detected within *FeatureIDE*. To benefit from this FeatureIDE's functionality, it is necessary to activate the automated feature-model analyses (cf. Fig. 8.2). In this example, we deactivated the analysis for the purpose of illustration. However, the feature model in Fig. 8.1 does not describe a single valid configuration.

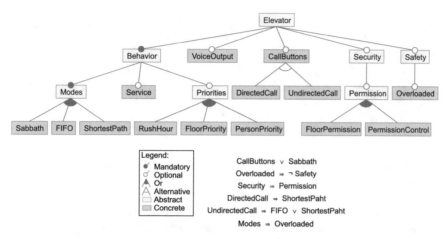

Fig. 8.1 The elevator feature model with an unnoticed, serious inconsistency

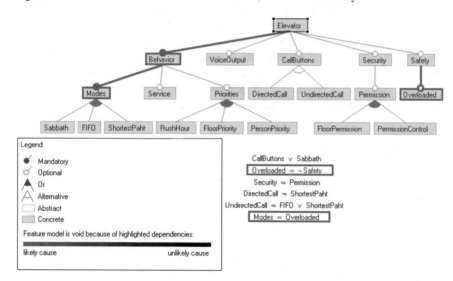

Fig. 8.2 The elevator feature model is *void* due to several cross-tree constraints

That is, opening a *Configuration Editor*, we were not able to derive a valid configuration for any choice of the selected features. That is why the feature model is called *void*. The reason for the inconsistency in this case is the last rather artificial constraint stating that we have two buttons to call the elevator at each floor (i.e., feature DirectedCall) and only one button independent of the direction (i.e., feature UndirectedCall). This constraint leads to an inconsistency as both features are modeled as alternative features in the hierarchy (i.e., at most one of them can be selected).

> **Instruction 8.2 (Activation and Deactivation of Analyses)**
>
> 1. Open the calculation submenu of the feature diagram by:
>   • Press *Set Calculations* in the context menu of any feature diagram
>   element except the constraints and legend
> 2. Select the desired calculation option

The inconsistency illustrated above is a rather trivial example. In practice, it frequently happens that several cross-tree constraints interact with each other, resulting in a *void* feature model. We give a slightly more complex interaction of cross-tree constraints in Fig. 8.2. In this diagram, *FeatureIDE* points us to the misleading cross-tree constraints. In detail, the second constraint is a contradiction to the tree structure (i.e., the feature Overloaded is dead; see the next section) and the last constraint increases the impact of this contradiction so that it affects the complete feature model. Whenever selecting the feature FIFO, ShortestPath, Service, or Sabbath, the feature Overloaded needs to be selected, too. However, it is not possible to select the feature Overloaded as it is a dead feature (see the next section for more details). Therefore, the feature model does not represent a product and, thus, the feature model is void. Removing one of the cross-tree constraints would turn the feature model into a non-void feature model.

Detecting Dead Features

A *void* feature model means that we can try out all feature combinations during configuration, but none of them is valid. A slightly different inconsistency is that when selecting a specific feature, there is no combination of other features leading to a valid configuration. Such a feature is therefore called *dead feature*, as it is not part of any valid configuration. The problem with *dead features* is that we may spend effort into a feature during all phases of the product line's life cycle, but in the end the effort is useless as it can never be selected (Kang et al. 1990).

Similar to a *void* feature model, a *dead feature* can be introduced with cross-tree constraints. In Fig. 8.3, we removed the last constraint of the void feature model presented in Fig. 8.2, which leads to a feature model that is non-void. As the characteristic of a void feature model cannot prohibit other feature-model analyses for this example anymore, *FeatureIDE* can now start to analyze the feature model in detail. Interestingly, the feature named Overloaded becomes a *dead feature* due to this change. The reason is an interaction with the second constraint and the tree structure. The selection of the feature Overloaded implies the selection of the feature Safety due to the *parent-child relationship* in the feature diagram and the second constraint does not allow to select the feature Safety at the same time. Thus, that these two features are selected at the same time conflicts with the constraint Overloaded $\Rightarrow \neg$ Safety. As a consequence, we only get invalid configurations

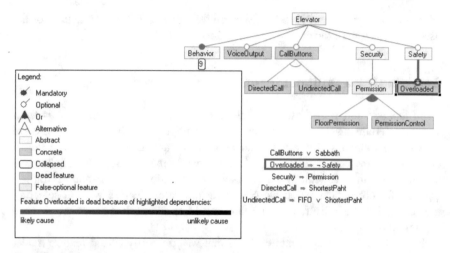

Fig. 8.3 Feature Overloaded is dead due to the second constraint

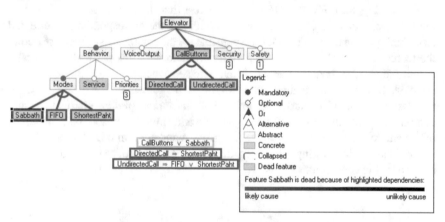

Fig. 8.4 Feature Sabbath is dead due to an incorrect mandatory relationship

whenever the feature Overloaded is selected, which is therefore called dead. Depending on the domain, a *dead feature* indicates that the diagram or cross-tree constraint must be corrected or that a feature is not needed and should be removed.

In our first example of a dead feature, we can remove the relevant constraint to allow configurations in which this feature is also available. By contrast, in Fig. 8.4, we present our elevator example in which all cross-tree constraints are identical to our final and correct version. However, the dead feature Sabbath is a result of an unintended structural change. *FeatureIDE* highlights the responsible constraint and presents further hints in constraint's tooltips to identify the primary reason for this dead feature. We identified the error in the mandatory relationship of the feature CallButtons. In detail, with a mandatory feature, CallButton, it is not possible to create an elevator without buttons, and, thus, the mode Sabbath is not possible.

With this example, we want to sensitize the reader to examine the intention of the used tree structure or the cross-tree constraint.

Detecting False-Optional Features

Dead features and *void* feature models are inconsistencies that prevent us from selecting certain or even all features during configuration. In contrast, there are other inconsistencies that are not so severe, but are at least smelly. A *false-optional feature*, for instance, is a feature that is marked as optional, but due to the constraints, it actually has a mandatory relation to its parent. While an optional feature indicates that we can select the parent feature without selecting the optional feature itself, one or more cross-tree constraints may forbid those configurations.

In Fig. 8.3, we use our feature model that was primarily a void feature model presented in Fig. 8.2. Since we removed the constraints that lead to a void feature model (cf. Fig. 8.2), *FeatureIDE* can also detect that the feature Permission is a false-optional feature. Thus, *FeatureIDE* highlights the corresponding feature and also highlights the constraint that is responsible for this characteristic when selecting the feature Permission (cf. Fig. 8.5). The problem with this particular constraint is that the feature Permission is always selected when the feature Security is selected. But then, the feature Permission is no longer optional and de facto mandatory although it is marked as optional. *False-optional features* indicate feature combinations which are actually not available and should therefore be avoided. In this example, we make the feature Permission mandatory. In this case, the change is considered a refactoring. However, in theory, it is also possible to remove the corresponding constraint.

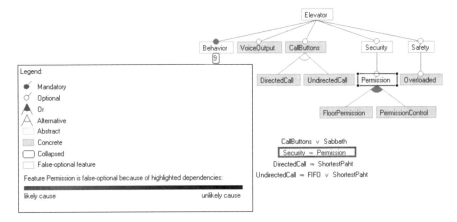

Fig. 8.5 Feature Permission is false optional due to the highlighted constraints

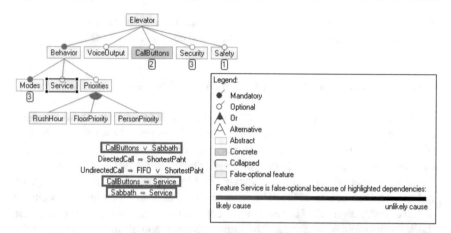

Fig. 8.6 Feature Service is *false optional* because of the last constraints

In Fig. 8.6, we present a more complex example of a false-optional feature. For the purpose of illustration, we added two constraints to our final elevator feature model (cf. Fig. 5.7 on Page 52). In detail, we add the constraint CallButtons⇒Service to ensure a service behavior if buttons exist and Sabbath⇒Service so that it is possible to stop the elevator for maintenance. However, both constraints lead to a false-optional feature, Service. The reason is that call buttons are only not available if the sabbath mode is selected. Therefore, the constraints also implement that in the cases of elevators with and without buttons, the service mode needs to be selected. By contrast to our first example, this inconsistency is the result of multiple constraints and, thus, not easy to detect without tool support. Again, *FeatureIDE* highlights the false-optional feature and also highlights the constraints that are responsible for this characteristic if the false-optional feature is selected.

Detecting Redundant Cross-Tree Constraints

Another smell in feature diagrams is caused by cross-tree constraints that have no influence on the valid combinations. Such a situation can happen if the constraint is entailed in the tree structure already or in any combination with other cross-tree constraints. That is, removing such a constraint does not change the valid feature combinations, which is therefore called *redundant constraint*. Redundant constraints make the feature model unnecessarily complex and can be removed in favor of brevity.

In our running example, we added the constraint FIFO ∨ ShortestPath ⇒ CallButtons as shown in Fig. 8.7. Even if it is not obvious, this new constraint is redundant to the constraint CallButtons ∨ Sabbath. Thus, *FeatureIDE* highlights the constraint and presents a tooltip to inform the user about possible reasons.

Removing a *redundant constraint* from a feature model is always a refactoring of the feature model, as it does not change the valid combinations of features.

Activating and Deactivating Automated Analyses

Although *FeatureIDE* applies state-of-the-art technology to detect these inconsistencies, they may take several seconds or minutes. Especially for feature models with more than 1000 features, we recommend to run these checks on demand and not after every change in the feature diagram. The default is that *FeatureIDE* checks for all these inconsistencies automatically. In Fig. 8.8, we show the context menu that can be used to turn off certain or all analyses depending on the user's choice (see also Instruction 8.2). However, not every analysis requires the same effort. The check for features is the fastest. The largest computation effort is required for the detection of redundant constraint.

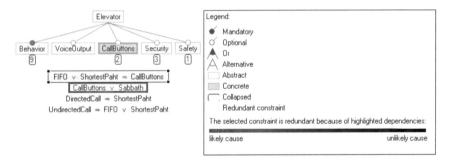

Fig. 8.7 The first cross-tree constraint is redundant to the second constraint

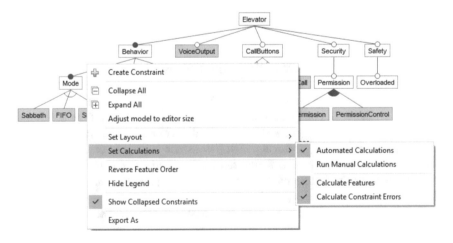

Fig. 8.8 Each feature-model analysis can be turned on automatically and be run on demand

8.2   Quality Assurance Based on FeatureIDE's Statistics View

Statistics often help to understand and to report variability. In *FeatureIDE*, we provide the view *FeatureIDE Statistics* that gives information about the variability (cf. Fig. 8.9). The view shows statistics about the current project. These are statistics on the feature model and statistics on the implementation, which we will explain in the subsequent chapters.

In this section, we investigate the statistics of the feature model. It contains several important information on the variability (see Fig. 8.9 that represents the statistics of Fig. 8.6), such as the number of concrete and abstract features. Furthermore, the feature model statistic also presents an overview on all results of feature-model analyses (e.g., dead features and false-optional features). Using the expansion mechanism, we present more details about the corresponding statistical value. For instance, if we expand the value *Number of false-optional features: <x>* (cf. Fig. 8.9), *FeatureIDE* shows all false-optional features of the current project. Furthermore, all statistics can be exported to a csv file using the export button on the top-right corner (see Instruction 8.3).

Besides the already presented analysis results of feature models, the view also presents further statistics that we cannot visualize in the *Feature Model Editor*. In

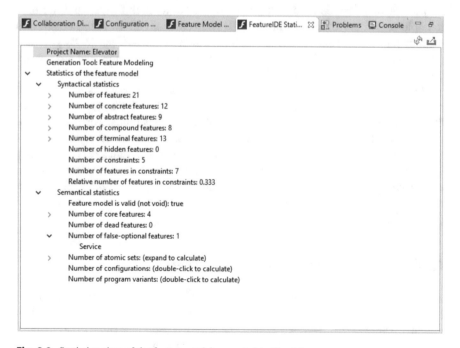

Fig. 8.9   Statistics view of the feature model presented in Fig. 8.6

the following, we will give a detailed overview on all statistics of *FeatureIDE* for feature models.

Instruction 8.3 (Export Statistics)

1. Open the export dialog by:
   - Press the button with the tooltip *Export to* *.*csv* in the upper-right menu toolbar of the *FeatureIDE* statistics view
2. Select the statistics which will be exported
3. Press *OK*

Feature Statistics About Direct Visible Aspects

The entry *Feature Statistics* includes all statistical values for features and the constraints between them. In detail, the entry presents statistics about the number of concrete and abstract features that we already introduced in previous parts of this book. Thus, *concrete features* are features with implementation artifacts, whereas *abstract features* can be used to structure the tree or to mark features that we plan to implement in the future (Thüm et al. 2011). In addition, the view also determines the number of *compound features*, which have at least one subfeature. By contrast, the number of *terminal features* represents the number of features that are located on the leaf nodes of the feature model tree.

Besides the statistics about features, *FeatureIDE* also provides statistics for constraints. In detail, *FeatureIDE* determines the number of constraints as well as the number of features that are involved in all these constraints. For instance, the feature model of Fig. 8.6 includes five constraints, whereas only seven different features are involved in these constraints. In addition, the value *relative number of features in constraints* determines the relation between features that are involved and features that are not involved in constraints. Therefore, *FeatureIDE* uses the number of all features to determine the relation and results for our example in 0.33 (cf. Fig. 8.9).

Feature Model Statistics About Analysis Results

As mentioned above, the view *FeatureIDE Statistics* also presents the results of the already introduced feature-model analyses of void feature models, dead and false-optional features. However, we cannot visualize the results of some other feature-model analyses and, thus, we present their results only in the statistics view. In detail, *FeatureIDE* also provides statistics about *core features*, *atomic sets*, and the *number of configurations* as well as the *number of program variants*.

The results of the analysis *core features* are one of the entries that are only available in the statistics view. In detail, core features are features that are included in all products of the product line (Trinidad and Ruiz-Cortés 2009). In our example of Fig. 8.6, the analysis results in four core features: `Behavior`, `Elevator`, `Modes`, and `Service`.

In general, an *atomic set* is a set of features in which all these features are completely included or completely absent in all products of the product line (Schröter et al. 2016). Therefore, the features can be considered as a unit and, thus, it is possible to replace all these features by a single feature. As this is not always possible because of the different position in the tree structure, the analysis of atomic sets often only considers mandatory features with their parent feature (Benavides et al. 2010; Zhang et al. 2004). By contrast, in a logical representation of feature models, we can profit by the more general description to improve the performance of all other feature-model analyses using a reduced size of features. Therefore, *FeatureIDE* determines all atomic sets based on the more general description and presents the results in the statistics view. For instance, using the feature model of Fig. 8.6, *FeatureIDE* determines all atomic sets with more than one feature. The result is a one set in which the features `Permission` and `Security` are included. A second set includes the features `Behavior`, `Elevator`, `Modes`, and `Service`, which at the same time represent the core features of the feature model.

Furthermore, the *FeatureIDE Statistics* view allows to calculate the number of configurations and program variants (Thüm et al. 2011). Whereas the *number of configurations* considers all features for the calculation of the number of products, the *number of program variants* only considers concrete features. Thus, the latter value is important if a user wants to know the number of products with different implementations of a product line.

8.3 Quality Assurance for Configurations

Besides the necessity to ensure the quality of feature models, it is also important that a user can rely on the correctness of configurations. Therefore, we present some insights to *FeatureIDE*'s facilities to ensure the quality of configurations.

FeatureIDE aims to keep the consistency of configurations to the feature model even if the feature model is changed. When saving the feature model, configurations are updated to a certain extent even if it is currently opened in an editor. For example, features are renamed accordingly, core and implied features are selected automatically, and the order is adjusted. However, the changes on the feature model may cause inconsistencies that cannot be solved automatically (e.g., if two selected features become alternative). Also the tree view of the open configuration editor is updated automatically if the feature model changes.

Furthermore, *FeatureIDE* provides further analyses outside of the *Configuration Editor* to present additional information to the configurations. If a configuration is *invalid* (e.g., because the feature model has changed), *FeatureIDE* shows this defect with an error marker at the corresponding configurations (represented in the *Package*

Explorer). Furthermore, *FeatureIDE* shows warnings on the usage of features at the configurations folder. We have two types of warnings on feature usage. The first type indicates whether a feature is never used in any configuration, but it is not dead. That means that there are implementations of the feature that are never actually used. The second type indicates whether a feature is used in all configurations, but it is not a core feature. This warning indicates that a feature is always used, which indicates an inconsistency of the feature model and its specification.

8.4   Quality Assurance by an Automatic Generation of Configurations

FeatureIDE provides several options to *automatically derive configurations* from the feature model. This functionality is useful for diverse reasons, such as *testing*, *static analysis*, and *export* of configured products. To automatically derive configurations and products, it is possible to use *FeatureIDE*'s product generator as explained in Instruction 8.4. In this section, we introduce the generation mechanism of configurations and describe the relevance on the product line implementation in Sect. 12.2 on Page 135 and Sect. 16.2 on Page 186.

Instruction 8.4 (Automatically Derive Configurations)

1. Open the build products dialog by:
   - Press *FeatureIDE* → *Product Generator* in the context menu of the Project/Package Explorer
2. Select a generation strategy (e.g., *All valid configurations*)
3. Optionally check *Run JUnit tests*
4. Press *Finish*

The dialog in Fig. 8.10 provides several ways to generate the products. The generation *strategy* defines what configurations are generated. For the generation, we can select *all valid configurations*, *all current configurations* (i.e., all configurations that are contained in the `config` folder), and *T-wise* configurations (i.e., to cover all interactions with a degree of T). If the *FeatureIDE* project is a modeling project, then the product generator creates configurations only; else the actual products with source code are generated (see Chaps. 12 and 16 for more details).

In the second drop-down box, we can define the tool used to generate T-wise configurations. *FeatureIDE* currently provides the algorithms *ICPL* (Johansen et al. 2011), *Chvatal* (Chvatal 1979), *CASA* (Garvin et al. 2011), and *IncLing* (Al-Hajjaji et al. 2016a). Furthermore, it is possible to *order configurations* in the third drop-down box to detect defects earlier. *Default* generates the products in the given order of the sampling tool. *Difference* compares the configurations and reorders them

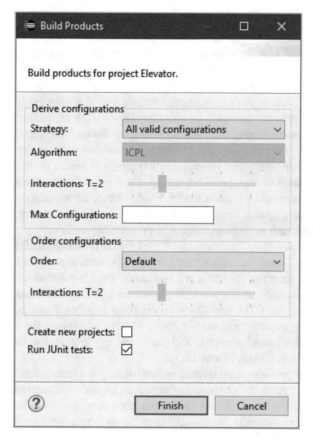

Fig. 8.10 Dialog to automatically generate configurations and according products based on a feature model

to cover more different configurations early (Al-Hajjaji et al. 2016c). *Interactions* counts the covered interactions of the configurations and reorders them to cover more interactions early and may also reduce the number of required configurations. With the bar below the degree of interactions can be defined that is used for the sampling algorithms. The maximum value changes according to the maximum T that the selected algorithm can generate ranging from 2 for IncLing and 3 for ICPL to 6 for CASA. With the check box *Create new projects*, we can define whether the generation result of the projects should be integrated into a folder inside of the FeatureIDE project (enables analyses) or exported as stand-alone products based on separate *Eclipse* projects. Furthermore, we can choose the additional option *Run JUnit tests* that is relevant for the quality assurance of product-line implementations. Therefore, we will focus this aspect in Chaps. 12 and 16.

8.5   Summary and Further Reading

As it is a hard task to create an errorless feature model that represents the desired products, *FeatureIDE* provides several mechanisms to support the creation process. In detail, *FeatureIDE* provides multiple feature-model analyses for the *Feature Model Editor* that can check the feature model during the creation process and highlight existing problem. In addition, *FeatureIDE* summarizes the analysis results and presents further statistics regarding the feature model in the *FeatureIDE Statistics* view. This can help the developer to examine whether the feature model satisfies their needs. Besides *FeatureIDE*'s facilities to ensure the quality of feature models, *FeatureIDE* also provides mechanisms to guarantee configurations that conform to the project's feature model. Furthermore, we introduced *FeatureIDE*'s mechanisms to generate configurations that can be used to ensure the quality of further aspects such as implementation of product lines.

A correct and desired feature model is the base for all subsequent steps to develop a product line. Therefore, the chapter introduced several aspects that we pick up in the remaining chapters. In detail, we introduced the view *FeatureIDE*'s *Statistics*, in which we focused on the modeling statistics of the product line. By contrast, in Chap. 12 on Page 131 and Chap. 16 on Page 183, we focus on the statistics of product-line implementation. Similarly, we also introduced the mechanism for the generation of configurations and focus on the impact for the product-line implementation in Chaps. 12 and 16.

FeatureIDE provides several mechanisms to analyze a feature model and, thus, to ensure a correct product-line modeling. However, a lot of additional analyses for feature models exist. Benavides et al. (2010) present a survey on the existing automated analyses of feature models. *FeatureIDE* implements the most common of them, such as a void feature model (Batory 2005; Kang et al. 1990), core features (Trinidad and Ruiz-Cortés 2009), dead features (Kang et al. 1990), false-optional features, atomic sets (Benavides et al. 2010; Zhang et al. 2004; Schröter et al. 2016), and number of products (Thüm et al. 2011). Furthermore, we also presented some integration of other tools that allow *FeatureIDE* to generate configurations T-wise or to order them. In detail, *FeatureIDE* includes the algorithms ICPL (Johansen et al. 2011), Chavatal (Chvatal 1979), CASA (Garvin et al. 2011), and IncLing (Al-Hajjaji et al. 2016a) for the T-wise generation. In addition, *FeatureIDE* also provides an algorithm to reorder configurations so that it covers more different configurations first (Al-Hajjaji et al. 2016c).

Part III
Tool Support for Conditional Compilation

Conditional Compilation with FeatureIDE

9

Implementing configurable software is a difficult task, especially if the implementation is not coupled with a representation of the domain. To solve these difficulties, we provide an integrated process in *FeatureIDE*. The process incorporates feature modeling, configuration, implementation, generation, and execution. In Part II, we discussed how *FeatureIDE* helps with feature modeling and product configuration. These mechanisms will also be used when actually implementing the source code in the form of conditional compilation as discussed in this part.

Conditional compilation is one of the most important and popular techniques to implement variable systems. Using *preprocessors*, code can be annotated with directives to include or exclude statements depending on feature selections. That way, products can be customized to the needs of a customer. Due to this mark-and-exclude principle, preprocessors are simple to use, easy to understand, and enable a fine-grained way to implement variability. Therefore, preprocessors gained popularity and are used in large highly-configurable systems, such as Linux.

In this chapter, we give a brief introduction to conditional compilation and introduce the main concepts of the integrated preprocessors *Antenna* and *Munge*. In detail, we give a short introduction to the concept of conditional compilation in Sect. 9.1. We introduce the general usage of the integrated preprocessors *Munge* and *Antenna* in Sects. 9.2 and 9.3, respectively. More details on how to use preprocessors in *FeatureIDE* are given in Chap. 10 on Page 105. How to trace features is explained in Chap. 11 on Page 123, and how *FeatureIDE* helps with quality assurance is discussed in Chap. 12 on Page 131.

9.1 Introduction to Conditional Compilation

We use a small configurable program to explain the basic functionalities of preprocessors. In Listing 9.1, we present a *Hello World* application that uses *preprocessor annotations* for customization. With the annotation #define (C style), we define the four features and their selections, namely, Hello, World, Beautiful,

© Springer International Publishing AG 2017
J. Meinicke et al., *Mastering Software Variability with FeatureIDE*,
DOI 10.1007/978-3-319-61443-4_9

Listing 9.1 *Hello World* product line using the C preprocessor

```
 1 #include <iostream>
 2
 3 #define Hello true
 4 #define Beautiful true
 5 #define Wonderful false
 6 #define World true
 7
 8 int main() {
 9    ::std::cout
10    #if Hello
11       << "Hello "
12    #endif
13    #if Beautiful
14       << "beautiful "
15    #endif
16    #if Wonderful
17       << "wonderful ";
18    #endif
19    #if World
20       << "world!"
21    #endif
22       << std::endl;
23 }
```

and `Wonderful` (Lines 3–5). We can use these definitions to include and exclude code artifacts using so-called ifdef blocks (i.e., an `#if` followed by a corresponding `#endif`). For instance, the preprocessor checks for the annotation `#if Hello` (Line 10) whether the feature `Hello` is defined and selected (i.e., true). As the value of `Hello` is assigned to `true`, the preprocessor includes Line 11 in the product. Similarly, the preprocessor checks the assignments for the other annotations and includes, respectively excludes, their annotated code. The preprocessor excludes the lines for features that are not selected, resulting in the source code shown in Listing 9.2, as the feature `Wonderful` is deactivated (i.e., false). Afterward, the generated source code for the configuration can be compiled that gives the program output *"Hello beautiful world!"*

Listing 9.2 Resulting program code after preprocessing the *Hello World* product line

```
1  int main() {
2    ::std::cout
3       << "Hello "
4       << "Beautiful "
5       << "World!"
6       << std::endl;
7  }
```

Considering our small *Hello World* example, some disadvantages of preprocessors can be observed. First, not all feature combinations are useful, which,
however, does not hinder the developer from defining an invalid feature combination
(e.g., the selection of mutually exclusive features is possible). The current program
allows us to create arbitrary feature combination, such as a configuration consisting
of no feature. Second, preprocessor annotations may have a negative impact on
the code structure and understandability. For preprocessor annotated code, it is
often not possible to perceive all combinations of annotated code fragments which
can result in program faults. For example, including Line 17 by selecting the
feature Wonderful results in a compiler error due to the additional semicolon. To
counteract the challenges of preprocessors and to ease their usage, *FeatureIDE*
provides a general concept to embed preprocessors in the development environment.
Among others, *FeatureIDE* helps to avoid invalid feature combinations using feature
models, eases to understand and trace the feature's implementations, and provides
analyses of the product line. In the following, we illustrate *FeatureIDE*'s concepts
using the Java preprocessors *Munge* and *Antenna*.

9.2   Preprocessor Munge

In this section, we give a first introduction to conditional compilation using the
preprocessor *Munge* and its integration into *FeatureIDE*. First, we give a brief
overview of the *Munge* preprocessor. Second, we introduce the details of *Munge*
projects in *FeatureIDE*.

Munge Overview

Munge is a purposely simple Java preprocessor.[1] The preprocessor uses the source
files and a list of selected features as input. Based on the given features, Munge
generates new source files which only contain the active lines. To annotate the
source code, *Munge* uses C-style comments (i.e., // and /* */) with the directives

---

[1] https://github.com/sonatype/munge-maven-plugin.

```
 1  public class Main {                         public class Main {
 2    public static void main(String[]            public static void main(String[]
           args) {                                       args) {
 3      /*if[Hello]*/
 4      System.out.print("Hello");                  System.out.print("Hello");
 5      /*end[Hello]*/
 6      /*if[Beautiful]*/
 7      System.out.print(" beautiful");             System.out.print(" beautiful");
 8      /*end[Beautiful]*/
 9      /*if[Wonderful]*/
10      System.out.print(" wonderful");
11      /*end[Wonderful]*/
12      /*if[World]*/
13      System.out.print(" world!");                System.out.print(" world!");
14      /*end[World]*/
15    }                                           }
16  }                                           }
```

Fig. 9.1 *Hello World* example using the Munge preprocessor. Annotated source file on the *left-hand side* and generated file on the *right*

if[tag], if_not[tag], else[tag], and end[tag] as shown in the left-hand code of Fig. 9.1. These conditions establish a mapping between features and source code, specifying whether the lines between these directives will be included into the generated source file. For the *Hello World* example, the preprocessor can be executed as follows:

```
Munge -DHello -DBeautiful -DWorld Main.java targetDir
```

We depict the generated source code in Fig. 9.1 on the right side.

Munge in FeatureIDE

Munge is completely integrated into the concept of *FeatureIDE* with a close integration to feature modeling, configuration, and product generation. We can use the general procedure (cf. Chap. 3 on Page 19) to create a *FeatureIDE* project based on *Munge*. *FeatureIDE* projects for *Munge* have custom mechanisms, specialized to the generation of *Munge*. In detail, this affects the project structure of *FeatureIDE* as well as the location for source files and generated files.

The project structure of *Munge* projects requires a specialized handling. In Fig. 9.2, we present the package explorer of *Eclipse*, in which the *Hello World* project of *Munge* is shown (see Sect. 3.2 on Page 20 to get detailed information on how to load an existing project). The project itself is a standard Java project of *Eclipse*. Thus, the files in the folder src are used for compilation. The additional folder source contains all annotated source-code files. The preprocessor *Munge* processes the files in source and generates the result in the folder src. As the preprocessor is fully integrated into *Eclipse*, the files are preprocessed and compiled

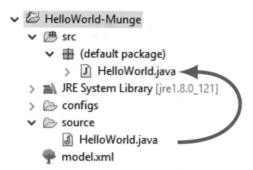

Fig. 9.2 The project structure of *Munge* with folder `source` as input folder

automatically after changes to the source files, and it is no longer necessary to call *Munge* via command line. All other artifacts of a *FeatureIDE* project are equal to the description of Sect. 3.7 on Page 27 (i.e., the `model.xml` and the configuration files).

9.3   Preprocessor Antenna

The preprocessor *Antenna* and the combination with *FeatureIDE* also come with some particularities that we want to introduce in this section. We start with a first overview on the preprocessor's concept. Afterward, we give some details of the preprocessor in *FeatureIDE*.

Antenna Overview

Antenna is a second preprocessor for Java,[2] available as command-line tool. Similar to *Munge*, *Antenna* uses the following directives to annotate optional code: `#if expression`, `#elif expression`, `#else`, and `#endif`. Additionally, a whole file can be annotated at once using the directive `#condition expression` in the first line of the file. In contrast to *Munge*, *Antenna* is tailored to the programming language Java and does not support other file extensions. The reason for this limitation is the output of the preprocessor. Instead of a removal of the specific lines, *Antenna* uses `//@` comments for the deactivation of code. Therefore, it is also possible for *Antenna* to use the same files as input and output. For example, the following application of *Antenna*

```
java Antenna Main.java Hello,World,Beautiful
```

---

[2]http://antenna.sourceforge.net.

```
 1  public class Main {                      public class Main {
 2    public static void main(String[]         public static void main(String[]
          args) {                                  args) {
 3      //#if Hello                              //#if Hello
 4      System.out.print("Hello");               System.out.print("Hello");
 5      //#endif                                 //#endif
 6      //#if Beautiful                          //#if Beautiful
 7      System.out.print(" beautiful");    //@ System.out.print(" beautiful");
 8      //#endif                                 //#endif
 9      //#if Wonderful                          //#if Wonderful
10  //@ System.out.print(" wonderful");         System.out.print(" wonderful");
11      //#endif                                 //#endif
12      //#if World                              //#if World
13      System.out.print(" world!");             System.out.print(" world!");
14      //#endif                                 //#endif
15    }                                        }
16  }                                        }
```

Fig. 9.3 *Hello World* example using the Antenna preprocessor

creates the source files for the product that consists of the features Hello, Beautiful, and World. In Fig. 9.3 on the left side, we depict the resulting source file, in which only the feature Wonderful is commented. By contrast, the application

    java Antenna Main.java Hello,World,Wonderful

uncomments the feature Wonderful and comments out the feature Beautiful (cf. Fig. 9.3 on the right side).

Antenna in *FeatureIDE*

FeatureIDE provides integrated support for *Antenna*. A developer can apply the general concept of *FeatureIDE* with the modeling, configuration, and product generation procedure (cf. Chap. 3 on Page 19). Due to the special characteristics of *Antenna*, in which source files are also generated files, *FeatureIDE* projects based on *Antenna* have a custom project structure.

In Fig. 9.4, we depict the project structure of the project *Hello World* for *Antenna*. Compared to other *FeatureIDE* generation mechanisms, *Antenna* projects do not have separate folders for source and generated files. Instead, the input and output files of *Antenna* are identical. Therefore, the project *Hello World* only contains one source folder, as the folder src that is also used as input for the compilation.

9.4   Summary and Further Reading

Conditional compilation is a popular way to implement variable software. In this chapter, we introduced the concept of preprocessors and how they can be used to implement variability in *FeatureIDE*. With *FeatureIDE*, we provide an integrated

Fig. 9.4 The project structure of *Antenna* with folder src as input and output

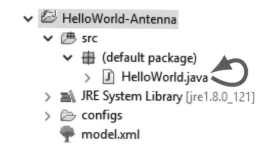

process for conditional compilation that incorporates feature modeling and product configurations (cf. Part II) with the actual implementation of the software. We further gave an introduction to the two integrated preprocessors *Munge* and *Antenna* including their main concepts and keywords. Finally, we gave a brief introduction on how both preprocessors are integrated into *FeatureIDE*.

The rest of this part will introduce *FeatureIDE*'s specialized functionalities for preprocessors based on *Antenna*. However, as *FeatureIDE* provides a general process for all preprocessors, the discussed details are similar to other preprocessors as well. In Chap. 10 on Page 105, we explain the details of how *Antenna* is integrated into *FeatureIDE*. By developing an elevator application, we introduce *FeatureIDE*'s functionalities that help developing configurable systems with preprocessors. Preprocessor annotated programs are harder to understand as the variability has to be considered as well (Melo et al. 2016). Thus, in Chap. 11 on Page 123, we introduce further concepts that help to understand preprocessor annotated code. As preprocessors can have a negative impact on software quality (Spencer and Collyer 1992; Le et al. 2011), we show in Chap. 12 on Page 131 how *FeatureIDE* helps to assure good software quality with specialized analyses.

Developing an Elevator with Conditional Compilation

10

In this chapter, we introduce the main support of *FeatureIDE* for conditional compilation. The chapter is designed that each part can be done hands-on. We explain the details of the functionalities using our running example of the elevator from Chap. 4. Using the initial example, we start with an elevator application without any variability. The elevator is implemented as a default Java project in *Eclipse* and only provides the functionality of the elevator's sabbath mode.

Using the base implementation, we will develop an elevator product line to explain the concepts of this chapter. First, we initialize the product line based on the preprocessor *Antenna*. Second, we add the optional feature Service and present setup as well as implementation details. Third, we include an alternative mode, FIFO, and show how to implement it with the support of *FeatureIDE*.

This chapter is designed as hands-on. However, to follow this chapter, if something goes wrong with the implementation, we provide the version of the elevator for each step in our example wizard. Thus, the reader can reproduce the descriptions in *Eclipse*. To check out a specific version of the elevator, follow Instruction 10.1.

Instruction 10.1 (Import the Specific Step of the Elevator Example)

1. Open the example wizard by any of the following options:
   - Press *New* → *Example* in the context menu of the Project/Package Explorer
   - Press *New* → *Examples* → *FeatureIDE* → *FeatureIDE Examples* in the upper-left menu toolbar of *Eclipse*
   - Press *File* → *New* → *Example* in the menu bar of *Eclipse*
2. Select *FeatureIDE Examples*
3. Press *Next*

(continued)

© Springer International Publishing AG 2017
J. Meinicke et al., *Mastering Software Variability with FeatureIDE*,
DOI 10.1007/978-3-319-61443-4_10

Instruction 10.1 (continued)
4. Select *Book Example* tab
5. Select the project *Part III* → *Chapter 10* → *<specific version>*
6. Press *Finish*

This chapter is based on the elevator version *"Elevator"*. To follow this chapter, check out the example project using the example wizard as described in Instruction 10.1.

10.1 Creating an Elevator Product Line Using Antenna

In Chap. 4 on Page 31, we described our initial elevator application. To allow a customization of this project, we need to convert it to a product line. Afterward, we can add new (optional) functionality, such as the feature Service (see the next section) that can be used to ease the maintainability of the elevator.

To initialize the elevator product line, we convert the Java project into a *FeatureIDE* project using the preprocessor *Antenna* as described in Instruction 10.2. As a result, the project structure is adjusted and an initial *feature model* (cf. model.xml on the left side of Fig. 10.1) and *configuration* (cf. configs/Elevator.config on the right side of Fig. 10.1) are created. As depicted in Fig. 10.1, the result of this initialization is a feature model with two features. The *root feature* is abstract and is named by the project itself (i.e., Elevator). The second feature is optional and is initially named Base. Furthermore, as the source and generation folder of the composer *Antenna* are identical, there will be no change on the source code during this transformation. Note that at this point, the transformation has no effect on the possible set of products as we did not introduce any variation points in the source code. Thus, we will get the same physical product for both configurations.

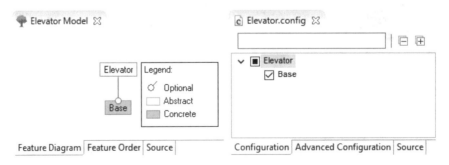

Fig. 10.1 Initial feature model as a result of using Instruction 10.2

Instruction 10.2 (Transformation to an Antenna Project)

1. Open the transformation wizard by:
   - Press *Configure → Convert to FeatureIDE Project...* in the context menu of the Project/Package Explorer
2. Select *Antenna* as composer
3. Press *Finish*

Fig. 10.2 From the initial to the desired feature model of our initial product line

After the product-line initialization, we can start editing the feature model according to our needs. The current source code of our initial elevator represents only the mode Sabbath. Therefore, we need to edit the feature model that contains an optional feature, Sabbath. To do so, we rename the feature Base to Sabbath. The transformation of the feature model is shown in Fig. 10.2. As a result, the feature model allows to optionally select the feature Sabbath. For more details on how to edit feature models, we refer the reader to Chap. 5 on Page 43.

After saving the feature model, the configuration files are automatically updated by *FeatureIDE*, according to our feature model changes (i.e., Base is renamed to Sabbath). In our case, the project only contains one configuration file that was automatically updated. When opening this configuration file with the configuration editor, we see the feature Sabbath is optional.

As the source code has some code artifacts belonging to the feature Sabbath, we can start to add preprocessor directives. This allows us to make this dependency more clear and to make the code optional. In particular, one source-code area in the class ControlUnit belongs to the feature Sabbath. The method calculateNextState of the class ControlUnit is responsible for the movement of the elevator. In our initial version of the elevator, this method only returns a state according to the Sabbath mode. The corresponding source code is depicted in Listing 10.1.

To make the code optional, we add an #if directive in Line 7. Note that the lines of the listings do not match with the lines in the actual file. Furthermore, we need to add a default return value for the case that the mode Sabbath is not selected. Therefore, we add #endif to finish the Service and return FLOORING as default value (cf. Lines 21 and 22).

To ease the use of preprocessor directives, *FeatureIDE* provides a *content assist for directives* that is in sync with the feature model. This content-assist mechanism

Listing 10.1 Class `ControlUnit` of the product line Elevator

```
1 public class ControlUnit implements Runnable{
2
3    // further source code
4
5    private ElevatorState calculateNextState() {
6      final int currentFloor = elevator.getCurrentFloor();
7      //#if Sabbath
8      switch (elevator.getCurrentState()) {
9      case FLOORING:
10       switch (elevator.getDirection()) {
11       case MOVING_DOWN:
12         return (currentFloor <= elevator.getMinFloor()) ?
13            ElevatorState.MOVING_UP :
                  ElevatorState.MOVING_DOWN;
14       case MOVING_UP:
15         return (currentFloor >= elevator.getMaxFloor()) ?
16            ElevatorState.MOVING_DOWN :
                  ElevatorState.MOVING_UP;
17       default:
18         return ElevatorState.MOVING_UP;
19       }
20     }
21     //#endif
22     return ElevatorState.FLOORING;
23   }
24 }
```

helps to find the right feature and to ensure a correct notation of it to prevent spelling errors. In Instruction 10.3, we present an overview on how to use the content assist for preprocessor annotations. We use the task of adding the preprocessor directive `#if Sabbath` to demonstrate the functionality in Fig. 10.3. Thus, after typing `#if` in the comment, the content assist shows us valid features to select. In our example, it is only the feature `Sabbath` as there are currently no further concrete features defined in the feature model. If there are other features available in the feature model, it is possible to type the first letters of the feature to reduce the number of proposed features.

Instruction 10.3 (Using Content Assist in Antenna)

1. Insert `//#if` or `//#condition`
2. Open the content assist by:
   - Press *Ctrl + Space*
3. Select a feature
4. Press *Enter*

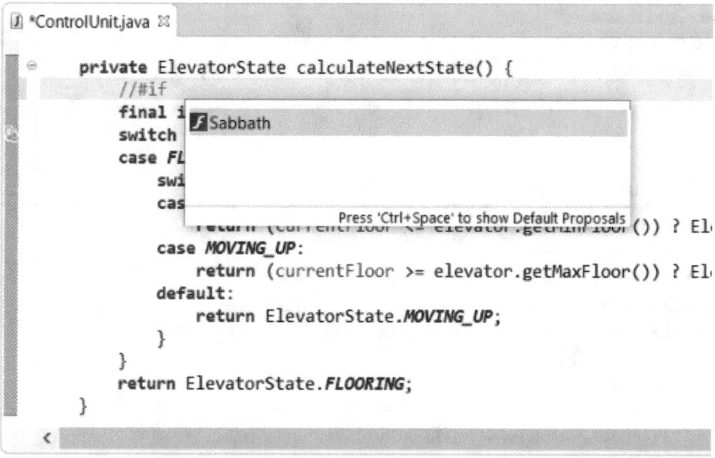

Fig. 10.3 Content assist for preprocessor annotations

At this point, we initialized the elevator product line. As described above, the product line consists of two possible elevator variants. The first product controls the elevator in the Sabbath mode. The second product actually does nothing at all (i.e., the elevator stays in the first floor and does not move). To execute the product described by this configuration, we use the default execution mechanisms of *Eclipse* (cf. Sect. 3.7 on Page 27).

10.2   Adding the Feature "Service" to the Elevator Product Line

In this section, we extend the elevator product line by an optional feature, Service. The idea of Service is to ease the maintainability of the elevator. For this purpose, a button should force that the elevator stops in the lowest floor and wait until the service operation is finished and the button is toggled again. As the development of this functionality requires effort and in a more expensive elevator, the functionality should be optional. As a result, we can tailor the elevator to the customer needs or to their financial resources.

To initialize the intended feature Service, we need to adapt the feature model. Therefore, we add the feature Service as an optional child feature of the root feature Elevator. The resulting feature model with an optional feature, Service, is depicted in Fig. 10.4. As a result of this feature-model edit, the feature Service is now available in the configuration editor. At this point, the feature model describes four products, for the two optional features Sabbath and Service.

After introducing the feature Service, we can start to add the functionality to the source code. Therefore, we first need to select the feature Service in the current configuration. This allows us to use the newly introduced methods for the feature Service which will be inactive otherwise (i.e., *Antenna* comments out the code).

Fig. 10.4 Add feature
`Service` to the initial
elevator feature model

Listing 10.2 Class `Elevator`

```
1  public class Elevator {
2    //#if Service
3    private boolean inService = false;
4    public boolean isInService() { return inService; }
5    public void setService(boolean mode) { this.inService =
         mode; }
6    //#endif
7
8    // further source code
9  }
```

To implement the feature `Service`, we need to adapt the source code of the
classes `Elevator`, `ControlUnit`, and `SimulationUnit`. In the following, we
present the detailed source-code changes. The resulting project is also available in
the example wizard.

Class Elevator To realize the functionality of the feature `Service`, we need to store
whether the elevator is in service. For this purpose, we use the class `Elevator`. In
detail, we extend the class `Elevator` by the boolean field `inService` (cf. Line 3
of Listing 10.2) and provide a corresponding getter (cf. Line 4) and setter method
(cf. Line 5). Furthermore, we need to add preprocessor annotations to ensure that
this functionality is only available if the feature `Service` is selected. Therefore, we
use our content assist for preprocessor annotations as described in Instruction 10.3.
We use this instruction to add the `#if Service` with the corresponding `#endif`
to the location in the class `Elevator` to surround the previously introduced source
code (cf. Lines 2–6).

Class ControlUnit As the class `ControlUnit` is used to determine and execute the
next state of the elevator, we also need to adapt the class to allow an optional service
behavior. In detail, the class `ControlUnit` needs to ensure that an elevator in service
is moved to the lowest floor and that it remains there until the elevator is no longer in
service. For this purpose, we only have to update the method `calculateNextState`
to support the service functionality.

In Listing 10.3, we depict the main control-flow changes of the method
`calculateNextState` (cf. Lines 5–19) to provide the service functionality. If the
elevator is in service, we calculate and return the next step accordingly (cf. Line 8–
14). Otherwise, the method's behavior is similar to the initial elevator that is based
on the `Sabbath` mode. Besides the control changes of the class `ControlUnit`, it is

Listing 10.3 Class ControlUnit

```
 1  public class ControlUnit implements Runnable {
 2
 3    // further source code
 4
 5    private ElevatorState calculateNextState() {
 6      final int currentFloor = elevator.getCurrentFloor();
 7      //#if Service
 8      if (elevator.isInService()) {
 9        if (currentFloor != elevator.getMinFloor()) {
10          return ElevatorState.MOVING_DOWN;
11        } else {
12          return ElevatorState.FLOORING;
13        }
14      }
15      //#endif
16
17      // implementation of Sabbath
18      return ElevatorState.FLOORING;
19    }
20
21    //#if Service
22    public boolean toggleService() {
23      elevator.setService(!elevator.isInService());
24      return elevator.isInService();
25    }
26    //#endif
27  }
```

also necessary to inform the elevator instance, which is stored in this class, about the service (de)activation. Therefore, the class also provides the corresponding method toggleService to forward the information to the elevator model (cf. Lines 22–25).

After our source-code changes to include the service functionality, we have to insert the preprocessor annotation to also allow us to remove the code belonging to the feature Service. In detail, we surround the optional code area in the method calculateNextState (cf. Lines 7–15). Additionally, we add preprocessor annotations to the newly introduced method toggleService (cf. Lines 21–26)

Class SimulationUnit At this point, we already integrated the logic to set the elevator in service mode. For the purpose of simulation of the feature Service, we also have to change the class SimulationUnit so that we are able to toggle whether the elevator is in service.

As stated with the initial version of the elevator (see Chap. 4 on Page 31), the simulation of the elevator will be represented on the console and by a graphical unit at the same time. Since the user of this simulation unit needs to interact with the elevator to toggle the service, we decided to extend the graphical unit by a toggle button. To avoid implementing a user interface, we provide the files containing the buttons. Therefore, follow Instruction 10.4 to adapt user interface. Thus, we only show how to initialize this unit and neglect the implementation details.

Instruction 10.4 (Adapting the User Interface for Service)

1. Copy the file MainWindow.java of the folder guiVersions / Service
2. Replace the file MainWindow.java of the source folder (src) with the new version.

After copying the class, an error appears as the class MainWindow calls the method toggleService of the simulation unit. To allow us to toggle the service by a graphical unit, we first need to allow the graphical unit to toggle the service mode. For this purpose, we introduce the method toggleService in the class SimulationUnit which is called by the service button of the graphical unit. As this functionality should be only available with the feature Service, we add the corresponding preprocessor annotations to the new code (cf. Lines 14–18 in Listing 10.4).

In addition to the previous source-code changes, it is necessary that the graphical unit holds an instance of this simulation unit to toggle the service functionality by the corresponding method call. For this purpose, we need to call different constructors of this graphical unit (i.e., with and without a parameter SimulationUnit)

Listing 10.4 Class SimulationUnit with the feature Service

```
 1 public class SimulationUnit {
 2   private static MainWindow simulationWindow;
 3
 4   public static void main(String[] args) {
 5     SimulationUnit sim = new SimulationUnit();
 6     //#if Service
 7     simulationWindow = new MainWindow(sim);
 8      //#else
 9      //@ simulationWindow = new MainWindow();
10      //#endif
11     sim.start(5);
12   }
13
14   //#if Service
15   public boolean toggleService() {
16     return controller.toggleService();
17   }
18   //#endif
19
20   // further source code
21 }
```

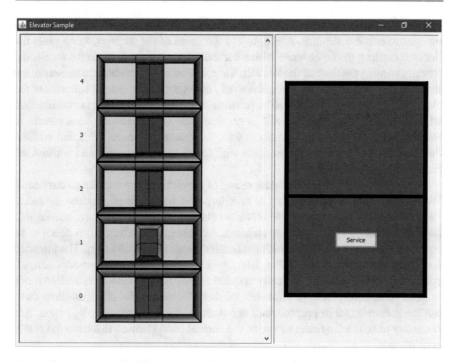

Fig. 10.5 Graphical unit of the elevator with the feature `Service`

depending on the selection of the feature `Service`. Therefore, we call the constructor with one parameter for the simulation unit for products with the feature `Service` (cf. Line 7) and without a parameter otherwise (cf. Line 9). Thus, we add the necessary preprocessor annotations using `#if Service` (cf. Line 6), `#else` (cf. Line 8), and `#endif` (cf. Line 10) to surround the code artifacts.

We finalized the necessary code changes to support the feature `Service`. We can select the features of interest in the configuration editor and execute the project. In Fig. 10.5, we show the graphical unit of the elevator if the features `Service` and `Sabbath` are selected. As a result, a toggle button named *Service* will appear in the elevator cabin.

10.3 Adding Feature "FIFO" to the Elevator Product Line

In the last sections, we described how to initialize a product line based on the preprocessor *Antenna* and how to add the optional feature `Service` using our running example of the elevator. Based on this starting point, we extend the elevator product line by a new feature to illustrate the main functionalities of *FeatureIDE* in a more complicated example. In detail, we add an additional feature, `FIFO`, as an alternative scheduling strategy to `Sabbath`. The feature `FIFO` requires a call button on each floor and one call button for each floor in the elevator cabin that allows the user to call the elevator. Analogous to the name of the strategy, FIFO visits the floors according to the order in which the calls occur. If there is no floor call, the elevator stays in the floor of the last call. Thus, in contrast to the feature Service, the feature FIFO is a real alternative and not only an interrupt of a default behavior of the elevator. Therefore, it should also be possible to use the feature FIFO in combination with the feature Service but *not* in combination with Sabbath. This results in four intended products: two products with the feature Sabbath with and without the feature Service and two products with the feature FIFO with and without the feature Service.

Again, we need to edit the feature model of the elevator product line to our needs. We want to add the feature FIFO as an alternative feature to the feature Sabbath. For this purpose, we also need to create an abstract compound feature, Modes, that holds both features as alternative children. As either Sabbath or FIFO needs to be contained in a configuration, we set the feature Modes to be mandatory. The intended feature model is presented in Fig. 10.6. As a result of this feature-model edit, all configuration files are automatically updated and we have to select the desired mode to get a *valid configuration*. Furthermore, these feature model changes allow us to use the feature FIFO in preprocessor annotations. As for the feature Service, it is necessary to select the feature FIFO in the current configuration to enable the newly created code.

To realize the feature FIFO, we need to adapt multiple classes, such as ControlUnit and SimulationUnit. Furthermore, we create a new class that can handle the floor requests, called Request. Besides these classes, we also create a new interface, ITriggerListener, and adapt the already existing interface ITickListener. In the following, we present the details of these source-code changes.

Class Request (New) To support the new elevator behavior FIFO, we create a new class, Request, which represents a request from a button call (cf. Listing 10.5). There are two ways to create a new class for *Antenna* projects. The first way is to use the *Eclipse "New Java Class"* wizard. Otherwise, *FeatureIDE* also provides a wizard to create Java classes. To create the class Request in the pack-

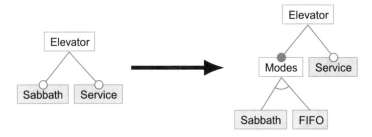

Fig. 10.6 Elevator product line with the feature FIFO

Listing 10.5 Class Request

```
 1 //#condition FIFO
 2 public class Request {
 3   private final int floor;
 4
 5   public int getFloor() {
 6     return floor;
 7   }
 8
 9   public Request(int floor) {
10     this.floor = floor;
11   }
12
13   public boolean equals(Object obj) {
14     return ((Request)obj).floor == floor;
15   }
16 }
```

age *de.ovgu.featureide.examples.elevator.core.controller* (i.e., the same package as ControlUnit), follow Instruction 10.5.

For FIFO, the class Request simply stores the floor of the request (cf. Line 3). In addition, the class also implements an equals method which is necessary if two requests to the same floor are called. As the class Request is only needed in products with the feature FIFO, we want to annotate the class accordingly. Therefore, we use the keyword #condition to enable the content assist and to assign the feature FIFO (cf. Line 1). In this case, we need no #endif or other annotations as this keyword automatically marks the complete file as conditional (i.e., #condition is equivalent of using #if and #endif around the whole file). Note that #condition needs to come in the first line of the file before the package declarations which are omitted in the listings.

Instruction 10.5 (Create a New Java Class File)

1. Open the *FeatureIDE* perspective if not active (cf. Instruction 3.1)
2. Open a class wizard by any of the following options:
   - Press *New → FeatureIDE Source File* in the context menu of the Package Explorer
   - Press *New → FeatureIDE → FeatureIDE Source File* in the upper-left menu toolbar of *Eclipse*
   - Press *File → New → FeatureIDE Source File* in the menu bar of *Eclipse*
3. Select a package
4. Enter a class name (e.g., Request)
5. Press *Finish*

eading-

Update UI Classes As for the feature `Service`, we need to update the UI to show buttons for the requests. To avoid manually updating the UI classes, we provide the updated versions. To update the UI classes *MainWindow.java* and *FloorComposite.java*, follow Instruction 10.6.

After copying the files, both classes have error markers as the referenced methods do not exist yet. In the following, we will introduce the required methods to link the UI with the rest of the program.

Instruction 10.6 (Adapting the User Interface for `FIFO`)

1. Copy the files `MainWindow.java` and `FloorComposite.java` of the folder `guiVersions / FIFO`
2. Replace the files `MainWindow.java` and `FloorComposite.java` of the source folder (`src`) with the new versions.

Interface ITickListener The interface `ITickListener` already exists in the initial version of the elevator product line. The interface is used to standardize all listener that should be informed if the next elevator step is executed. For the graphical unit, it is also necessary to know whether a request is handled to reset the button states. This listener call will then enable a button again after the request was handled. To this end, we add the method `onRequestFinished` to this interface `ITickListener` and to its implementation in the class `SimulationUnit`. The new version of `MainWindow` already contains the method. As this method is only necessary for products with the feature `FIFO`, we again surround the code artifact with directives for the feature `FIFO` (cf. Listing 10.6, Lines 4–6).

New Interface ITriggerListener To trigger a request by a button push, we need to introduce a new listener interface, `ITriggerListener`. This listener informs the `ControlUnit` whenever a new request occurred. To create the new Java interface `ITriggerListener` in the controller package, follow Instruction 10.7.

To trigger a request, we create a method in the interface called `trigger` with a `Request` as a parameter. As the interface should be only available if the feature

Listing 10.6 Interface `ITickListener`

```
1 public interface ITickListener {
2     void onTick(Elevator elevator);
3
4     //#if FIFO
5     void onRequestFinished(Elevator elevator, Request
          request);
6     //#endif
7 }
```

Listing 10.7 Class `ITriggerListener`

```
1  //#condition FIFO
2  public interface ITriggerListener {
3    void trigger(Request request);
4  }
```

FIFO is selected, we use the directive #condition to assign the whole file to the feature FIFO. The resulting interface is shown in Listing 10.7.

Instruction 10.7 (Create a New Java Interface File)

1. Open the *FeatureIDE* perspective if not active (cf. Instruction 3.1)
2. Open a class wizard by any of the following options:
   - Press *New → FeatureIDE Source File* in the context menu of the Package Explorer
   - Press *New → FeatureIDE → FeatureIDE Source File* in the upper-left menu toolbar of *Eclipse*
   - Press *File → New → FeatureIDE Source File* in the menu bar of *Eclipse*
3. Select a package
4. Enter a class name (e.g., Request)
5. Check interface
6. Press *Finish*

Class ControlUnit After this preliminary work to initialize the mode FIFO, we can add the new control logic for FIFO in the class ControlUnit. First of all, the class ControlUnit needs to implement the interface ITriggerListener as it will handle the request. In Listing 10.8, we depict the necessary class changes. The class needs to optionally implement the interface depending on the selection of FIFO (cf. Lines 2–4). As this interface provides the method trigger, we also need to implement the method depending on FIFO. The method trigger will be called whenever a button is pressed and a request is performed. Thus, we also create a queue to store the requests (cf. Line 7). For FIFO, it is sufficient to use a LinkedList as queue implementation. Whenever trigger is called, the request is added to the queue if it is not contained yet.

As we want to avoid that a request is added to the queue if the elevator is already in the same floor, we add the method getCurrentFloor (cf. Line 15). This method is used by the UI classes to check whether the current floor is equivalent to the requested floor.

Listing 10.8 Implementing the interface `ITriggerListener` in the class `ControlUnit`

```
 1 public class ControlUnit implements Runnable
 2 //#if FIFO
 3 , ITriggerListener
 4 //#endif
 5 {
 6   // #if FIFO
 7   private Queue<Request> requests = new LinkedList<>();
 8
 9   public void trigger(Request request) {
10     if (!requests.contains(request)) {
11       requests.offer(request);
12     }
13   }
14
15   public int getCurrentFloor() {
16     return elevator.getCurrentFloor();
17   }
18   //#endif
19
20   // further source code
21 }
```

The necessary changes to implement the actual control logic for FIFO are depicted in Listing 10.9. To implement the control logic, we again need to change the method `calculateNextState`. The control logic for FIFO works as follows. As long as there is request in the queue, the controller checks whether the requested floor is reached. If the requested floor is above of the current floor, the elevator will move upward. Else if the floor is below, the elevator will move downward. When the floor is reached, the elevator will remove the request from the queue (cf. Line 19) and will open the doors by returning the FLOORING state (cf. Line 23).

To communicate that the elevator has reached its target, we use the method `onRequestFinished` of the interface `ITickListener`. Therefore, we implement the new method `requestFinished` depending on the feature FIFO (cf. Lines 27–31). This listener call will tell the UI that the floor is reached and that the button can be released again.

Class SimulationUnit   Similar to the inclusion of the feature Service, the feature FIFO is also based on user interactions. Therefore, the SimulationUnit (cf. Listing 10.10) needs to forward the information from the graphical unit to the class ControlUnit. Therefore, the graphical unit MainWindow needs a reference to the instance of the simulation unit. Thus, the source code of the main method is identical to the description of the last section in which we added the feature Service. However, we only have to edit the preprocessor annotation (cf. Line 4) so that the surrounded source code is activated if the feature Service or FIFO is selected.

Listing 10.9 Implementing the control logic for `FIFO` in the class `ControlUnit`

```
1  public class ControlUnit implements Runnable
2
3     // further source code
4
5     private ElevatorState calculateNextState() {
6        final int currentFloor = elevator.getCurrentFloor();
7        // implementation of Service
8        // implementation of Sabbath
9
10       // #if FIFO
11       if (!requests.isEmpty()) {
12          Request nextRequest = requests.peek();
13          int floor = nextRequest.getFloor();
14          if (floor > currentFloor) {
15             return ElevatorState.MOVING_UP;
16          } else if (floor < currentFloor) {
17             return ElevatorState.MOVING_DOWN;
18          } else {
19             requestFinished(requests.poll());
20          }
21       }
22       // #endif
23       return ElevatorState.FLOORING;
24    }
25
26    // #if FIFO
27    private void requestFinished(Request request) {
28       for (ITickListener listener : this.tickListener) {
29          listener.onRequestFinished(elevator, request);
30       }
31    }
32    //#endif
33 }
```

We already talked about the necessity to forward the information from the graphical parts to the control unit. In the case of the feature FIFO, we need to forward the floor requests. For this purpose, we created the interface ITriggerListener from which the class ControlUnit is a concrete implementation (cf. Lines 13–15). We create the method floorRequest to forward the request to the control unit.

As discussed before, the graphical unit needs to know whether the elevator is in the same floor as the requested floor. Therefore, we create the method getCurrentFloor which forwards the floor variable of the elevator.

Listing 10.10 Class `SimulationUnit` with the feature `FIFO`

```
 1  public class SimulationUnit {
 2    public static void main(String[] args) {
 3      SimulationUnit sim = new SimulationUnit();
 4      //#if FIFO | Service
 5      simulationWindow = new MainWindow(sim);
 6      //#else
 7      //@ simulationWindow = new MainWindow();
 8      //#endif
 9      sim.start(5);
10    }
11
12    //#if FIFO
13    public void floorRequest(Request floorRequest) {
14      controller.trigger(floorRequest);
15    }
16
17    public int getCurrentFloor() {
18      return controller.getCurrentFloor();
19    }
20    //#endif
21
22    // further source code
23  }
```

After finishing the implementation of the `SimulationUnit`, we can try out the elevator product line. To check out the result, simply run the project as Java Application. In Fig. 10.7, we depict an exemplary execution of the elevator with the feature `FIFO` and without the feature `Service`. Using the floor buttons, it is possible to call the elevator and to use the implemented behavior of the mode `FIFO`.

10.4   Summary and Further Reading

The development of a product line with conditional compilation as well as the transformation of an existing product into a product line can be an error-prone task with several pitfalls. To support the developer, *FeatureIDE* provides several mechanisms that we illustrated on our running example (cf. Chap. 4 on Page 31). Especially, the automated integration of preprocessors into *Eclipse* makes preprocessors easy to use. With the use of a feature model, the features and their dependencies can be designed, and with the configuration editor, the products can be configured easily. The actual call of the preprocessor is oblivious to the user as it is integrated and called automatically.

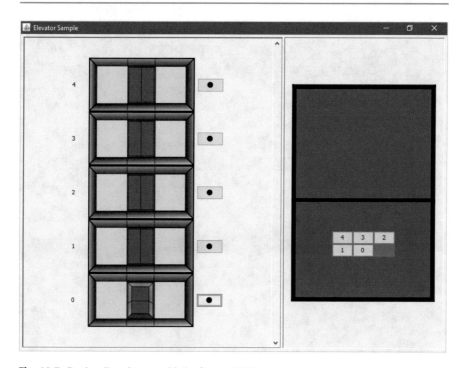

Fig. 10.7 Product line elevator with the feature FIFO

FeatureIDE provides a simple mechanism to transform a single product into an initial product line. After this transformation, we can use the default procedure of *FeatureIDE* given in Chap. 3 on Page 19 to configure or execute the resulting product(s). Based on this product-line initialization, it is easy to extend the product line. We can add new features to the feature model, and it is possible to use this feature in a subsequent feature implementation. Looking at preprocessors, *FeatureIDE* provides a content assist to support the developers during the annotation of preprocessor directives.

In the remaining chapters for conditional compilation, we use our extended running example of the elevator product line to present the advanced tool support that *FeatureIDE* provides. First, we show in Chap. 11 on Page 123 how *FeatureIDE* helps to handle and trace features in larger programs. In Chap. 12 on Page 131, we then show mechanisms that help to ensure the quality of product lines with conditional compilation.

Feature Traceability for Conditional Compilation

11

A common task during software development, in general, and feature-oriented software development, in particular, is to locate features in domain artifacts. Whereas in Chap. 7 we have already discussed how to trace features in feature modeling and in the configuration process, this chapter is devoted to the feature traceability problem for domain artifacts. That is, we discuss how to trace features that are implemented using conditional compilation.

Feature traceability is especially challenging for conditional compilation, as features used in *preprocessor annotations* are often scattered over multiple locations and files. Locating all artifacts for a certain feature is typically referred to as the *feature traceability problem*. We argue that tool support is required to ease the process of tracing features. With FeatureIDE, we aim to ease the implementation with preprocessors with several views and mechanisms that help to locate features and provide an overview on their implementation and usage.

In this chapter, we present the *FeatureIDE*'s support for feature traceability in the presence of preprocessor annotations. That is, we give insights into multiple views and editors that ease feature traceability. In particular, we present how features are identified with the help of *Project Explorer*, *Java Editor*, *FeatureIDE Outline*, and *Collaboration Diagram*. Across all such views, FeatureIDE relies on the user-guided coloring of features, as presented in Chap. 7 on Page 73. FeatureIDE provides a palette of predefined colors that can easily be distinguished by humans, and each feature can but does not have to be assigned to one of those colors.

11.1 Tracing Features in Project Explorer

Conditional compilation is a flexible technique to map features to parts of domain artifacts. However, this flexibility also results in features being hard to be identified in artifacts. During development, developers might know that their maintenance is

© Springer International Publishing AG 2017
J. Meinicke et al., *Mastering Software Variability with FeatureIDE*,
DOI 10.1007/978-3-319-61443-4_11

devoted to one or some specific features. For large projects, it can be a real challenge to manually identify all folders and files that are relevant for a specific feature.

With FeatureIDE, we visualize relevant parts by means of colors, whereas the developer decides which features are of interest. Such relevant features are assigned to colors as described in Chap. 7 on Page 73. In maintenance, developers can concentrate on those relevant features and identify their location as we explain below.

Using our running example of the elevator, we take a look at the facilities of *FeatureIDE* to trace features in domain artifacts. Please follow Instruction 11.1 to open the example project in *FeatureIDE*.

Instruction 11.1 (Import the Elevator-v1.4 Example)

1. Open the example wizard by any of the following options:
   - Press *New* → *Example* in the context menu of the Project/Package Explorer
   - Press *New* → *Examples* → *FeatureIDE* → *FeatureIDE Examples* in the upper-left menu toolbar of *Eclipse*
   - Press *File* → *New* → *Example* in the menu bar of *Eclipse*
2. Select *FeatureIDE Examples*
3. Press *Next*
4. Select *Book Example* tab
5. Select the project *Part III* → *Chapter 11* → *Elevator-Antenna-v1.4*
6. Press *Finish*

In the example project, we assign colors to features as known from Chap. 7. On the right side of Fig. 11.1, we illustrate how the feature model looks like after assigning a different color to each concrete feature. On the left side, it can be seen how *FeatureIDE* visualizes which packages and classes refer to those eight features.

In the Project Explorer, there is a small box for each of the ten colors in front of every class and package. The box is empty (i.e., white) if no feature is assigned to that color. It is also white if none of the features assigned to that color is contained in the package or class. Otherwise, the color indicates that at least one of the colored features is contained in the artifact. Hence, this scales also to large feature models with thousands of features, as developers can assign multiple features of interest to the same color.

The example shown in Fig. 11.1 allows some interesting remarks. First, the feature ShortestPath is only contained in the class Request, whereas the feature CallButtons is distributed over numerous classes and packages. Second, some classes do not reference features at all, whereas others contain almost all features. In our experience, larger projects typically lead to the fact that features are included in a significantly lower percentage of classes and packages. Also, classes do not tend

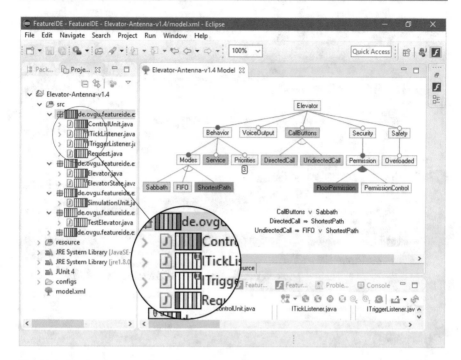

Fig. 11.1   Tracing features using colors in the *Project Explorer*

to contain all features if there are many features. In any case, the project explorer is a good starting point to identify resources to work on, especially for large product lines.

11.2   Tracing Features in Java Editor

With conditional compilation, a mapping from features to domain artifacts is given at fine grain. Developers can annotate single or consecutive lines with preprocessor directives. As a result, a given source file may contain several of those directives, and identifying the relevant part of a file during maintenance is challenging.

Since *FeatureIDE* uses default editors for the representation of specific source files, we take a look at the Java Editor with which we open the class ControlUnit. For the sake of an example, assume we are interested in all source code of the feature Service in this class. Therefore, we assigned the color *green* to the feature Service in the *Feature Model Editor*. The resulting *Java Editor* is shown in Fig. 11.2.

As a result of this color assignment, we can find code artifacts of the feature Service more efficiently using this color in two different ways. First, *FeatureIDE* highlights the code of the feature Service and all other colored features using *background colors*. Second, *FeatureIDE* uses the color to mark the specific file area

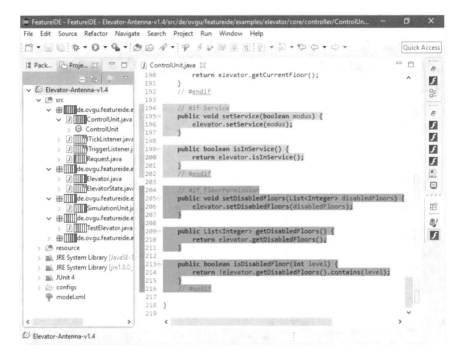

Fig. 11.2 Highlighted source code of features in the class ControlUnit

in the sidebar of the editor (cf. right side of the figure close to the slider in Fig. 11.2). In the sidebar, we can see that there are two occurrences of the feature Service's code in that class and we can access them simply by clicking on the color at the sidebar.

There are certain mappings of features to the source code that often hinder efficient development. First, typical files do usually not fit onto a single screen. While editors always support scrolling, developers can easily miss beginning or end of a preprocessor directive. With the color assignment, developers can even recognize beginning and end of relevant features if only an excerpt of the code is shown on the screen.

A common source of errors is that preprocessor directives can be nested. Nesting results in the fact that certain lines are only included if all surrounded preprocessor directives evaluate to true. A potential problem with nesting is that it may stay unnoticed if the beginning of the file is not visible on the screen.

Besides the highlighting mechanism of a single feature, *FeatureIDE* also supports nested source code of different features. To illustrate this scenario, we assigned the color purple to the feature CallButtons, yellow to ShortestPath, cyan to DirectedCall, and orange to FIFO. All these features are referenced in the class Request, and it is easy to find the corresponding source-code location based on these colors. In Fig. 11.3, we depict the relevant source code. As *Antenna* is an in-

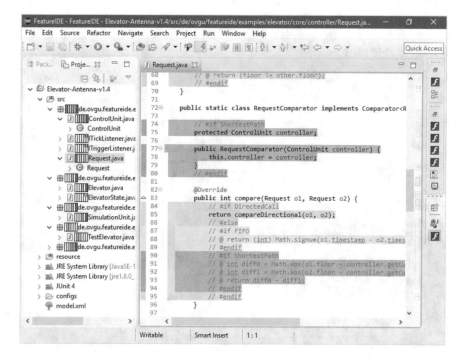

Fig. 11.3 Coloring of nested features in the class Request

place preprocessor (cf. Chap. 9 on Page 97), comments starting with "//@" indicate that those lines are removed in the current configuration.

Basically, *FeatureIDE* uses the first character of each line, which is typically a tabulator, to depict the outer feature definition and the remaining characters for inner feature definitions. For instance, *FeatureIDE* visualizes that the source code of the feature ShortestPath is nested inside of the source code for the feature CallButtons. As only one color is visible in the sidebar of the editor, *FeatureIDE* depicts the inner feature definition (cf. right side of Fig. 11.3).

11.3 Tracing Features in FeatureIDE Outline

Besides the tracing of features using the editor itself, it is also possible to use the outline view of the Java Editor to browse the source code. As known from standard Java programming, the outline lists all fields and methods of the currently edited class. Hence, the outline is often used to identify and locate members of interest.

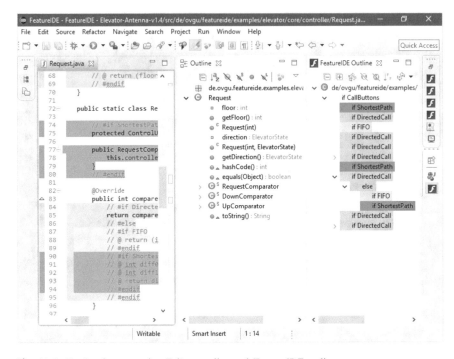

Fig. 11.4 Tracing features using *Eclipse* outline and *FeatureIDE* outline

In the middle of Fig. 11.4, we show the default outline of the Java Editor. As we can see, this outline presents all members of the class ControlUnit and allows us to jump into their definition using a double-click. However, this outline is not aware of the existing variability inside of this source code. In particular, only fields and methods are shown that are not in comments and thus depend on the currently selected configuration (cf. Sect. 6.1 on Page 64).

Besides this *Eclipse* standard view, *FeatureIDE* also provides an outline dedicated to the specific needs of conditional compilation. On the right side of Fig. 11.4, the *FeatureIDE Outline* is shown for the class ControlUnit. Instead of the list of members, it provides a tree of preprocessor directives according to their nesting in the source code. In our example, the complete class is annotated with the feature CallButtons (colored with purple), and therein several other features are mapped to parts of the class. Similar to the *Eclipse* outline, the *FeatureIDE* outline enables to jump to the declaration by clicking on an element of the tree view. Hence, the *FeatureIDE* outline helps developers to understand the nesting and occurrences of preprocessor directives with a class.

11.4   Tracing Features in Collaboration Diagram

The mapping of features to the source code can be quite complex due to nesting and that features may be used in logical formulas as preprocessor directives. The mapping can be accessed with Project Explorer and *FeatureIDE* Outline, but the overview can be hard to establish. Hence, *FeatureIDE* also provides what is called a Collaboration Diagram, a view giving an overview of all preprocessor directives within a *FeatureIDE* project. The view is part of the *FeatureIDE* perspective (cf. Sect. 3.1 on Page 19).

In Fig. 11.5, we give an example using the *Collaboration Diagram*. It is basically a table, whereas each row is devoted to a feature occurring in preprocessor directives and each column is devoted to a file containing preprocessor directives. If there is a cell in a certain column and row, it means that at least one *preprocessor annotation* within that file (column) contains the feature (row).

Collaboration diagrams tend to get large, due to the number of features and files within a project. Already for our example project, the whole collaboration diagram is too huge to be shown in this book. *FeatureIDE* enables to filter the table by columns, rows, or combinations thereof. In the example, we only show the features Sabbath, Service, and FloorPermission and for those only three files of interest for a particular maintenance. Another option is to hide feature not

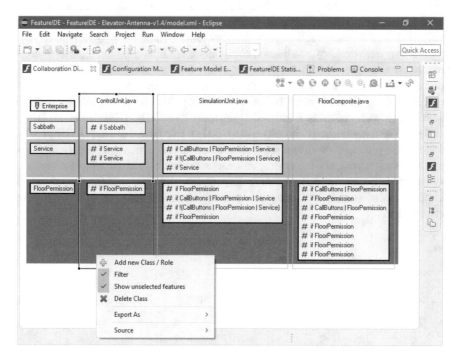

Fig. 11.5 Tracing features using the collaboration diagram

selected in the current configuration, as those features are typically not of interest during development. The view does not only serve to give an overview but also allows developers to navigate to a particular preprocessor directive by means of a double-click.

11.5   Summary and Further Reading

In product lines with conditional compilation, feature traceability is hard to establish manually for developers. *FeatureIDE* provides a variety of views based on the concept of coloring features of interest and identifying those features by their colors in domain artifacts. Project Explorer, Collaboration Diagram, and Statistics View help to identify relevant files for maintenance. Then, coloring in the Java Editor and *FeatureIDE* Outline support developers in finding relevant parts thereof. Without all those views, developers are likely to be overcharged by the process of feature location.

Feature traceability has already been discussed in Chap. 7 on Page 73, but only for feature modeling and during configuration. *FeatureIDE*'s tool support for conditional compilation builds on that basis for assigning colors to features. Although feature location should be easier with the above-described tool support, it is still likely that developers introduce defects in some or all configurations. Hence, the next chapter will introduce techniques for quality assurance. In contrast to conditional compilation, Part IV focuses on techniques to modularize all domain artifacts for each feature and thereby simplify feature traceability significantly.

The expressiveness of conditional compilation leads to complex feature-to-code mappings (Liebig et al. 2010; Queiroz et al. 2017; Rodrigues et al. 2016). In particular, the complexity of preprocessors increases the likelihood to introduce defects during maintenance (Thüm et al. 2016). The idea of enabling feature traceability with colors is borrowed from tools like *CIDE* (Kästner et al. 2008) and *FeatureCommander* (Feigenspan et al. 2011). In contrast to *FeatureIDE*, *CIDE* follows the principle of virtual separation of concerns, which completely replaces preprocessor statements by storing color annotations that align with the abstract syntax tree (Kästner and Apel 2009). Experiments indicate that the use of colors improves some aspects of program comprehension during maintenance (Feigenspan et al. 2013).

Quality Assurance for Conditional Compilation

12

Preprocessors can help to implement better quality software as they prevent to copy and adapt an existing system multiple times. However, preprocessor annotated software also comes with problems for code comprehension and failure detection. We already showed how *FeatureIDE* helps to implement variable software using conditional compilation (cf. Chap. 10 on Page 105). We further discussed how *FeatureIDE* helps to understand variability in preprocessor annotated code using specialized views and background colors (cf. Chap. 11 on Page 123).

Preprocessors are a relatively easy approach to implement variability in software. However, preprocessor annotations have a negative impact on code understanding, and it is often hard to reason about the correct usage of features in annotations. In this chapter, we show how *FeatureIDE* helps to improve code quality by providing specialized analyses for conditional compilation.

In detail, features used in preprocessor annotations need to be consistent with the feature model as inconsistencies can cause dead or superfluous code. Thus, in Sect. 12.1, we show how these inconsistencies can be prevented using *FeatureIDE*. Second, different configurations include and exclude the source code; thus, some failures may only appear for certain combinations of features, known as feature interactions. *FeatureIDE* provides specialized analyses to detect such feature interaction faults using automated product-based analyses (cf. Sect. 12.2). Finally, in Sect. 12.3, we show how code metrics can help understanding the complexities of annotations to detect error-prone code.

To recreate the problems that can appear with conditional compilation, check out the example project as described in Instruction 12.1. The example project already contains faults which will be resolved in this chapter using *FeatureIDE*.

© Springer International Publishing AG 2017
J. Meinicke et al., *Mastering Software Variability with FeatureIDE*,
DOI 10.1007/978-3-319-61443-4_12

Instruction 12.1 (Import the Elevator-Antenna-v1.2 Example)

1. Open the example wizard by any of the following options:
   - Press *New → Example* in the context menu of the Project/Package Explorer
   - Press *New → Examples → FeatureIDE → FeatureIDE Examples* in the upper-left menu toolbar of *Eclipse*
   - Press *File → New → Example* in the menu bar of *Eclipse*
2. Select *FeatureIDE Examples*
3. Press *Next*
4. Select *Book Example* tab
5. Select the project *Part III → Chapter 12 → Elevator-Antenna-v1.2*
6. Press *Finish*

12.1   Consistency Checking for Preprocessors

Feature models define the features and their relations. As we use features in preprocessor directives, it is necessary to check that the features defined in the model are consistent to the features used in the directives. Furthermore, relations among features can be implemented with directives (e.g., by nesting multiple #if directives). Inconsistent use of features in directives can cause multiple defects. *FeatureIDE* automatically checks these inconsistencies and reports using error markers. Specifically, *FeatureIDE* can detect the following inconsistencies:

- Use of undefined features in directives (e.g., due to spelling mistakes).
- Combination of features is a tautology which causes the corresponding code to be included despite the feature selections. Thus, the annotation is redundant and could be removed.
- Combination of features is a contradiction which causes the corresponding code to be dead (i.e., the code is never active in any configuration).

In the screenshots of Fig. 12.1, we show examples for the three types of inconsistencies. The first warning of Fig. 12.1a points out that the feature `DirectionalCall` is not defined in the feature model. Thus, the feature can never be selected, causing the directive to be invalid and the corresponding code to be dead.

Features can be used in arbitrary combinations in multiple if directives. This can cause wrong combination of features, especially as their relation in the feature model is not always obvious. In Fig. 12.1b, c, we show examples for defects caused by inconsistent combinations of feature directives. First, in Fig. 12.1b, the feature `CallButtons` is nested in the feature `DirectedCall`. However, as defined in the feature model, the feature `DirectedCall` already implies `CallButtons`. Thus, the

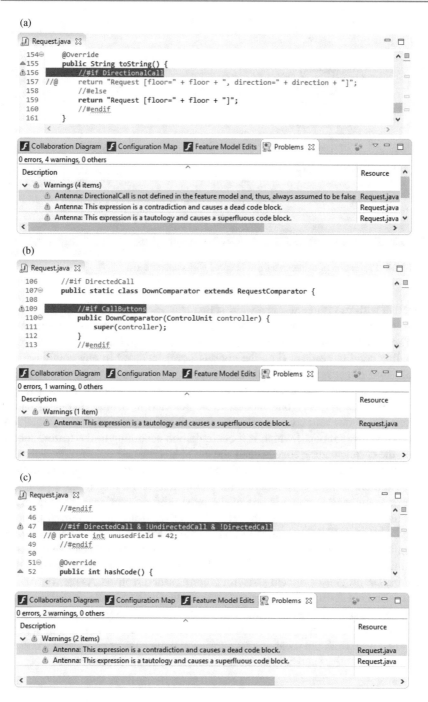

Fig. 12.1 Quality assurance for preprocessor annotated code in *FeatureIDE* ensuring consistent usage of features. (**a**) Detection of undefined features used in preprocessor directives. (**b**) Detection of superfluous preprocessor directives. (**c**) Detection of contradicting preprocessor directives

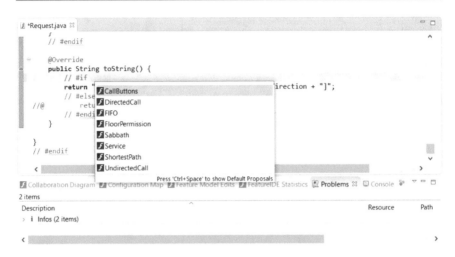

Fig. 12.2 Prevention of using undefined features with content assist

directive with `CallButtons` is always active if `DirectedCall` is selected. As this
dependency makes the second directive redundant, the directive should be removed.

The second combination of features, depicted in Fig. 12.1c, causes the corresponding code to be dead (i.e., the code is never included in any configuration).
Again two directives are nested, `CallButtons` and `Sabbath`. In this example,
`Sabbath` can never be selected, because `CallButtons` implies either `FIFO` or
`ShortedtPath`. As only one mode can be selected at a time, `Sabbath` cannot
be selected if `CallButtons` is selected. The actual expression of the directive is
`CallButtons`∨`Sabbath`, which is a contradiction according to the feature model.
Thus, the corresponding code is dead and could be removed.

Beyond pointing out these inconsistencies with error markers, *FeatureIDE* helps
to avoid them using a content assist for annotations and a refactoring to correctly
rename features. Renaming is one of the most used refactorings. When changing
a feature's name in the feature model, all directives using this feature need to be
adapted. *FeatureIDE* automatically updates the feature names in directives when
renaming a feature. With this renaming refactoring inconsistencies and manual
renaming can be avoided. To further avoid inconsistencies due to naming conflicts,
FeatureIDE provides a content assist for preprocessor directives. As known from the
Eclipse content assist in the source code, the content assist provides possible content
that can be placed, however, within comments. When the assist is activated (using
ctrl + space) after a directive, *FeatureIDE* shows the features that can be inserted
(cf. Fig. 12.2). Both the renaming refactoring and the content assist ease the use of
features in directives and help to ensure consistency to the feature model.

12.2   Product-Based Analyses for Preprocessors

Defects in configurable software may only occur in certain configurations due to defects in certain features or due to feature interactions. Manually generating and analyzing single configurations is a time-consuming task. To support ease of *product-based analyses* (i.e., analyses of single configurations), *FeatureIDE* provides automated derivation and analysis of configurations. Automated derivation of configurations with *FeatureIDE* is already described in Sect. 8.4 on Page 92. To analyze the generated configurations, the generation process is extended by the generation of the corresponding source code and the analysis thereof.

Due to scalability and the possibly large number of possible configurations, it is useful to run the generation on sample sets only, such as the manually defined configurations or configurations that only cover pairs of feature interactions. The strategy which set of configurations should be generated to analyze can be selected in the product generation dialog.

After generating single configurations, it is possible to apply analyses from single systems. *FeatureIDE* currently integrates *static analysis* provided by the compiler and *testing* of the generated products with *JUnit*. Thus, after the generation of the preprocessed source code, *FeatureIDE* automatically compiles the variants. If a defect is found by the compiler, an error marker is created on the corresponding file. As the products are generated in a separate place than the source folder, *FeatureIDE* propagates the markers back to the original source files. Thus, the fault can be directly seen in the source file even if the corresponding line is inactive (i.e., commented out for Antenna). In Fig. 12.3, we exemplary show a defect that only occurs in certain configurations. As shown, Line 30 is not included in the current product. However, the configuration generator created a configuration containing the line and the corresponding product with the fault.

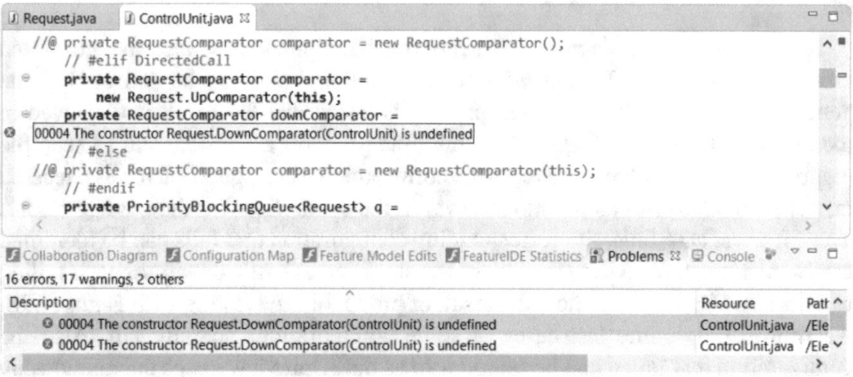

Fig. 12.3 Detection of configuration-specific faults with *FeatureIDE*

Fig. 12.4 Product-based testing with *FeatureIDE*, preventing fault configuration relationship

In a further step, *FeatureIDE* supports to automatically test the generated products using JUnit. Testing with JUnit is optional and can be activated in the generation dialog. Each generated product is tested and the result is displayed in the original JUnit view. However, as multiple products are tested, and to keep the mapping of the executed test case to the corresponding configuration it was executed in, *FeatureIDE* shows an additional level in the JUnit view for the configurations. Thus, if a test case fails, the corresponding configuration that fails can be identified easily. As known from the JUnit view, the stack trace is still shown for each failing test case. In Fig. 12.4, we show the result of product-based testing with *FeatureIDE*. As shown, only some test cases of some configurations actually fail. Also the configuration that failed can be reproduced as the JUnit view keeps the relationship to the configuration.

12.3   Code Metrics for Preprocessors

Understanding how preprocessor annotations are used to implement variability is necessary to identify probably error-prone code. To help to understand the variability of the program, *FeatureIDE* provides a statistics view that shows information on the system. The *FeatureIDE Statistics* view should be already open in *Eclipse* as it is part of the *FeatureIDE* perspective. However, if it is not open yet, follow Instruction 12.2.

Instruction 12.2 (Open the Statistics View)
Open the statistics view by any of the following options:

- Press *FeatureIDE Statistics* in the lower part of *Eclipse* next to the other *FeatureIDE* views
- Press *Window* → *Show View* → *FeatureIDE Statistics* in the menu bar of *Eclipse*

For preprocessor annotated programs, the statistics view shows the following metrics:

- Number of if-defs per file
- Nesting depth of if-defs
- Number of involved features

There are more metrics for preprocessor (Liebig et al. 2010). Though, the three metrics are easily understandable and give an impression whether a file is highly using if-defs and whether it is error prone. These metrics indicate whether the project needs to be restructured.

As there is no maximum nesting of preprocessor directives and, in principle, all features can be referenced within the same preprocessor directive, product lines with conditional compilation can become arbitrarily complex. Identifying extreme cases in the mapping is hardly possible with the previously mentioned views. Hence, *FeatureIDE* provides a view for that particular case, called Statistics View. In Fig. 12.5, we present some of the statistics currently available within *FeatureIDE*, whereas files can typically be opened by means of a double-click.

In particular, we can see that the class with the most preprocessor directives is `FloorComposite`. Hence, this class is likely to be hard to understand. Interested readers may want to have a look at the file, and experienced programmers will find ways to simplify the mapping by reorganizing the content of the file. In contrast, the preprocessor directive with the most features is given in the class `MainWindow`. While three features are not that much, industrial projects tend to have many features involved and they can often be simplified. Also, if such expressions contain quite

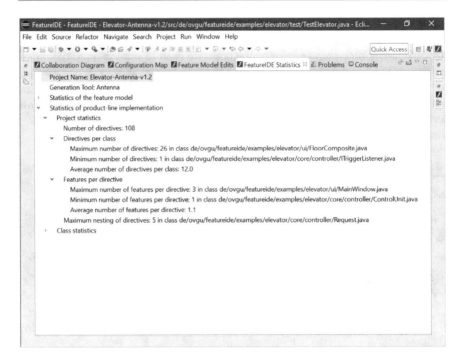

Fig. 12.5 Identifying complex feature-to-code mapping with the statistics view

often, they could indicate that rather a new feature should be created as a domain abstraction in the feature model.

12.4   Summary and Further Reading

Preprocessors are powerful tools to implement fine-grained variability in software. Though, these fine-grained variations in the source code not only come with challenges for code comprehension but also hinder quality assurance. Default analyses, such as testing, can only check one product at once. As there are up to exponentially many products to the number of features, it is usually impractical to analyze all products manually.

To handle the variability, *FeatureIDE* provides automated mechanisms to analyze preprocessor annotated programs. First, *FeatureIDE* checks whether the annotations are correctly used according to the feature model. This analysis ensures that the features are used correctly to not introduce dead or superfluous code. Second, we allow to analyze large configuration spaces by generating and checking products automatically. To increase the detection rate, *FeatureIDE* allows to use T-wise configurations that cover all interactions among T features. Finally, *FeatureIDE* provides metrics about the variability in the statistics view. Using this metric, it is possible to reason about how variation is implemented. This can help to detect possibly error-prone code, for example, with a high number of nested directives.

In Chap. 8 on Page 81, we described how *FeatureIDE* supports domain analysis and ensures valid feature dependencies. In this section, we connected this analysis with the actual source code. Thus, *FeatureIDE* helps to ensure that the implementation actually represents the previously designed variability model. In Chap. 11 on Page 123, we showed how *FeatureIDE* helps to understand the variations in the program. Both code comprehension and software analysis for preprocessors help to implement better software with variability and should be always used in concert.

Product-based analyses usually only allow to analyze a representative subset of products. With variability-aware analysis, it is possible to analyze all configurations anyhow. These kinds of analyses lift a standard analysis (e.g., type checking) to be able to handle variability. For example, TypeChef (Kästner et al. 2011) is able to type check Linux kernel with thousands of configuration options.

Part IV

Tool Support for Feature-Oriented Programming

Feature-Oriented Programming with FeatureIDE

13

In the previous parts, we showed how *FeatureIDE* helps to model the domain using feature models (cf. Chap. 5 on Page 43), how to configure products (cf. Chap. 6 on Page 63), and how to implement variability using conditional compilation (cf. Part III on Page 95). For conditional compilation, we introduced a general process to implement software product line in *FeatureIDE* (cf. Chap. 9 on Page 97), how to implement a software product line (cf. Chap. 10 on Page 105), how to trace features in source code (cf. Chap. 11 on Page 123), and how to ensure good software quality (cf. Chap. 12 on Page 131). In this part, we introduce the same concepts specialized to *feature-oriented programming*.

Feature-oriented programming is a specialized form of generative programming (Prehofer 1997). A specialized composition mechanism generates program variants out of code fragments. In contrast to conditional compilation, this approach allows to realize separation of concerns, meaning that features are implemented in isolation, while features in preprocessor annotated code intermix with each other.

In this chapter, we introduce *feature-oriented programming* and the general process of how *FeatureIDE* helps to implement software product lines using this approach (cf. Sect. 13.1). We introduce the three integrated composition tools *FeatureHouse*, *AHEAD*, and *FeatureC++* in Sects. 13.2, 13.3, and 13.4, respectively. Finally, in Sect. 13.5, we give a brief introduction on how to use these tools in *FeatureIDE*.

13.1 Feature-Oriented Programming

The main goal when implementing software product lines is *separation of concerns*, meaning that separate features (i.e., concerns) are also physically separated, for example, into different files. When implementing with conditional compilation, features usually intermix with multiple files and other features, thus making the development and traceability of features hard. FOP aims to separate each feature into a separate module to realize separation of concerns. FOP was initially designed

© Springer International Publishing AG 2017
J. Meinicke et al., *Mastering Software Variability with FeatureIDE*,
DOI 10.1007/978-3-319-61443-4_13

as an extension of object-oriented programming in which the system is decomposed into feature modules (Prehofer 1997). It has been generalized as a concept that can be uniformly applied to multiple host languages and even non-code artifacts (Batory 2006; Apel et al. 2013b).

Starting from a base program, each feature module can be seen as an increment of functionality realizing a certain feature. For object-oriented languages, such as Java, a feature module can introduce new classes, methods, or fields to the program. Additionally, a feature module can change existing classes by replacing or refining its methods and fields. For this purpose, a feature module consists of class fragments that are mapped to features. A variant can be generated by an FOP composer that composes a set of feature modules by merging them according to certain composition rules as explained in the following example.

In Listing 13.1, we use a product line that prints a variation of *Hello World* to illustrate the principle of feature-oriented programming. In this example, we have four different feature modules in which we include the corresponding source code of each feature. The first feature module `Hello` (cf. Lines 1–8) contains the class

Listing 13.1 Feature modules of the *Hello World* product line

```
 1  public class Main {                           feature module Hello
 2    public static void main(String[] args){
 3      new Main().print();
 4    }
 5    public void print() {
 6      System.out.print("Hello");
 7    }
 8  }
```

```
 9  public class Main {                           feature module Beautiful
10    public void print(){
11      original();
12      System.out.print(" beautiful");
13    }
14  }
```

```
15  public class Main {                           feature module Wonderful
16    public void print(){
17      original();
18      System.out.print(" wonderful");
19    }
20  }
```

```
21  public class Main {                           feature module World
22    public void print(){
23      original();
24      System.out.print(" world!");
25    }
26  }
```

Main with the methods main and print. The method main initializes an object of this class to call the method print of our *Hello World* program. Additionally, the method print writes *Hello* to the console. In addition to this first feature module Hello, we can define refinements of this class using further feature modules. In detail, we can add new methods and fields, functionality to existing methods, or we can redefine the value of existing fields. For instance, the feature module World defines the same class Main, thus refining it (cf. Line 21). Furthermore, this class refinement also defines a method called print. We intend to add additional functionality to this already existing method (i.e., the method already exists in the base implementation). Rather than replacing its implementation, we use the keyword original to call the initial functionality (cf. Line 23). This original call is similar to the super call in object-oriented programming for inheritance. Without this additional call to the original implementation, the previous code would be overwritten by the new method. In the same way, we also implement the feature modules of Beautiful (cf. Lines 9–14) and Wonderful (cf. Lines 15–20).

To generate a program variant for a certain configuration, we can run the composer (in the case of our example *FeatureHouse*). The composer takes the modules of the selected features as input and combines them to a standard program without variation. For example, the composition of the feature modules Hello, Wonderful, and World generates a program that prints the sentence *"Hello wonderful world!"*. We show the generated source code in Listing 13.2.

For the composition of feature modules, different orders can generate different programs. For example, composing {Hello, World, Beautiful} would create a program that prints *"Hello world! beautiful"*. Thus, for FOP, it is necessary to explicitly define the order in which features are composed. Furthermore, it is possible to create invalid variants that do not compile. For example, the configuration {Beautiful, Hello} is invalid as the original call in the method print of the module Beautiful does not point to a base module. Thus, it is also necessary to

Listing 13.2 Composition of the features Hello, Wonderful, and World

```
1  public class Main {
2    public static void main(String[] args){
3      new Main().print();
4    }
5    public void print__wrappee__Hello() {
6      System.out.print("Hello");
7    }
8    public void print__wrappee__Wonderful() {
9      print__wrappee__Hello();
10     System.out.print(" wonderful");
11   }
12   public void print(){
13     print__wrappee__Wonderful()
14     System.out.print(" world!");
15   }
16 }
```

define constraints among features representing valid feature combinations. In the following of this part, we will show how the integration of FOP in *FeatureIDE* with feature models that explicitly define the constraints of the feature order helps preventing these issues.

There are several tools for feature-oriented programming that slightly differ in their syntax used to define feature modules and in details of the composition mechanism. In *FeatureIDE*, we support the user during the implementation, by providing an integration of several tools for feature-oriented programming, namely, *AHEAD*, *FeatureHouse*, and *FeatureC++*. For all these tools, *FeatureIDE* helps to model the domain, implement the modules, configure the variants, and automatically generate the products. Furthermore, *FeatureIDE* provides several mechanisms to analyze the product line's implementation. In the following, we provide a general overview on the functionality for the supported composition tools and illustrate their integration into *FeatureIDE*. We give an overview on further tool support for other languages in Chap. 17 on Page 199.

13.2   Feature Modules with FeatureHouse

In this section, we introduce the details of the composition tool *FeatureHouse*, which we already used in the previous example. In the following, we give a short introduction to the general idea of FeatureHouse and give an overview to its general functionality and integration into *FeatureIDE*.

FeatureHouse Background

In feature-oriented programming, a variant is built by composing a set of *feature modules*. A possible approach for the composition of features is the superimposition of *feature structure trees*. *FeatureHouse* is a software-composition tool based on this idea that can be used to compose feature modules containing software artifacts written in various languages including Java.

A feature structure tree (FST) is a hierarchical representation of the structural elements of a feature module. In the case of Java, these elements are packages, classes, fields, and methods. Each node in an FST must have a name and a type. We distinguish between terminal nodes (i.e., nodes without children, such as methods and files) and nonterminal nodes (i.e., nodes with children, such as packages and classes).

FeatureHouse composes feature modules by superimposing their FSTs. By merging the corresponding nodes of the FSTs of two features based on their names, types, and relative positions, *FeatureHouse* creates a new FST containing the merged nodes. The resulting FST can then be composed with a third FST, and so on. Two corresponding terminal nodes are merged following language- and type-specific composition rules. In the case of feature-oriented programming for Java,

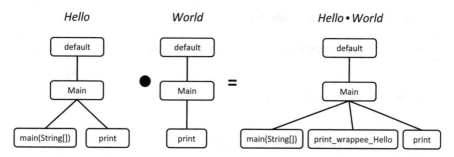

Fig. 13.1 Superimposition of FSTs with *FeatureHouse*

Listing 13.3   The content of the configuration file helloWorld.features

```
1  Hello
2  Wonderful
3  World
```

the rules define how methods are refined by using the keyword `original` and how fields are overwritten.

Superimposition can be applied to all tree-like structures. The general algorithm only requires each node to be given a unique combination of name and type and can be enriched with arbitrary composition rules for terminal nodes. Thus, *FeatureHouse* is considered as a general approach for software composition and can be used for several languages such as Java, C#, C, Haskell, JavaCC, Alloy, and UML. In Fig. 13.1, we exemplary illustrate the superimposition for the features `Hello` and `World` of the previous example.

Using *FeatureHouse*

FeatureHouse is deployed as command-line tool. In the following, we give an overview on how to use it to compose feature modules. A tutorial can also be found on the developers website.[1]

To select the modules that should be composed, you need to specify the feature modules that are supposed to be composed. Therefore, *FeatureHouse* expects a path to a called configuration file that contains a list of the features. The order of features in the configuration file also defines the order in which the feature modules are composed (cf. Listing 13.3).

As introduced in the previous section, *FeatureHouse* uses the keyword `original` to call the previous implementation of a method. In *FeatureHouse*, the feature modules contain a set of files. To compose the feature modules of the features `Hello`

---

[1] http://www.infosun.fim.uni-passau.de/spl/apel/fh/.

and `World`, we can execute *FeatureHouse* as follows:

```
java -jar FeatureHouse.jar -expression helloWorld.features
```

As result of composition, regular Java files are created.

13.3   Feature Modules with AHEAD

In this section, we give an overview on feature-oriented programming using *AHEAD* (Batory 2003, 2006). First, we give an overview on the background of the tool *AHEAD* and introduce its general functionality.

AHEAD Background

The composition tool *AHEAD* has been developed as an implementation of a fundamental architectural model for feature-oriented programming (Batory 2003, 2006). In AHEAD, a software product line is considered as a so-called algebraic structure in which operations correspond to the features that change or add functionality. This means that individual products are represented by unique compositions of feature modules. This universality of this rather abstract concept enables the uniform composition of code and non-code artifacts in different languages. Each *feature module* defines a set of refinements that are to be applied to all these different representations simultaneously. Considering the Elevator example, each feature might refine multiple classes.

To explain how *AHEAD* composed feature modules, we again use a simple hello world example. The classes for the features `Hello` and `World` are shown in Listing 13.4. As shown, there are two differences compared to *FeatureHouse*. First, to call the refined method, the keyword `Super()` is used, similar to inheritance in Java (cf. Line 11). Additionally, it is necessary to reference the method that should be called (e.g., the method `print`). The second difference is that refining classes need to be explicitly marked with the keyword `refines` (cf. Line 9).

Listing 13.4 Feature modules of the *Hello World* product line for *AHEAD*

```
1 public class Main {                          feature module Hello
2   public static void main(String[] args) {
3     new Main().print();
4   }
5   public void print() {
6     System.out.print("Hello");
7   }
8 }
```

```
 9 public refines class Main {                    feature module World
10    public void print(){
11       Super().print();
12       System.out.print(" world");
13    }
14 }
```

Listing 13.5 Composition of the features Hello and World with *AHEAD* with *Mixin*

```
 1 abstract class Main$$Hello {
 2    public void print() {
 3       System.out.print("Hello");
 4    }
 5    public static void main(String[] args) {
 6       new Main().print();
 7    }
 8 }
 9 public class Main extends Main$$Hello {
10    public void print() {
11       super.print();
12       System.out.print(" world!");
13    }
14 }
```

Listing 13.6 Composition of the features Hello and World with *AHEAD* with *Jampack*

```
 1 public class Main {
 2    public static void main(String[] args) {
 3       new Main().print();
 4    }
 5    public final void print$$Hello() {
 6       System.out.print("Hello");
 7    }
 8    public void print() {
 9       print$$Hello();
10       System.out.print(" world!");
11    }
12 }
```

AHEAD provides two different approaches to compose the feature modules, namely, *Mixin* and *Jampack*. Mixin uses Java inheritance to refine classes. Thus, the Super() keyword is just replaced by super calling the extended class. If the previous method is not called with Super, then the method is overwritten. In Listing 13.5, we show the result of Mixin for the Hello World example. The class of the feature Hello is set abstract and is extended by the class of the feature World. Thus, when calling the main method, the program will call the extended print method.

The second composition mechanism Jampack is similar to the composition with *FeatureHouse*. The resulting code for Jampack is depicted in Listing 13.6. All

methods are in the same class and the refinement is realized by renaming and calling
the original method. Thus, the method `print` of the feature `Hello` is renamed to
`print$$Hello`. This renamed method is called by the refining print method of
feature `World`.

Using *AHEAD*

In the following, we explain how to use AHEAD outside of *FeatureIDE* to perform
the composition of feature modules to generate products. The *AHEAD* tool suite
is a set of command-line tools including the *AHEAD* composer for software
composition (Batory 2003, 2006). A comprehensive tutorial on how to use the
AHEAD command-line tools already exists, and we refer the reader to this tutorial
to get more detailed information (Batory 2003, 2006). We will summarize the
information based on this tutorial to give some insights into *AHEAD*'s functionality.

The *AHEAD* composer uses a set of feature folders that represent feature modules
as input and combines the underlying source files according to the concept of
feature-oriented programming explained above. It supports an extension of Java
1.4 with additional keywords to define the relation between feature modules.
In AHEAD, feature folders contain a set of `jak` files with the file extension
.jak. Jak is a convention of *AHEAD* as the files contain non-Java keywords. To
compose the feature modules of the features `Hello` and `World` that are located
in the corresponding folders by a set of `jak` files, we can execute *AHEAD* as
follows (Batory 2003, 2006):

```
composer   --target=HelloWorld   Hello   World
```

The result of this execution is a new feature module (i.e., folder) `HelloWorld` with
the composed `jak` files of the input folders `Hello` and `World`.

After the composition, we can use a second tool called *jak2java* to generate Java
files based on it (Batory 2003, 2006):

```
jak2java   *.jak
```

The resulting Java files only contain ordinary Java syntax, and we can compile
the sources in an ordinary manner using the Java compiler *javac*.

13.4   Feature Modules with FeatureC++

Similar to *FeatureHouse* and *AHEAD*, *FeatureC++* is a composition tool for
feature-oriented programming. *FeatureC++* is an extension of C++ to realize
modularity (Apel et al. 2005).

FeatureC++ Background

As all approaches for FOP, each feature has an own module containing the source files that are used for composition. In the case of *FeatureC++*, the files are header files with the file extension .h.

In Listing 13.7, we show the Hello World example *FeatureC++*. The code for the feature module Hello is standard C++ code that is used as base implementation. The program provides a method called run that prints *"Hello"* to the console. The second listing for the module of World refines the class Main and refines its method run. To refine a class, *FeatureC++* introduces the keyword refines, similar to *AHEAD* (cf. Line 9). To call the refined method, the keyword super is used. By calling super::run(), the module of World can call the method of the module Hello (cf. Line 12).

When composing the *feature modules* with *FeatureC++*, the refined methods are renamed and called by the refining method if there is an explicit super call. In Listing 13.8, we show the result of composing the modules of Hello and World. The method run of the module Hello is renamed to Hello_run (cf. Line 4). This method is called by the refining method of the feature World (cf. Line 11). Additionally, the keyword inline will tell the compiler to inline the method Hello_run into the method run (cf. Line 4).

Using *FeatureC++*

As the other tools, *FeatureC++* is deployed as command-line tool. The composer takes a configuration file with the file extension .equation which needs to be in the

Listing 13.7 Feature modules of the *Hello World* product line for *FeatureC++*

```
 1  #include <stdio.h>                          feature module Hello
 2  class Main {
 3    public:
 4      int run() {
 5        printf("Hello");
 6        return 0;
 7      }
 8  };
```

```
 9  refines class Main {                         feature module World
10    public:
11      int run() {
12        int res = super::run();
13        if (res!=0)
14          return res;
15        printf(" World!");
16        return 0;
17      }
18  };
```

Listing 13.8 Composition of the features `Hello` and `World` with *FeatureC++*

```
1 #include <stdio.h>
2 class Main {
3   public:
4     inline int Hello_run() {
5       printf("Hello");
6       return 0;
7     }
8
9   public:
10    int run() {
11      int res = Hello_run();
12      if (res!=0)
13        return res;
14      printf(" World!");
15      return 0;
16    }
17 };
```

Listing 13.9 The content of the configuration file HelloWorld.equation

```
1 Hello
2 World
```

root folder as input. The configuration file contains the names of the features that should be composed as input as shown in Listing 13.9.

FeatureC++ can be executed as follows:

$$\texttt{fc++ -gpp HelloWorld}$$

As *FeatureC++* provides further functionalities, as well as support for aspect-oriented programming, we refer to its website.[2]

13.5   Feature-Oriented Programming with FeatureIDE

In the previous section, we introduced how composition tools for FOP work, what their keywords are, and how they can be used. As illustrated, all tools can only be used via command line. Thus, their usability is limited and causes further challenges for the correctness and implementation of the product lines.

With *FeatureIDE*, we aim to solve these challenges by providing these tools in an integrated development environment. *FeatureIDE* automates the call to the composition tool, so that the usage of the feature-oriented programming is

---

[2]http://wwwiti.cs.uni-magdeburg.de/iti_db/fcc/.

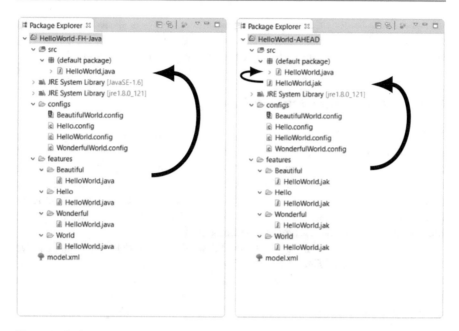

Fig. 13.2 Project structures for feature-oriented programming with *FeatureHouse* (*left*) and *AHEAD* (*right*)

convenient. Furthermore, with the integration of feature models and configuration support, the design of the domain and the products is eased. The standard procedure to create projects with *FeatureIDE* is discussed in Chap. 3 on Page 19. To check out another composition tool, the tool can be chosen in the new project wizard.

After initializing the project, you would typically create the feature model for your product line. As explained above, in feature-oriented programming, the composition order matters. Thus, in addition to the set of features and its dependencies, the feature order can be defined in the feature model editor (cf. Chap. 5 on Page 43). By default, the feature order is derived from the structure of the feature model (pre-order). As the order typically depends on implementation details, it can be changed at any point during development in the order page of the Feature Model Editor.

In Fig. 13.2, we depict the details of *FeatureIDE*'s project structure for projects based on *FeatureHouse* (left) and *AHEAD* (right). For *FeatureC++* projects, the structure is similar to projects with *FeatureHouse*. The folder feature contains all feature modules (i.e., folders with the names of concrete features) of the product line. The feature folders are used as input for the composition, depending on the selected features of the current configuration (i.e., the configuration file marked with a green pencil). The folder src is used as output folder of the composition. For *AHEAD*, it also contains the resulting jak files of the composition process, which are then translated to Java. All the generation processes are automated in *FeatureIDE*. Thus, the user does not need to handle the composition. If a file is changed in the folder features, the generation process is started automatically. As the output folder of the composition is also the source folder of the underlying *Eclipse* project, *Eclipse* automatically compiles the project after composition.

13.6   Summary and Further Reading

In this chapter, we introduced the basics of using feature-oriented programming with FeatureIDE. First, we explained the main concept of FOP and how it realized separation of concerns. Second, we introduced the three integrated composition tools for FOP, namely, *FeatureHouse*, *AHEAD*, and *FeatureC++*. We have shown that all these tools have the main drawbacks that they are only available as command-line tools. Thus, we showed how *FeatureIDE* solves the issues with these tools as an integrated development environment.

In this chapter, we only gave a general overview on FOP. In Chap. 14, we explain the concepts of *FeatureIDE* for FOP in detail. In that chapter, we extend the running elevator example of Chap. 4 on Page 31 into a software product line using *FeatureHouse* in *FeatureIDE*. Further functionalities for feature traceability and quality assurance are explained in Chap. 15 on Page 173 and Chap. 16 on Page 183, respectively.

In this chapter, we only gave a brief overview on FOP. For more specific information on the FOP, we refer to the literature of the three compositional tools *AHEAD* (Batory 2003, 2006), *FeatureHouse* (Apel et al. 2009), and *FeatureC++* (Apel et al. 2005). A general overview on feature-oriented software product lines including FOP can be found in the book of Apel et al. (2013a).

Developing an Elevator with Feature-Oriented Programming

14

In this chapter, we illustrate how to implement software product lines with *feature-oriented programming* in *FeatureIDE*. The goal of this chapter is to illustrate and practice how feature-oriented programming works in detail and how the workflow of *FeatureIDE* implements the product line. In this chapter, we assume that the *FeatureIDE* perspective is active.

We use our running example of the elevator product line (cf. Chap. 4 on Page 31) and extend it with features for control logics Sabbath and FIFO and with an optional Service feature. In the initial version of the project, the elevator uses the sabbath mode, in which no user input is required and all levels are reached periodically. As a first step, we show how to transform this project to a *FeatureIDE* project based on feature-oriented programming using *FeatureHouse*. This step also includes a first separation of functionality, because the base version contains not only the main functionality of the elevator but also the realized behavior of the sabbath mode. In a second step, we introduce an optional feature, Service, that should allow authorized persons to easily maintain the elevator. In a last step, we implement an alternative control logic, FIFO.

To allow readers to skip steps or to compare their implementation with our solution, we provide all intermediate results in *FeatureIDE*'s example wizard. In Instruction 14.1, we present how to access those solutions.

14.1 Creating an Elevator Product Line

In this first step, we describe the procedure on how to create an initial *FeatureIDE* project based on feature-oriented programming with a subsequent separation of concern. As a result of this section, we get a small product line with two features: the root feature Elevator and the optional feature Sabbath.

© Springer International Publishing AG 2017
J. Meinicke et al., *Mastering Software Variability with FeatureIDE*,
DOI 10.1007/978-3-319-61443-4_14

Instruction 14.1 (Import the Specific Step of the Elevator Example)

1. Open the example wizard by any of the following options:
   - Press *New* → *Example* in the context menu of the Project/Package Explorer
   - Press *New* → *Examples* → *FeatureIDE* → *FeatureIDE Examples* in the upper-left menu toolbar of *Eclipse*
   - Press *File* → *New* → *Example* in the menu bar of *Eclipse*
2. Select *FeatureIDE Examples*
3. Press *Next*
4. Select *Book Example* tab
5. Select the project *Part IV* → *Chapter 14* → *<specific version>*
6. Press *Finish*

At first, we need to check out the basis elevator application. Therefore, check out the example called "Elevator SPL_FOP" using the example wizard (cf. Instruction 14.1). This base version is a standard *Eclipse* Java project that we will transform to a product line using *FeatureIDE*.

Next, we need to initialize the product line by transforming the project to a *FeatureIDE* project as explained in Instruction 14.2. This transformation automatically adapts the project structure. In detail, it creates an initial version of the feature model (cf. `model.xml`) with two features, a root feature `ElevatorSPL_FOP` and a feature `Base`, and a corresponding default configuration (cf. `configs/default.config`) as shown in Fig. 14.1. Furthermore, the conversion will automatically move the Java files from the source folder to the base module in a new folder called *features*. The composition process with the selected composer is automatically activated, in our case *FeatureHouse*. Thus, the code will be generated into the source folder again, which can be executed as Java Application as usual.

Instruction 14.2 (Transformation to a FeatureHouse Project)

1. Open the transformation wizard by:
   - Press *Configure* → *Convert to FeatureIDE Project...* in the context menu of the Project/Package Explorer
2. Select *FeatureHouse* as composer
3. Press *Finish*

Fig. 14.1 Initial feature model as a result of using Instruction 14.2

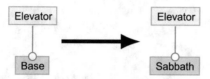

Fig. 14.2 From the initial to the desired feature model of our initial product line

After the transformation into an *FeatureIDE* project, we want to separate the functionality of Sabbath. Thus, we have to change the feature model so that the feature Sabbath is optional. In Chap. 5 on Page 43, we give more details on how to edit feature models. To ensure that the source code is located in our desired feature, we assume that the feature model is changed as follows (cf. Instruction 14.3). First, the feature Base is renamed to Elevator. Second, the concrete feature Sabbath is added as an optional child feature of the feature Elevator. Third, the root feature ElevatorSPL_FOP is removed. We depict the resulting feature model in Fig. 14.2. As a result, the existing configuration files (cf. configs/default.config) will be changed automatically. Furthermore, *FeatureIDE* automatically renames the feature module *Base* to elevator and creates a new feature module for Sabbath. This process is necessary to ensure that the root feature, now called Elevator, contains all the class files.

Instruction 14.3 (Initial Modification of the Feature Model)
Perform the following operations on the feature diagram:

1. Rename the feature Base to Elevator (cf. Instruction 5.3)
2. Add a new optional concrete feature Sabbath below Elevator (cf. Instruction 5.4)
3. Remove the abstract root feature (the feature on the top)

As a next step, we can start to separate the feature Sabbath. In detail, we extract the method calculateNextState, which currently realizes the sabbath mode. Therefore, we refactor this method into the feature module Sabbath. Using Instruction 14.4, we first create a new source file of the class ControlUnit in the feature module Sabbath. To refine the original class ControlUnit, the package declaration needs to match as well (i.e., select the package `de.ovgu.featureide.examples.elevator.core.controller`). The wizard will automatically create an empty class file for `ControlUnit` in the feature module `Sabbath`.

Instruction 14.4 (Add FeatureIDE Source File)

1. Open the *FeatureIDE* perspective if not active (cf. Instruction 3.1)
2. Open a class wizard by any of the following options:
   - Press *New → FeatureIDE Source File* in the context menu of the Package Explorer
   - Press *New → FeatureIDE → FeatureIDE Source File* in the upper-left menu toolbar of *Eclipse*
   - Press *File → New → FeatureIDE Source File* in the menu bar of *Eclipse*
3. Select a package
4. Enter a class name (e.g., Request)
5. Optionally check interface
6. Press *Finish*

Hint: using the menu on the file that should be refined will automatically fill the entries for package and class name.

Finally, we can extract the functionality for the feature `Sabbath`. The resulting source code of the two modules is depicted in Listing 14.1. To make the implementation of the method `calculateNextState` optional, we first move the complete method to the new class declaration of `Sabbath`. As `Sabbath` is optional, we need to have a default implementation in the module `Elevator`. This default implementation simply returns the `FLOORING` state which essentially leaves the elevator in the current floor. The method `calculateNextState` in the module `Elevator` is now refined by the implementation of `Sabbath` as both methods have the same signature. To call the default behavior of the elevator if `Sabbath` is selected, we return `original` in the module `Sabbath` (cf. Line 25)

Listing 14.1 Class fragment `ControlUnit` of the feature modules `Elevator` and `Sabbath`

```
 1 public class ControlUnit {                        feature module Elevator
 2
 3    // ... further source code
 4
 5    private ElevatorState calculateNextState() {
 6       return ElevatorState.FLOORING;
 7    }
 8 }
```

```
 9 public class ControlUnit {                        feature module Sabbath
10    private ElevatorState calculateNextState() {
11       final int currentFloor = elevator.getCurrentFloor();
```

```
12    switch (elevator.getCurrentState()) {
13    case FLOORING:
14      switch (elevator.getDirection()) {
15      case MOVING_DOWN:
16        return (currentFloor <= elevator.getMinFloor()) ?
17          ElevatorState.MOVING_UP :
                ElevatorState.MOVING_DOWN;
18      case MOVING_UP:
19        return (currentFloor >= elevator.getMaxFloor()) ?
20          ElevatorState.MOVING_DOWN :
                ElevatorState.MOVING_UP;
21      default:
22        return ElevatorState.MOVING_UP;
23      }
24    }
25    return original();
26  }
27 }
```

As there are multiple files with the same name (e.g., of *ControlUnit.java*), it might be confusing to know which file is currently open in the editor. *FeatureIDE* helps identifying the module by showing the feature name in the editors tab name. In Fig. 14.3, we show how the editor tabs for the three versions of the class ControlUnit are renamed. The two editors on the left belong to the features Elevator and Sabbath. This relation is emphasized using square brackets (e.g., [Sabbath]). The editor on the right contains the composed source file. This relation is emphasized by "<configuration name>" which refers to the configuration the file is built with. We recommend not to modify the generated file as it will be replaced when the modules are composed again.

As a result of our initialization step, we get a *FeatureIDE* project with the composer *FeatureHouse* in which different concerns are separated in different feature modules. The product line consists of two features, representing two products, even though an elevator that cannot move is not desirable (i.e., if Sabbath is not selected). By modifying the current configuration, we can create both program variants. For example, select the feature Sabbath in the configuration editor of the current configuration. After saving the configuration, the source code is automatically composed and compiled. Note that the program is also composed if the files in the feature modules are changed. The program can be executed using *Eclipse*'s *run as Java Application*.

14.2   Adding Feature "Service" to the Elevator Product Line

After the initialization of the elevator product line, we can now add an additional optional feature. In detail, we implement a new feature, Service, that allows authorized persons to maintain the elevator. The Service feature will send the elevator to the lowest floor if the corresponding button is activated. As this

Fig. 14.3 Identifying the relation of the open source file

Fig. 14.4 From the initial to the desired feature model of our initial product line

functionality is not necessarily needed in the final product, we add it as an optional feature.

To initialize the feature `Service` and the corresponding feature module, we first need to edit the feature model. As `Service` has no constraints with other features, we simply add it as an optional concrete feature under the root feature `Elevator`. Again, we refer the reader to Chap. 5 on Page 43 to get detailed information on how to add a feature. In Fig. 14.4, we show the desired feature model. After saving the feature model, *FeatureIDE* automatically creates a new empty feature module for `Service`.

At this point, we initialized the feature `Service` and, thus, we can start to implement the source code to realize the feature. Therefore, we will refine the classes `Elevator`, `ControlUnit`, and `SimulationUnit`. In the following, we discuss all the necessary changes.

Class Elevator To know whether the elevator is in the service mode, we have to add this information to its model class (i.e., the class `Elevator`). However, we only

Listing 14.2 Class fragment `Elevator` of the feature module `Service`

```
 1  public class Elevator {                          feature module Service
 2    private boolean inService = false;
 3
 4    public void setService(boolean mode) {
 5      this.inService = mode;
 6    }
 7
 8    public boolean isInService() {
 9      return inService;
10    }
11  }
```

want to store this information if the feature `Service` is selected. To realize this optional functionality, we create a new refinement of the class `Elevator` for the feature `Service` (cf. Instruction 14.4).The final class refinement of `Elevator` is depicted in Listing 14.2. In that class fragment, we define the field `isService` to store the information (cf. Line 2), add the method `setService` to change the stored value (cf. Lines 4–6), and add the method `isInService` to access the service information (cf. Lines 8–10).

Class ControlUnit The feature `Service` modifies the control logic of the elevator if the elevator is in service mode. Thus, we have to interrupt the current scheduling mechanism and send the elevator to the first floor. To change the behavior of the elevator, we again create a new class fragment for `ControlUnit` in the feature module `Service`. Afterward, we can refine the scheduling functionality of the class `ControlUnit`. The resulting code is depicted in Listing 14.3. In detail, the control logic is implemented in the method `calculateNextState` which already exists in the other modules. In the case of the feature `Service`, we have to refine the method so that the initial behavior is called if the service is not active (cf. method call `original` of Line 11). If the service is active, we calculate the next state so that the elevator is controlled to the first floor.

The method refinement illustrates how the order of feature composition can have an effect on the functionality. In the example, it is necessary that the feature `Service` is composed after other scheduling mechanisms. For example, composing the feature `Sabbath` after `Service` would cause a faulty behavior; when the service button is activated, the elevator moves to the first floor and then repeatedly moves back to the second floor again. To change the order in which the features are composed, either the order in the model can be changed by moving features in the model or the order can be explicitly defined using the *Feature Order* page of the feature model editor (cf. Sect. 5.6).

Class SimulationUnit As we now have implemented the model and the logic for the service behavior, we can couple it with the user interface. Therefore, we have

Listing 14.3 Class fragment `ControlUnit` of the feature module `Service`

```
 1 public class ControlUnit {                              feature module Service
 2   private ElevatorState calculateNextState() {
 3     final int currentFloor = elevator.getCurrentFloor();
 4     if (elevator.isInService()) {
 5       if (currentFloor != elevator.getMinFloor()) {
 6         return ElevatorState.MOVING_DOWN;
 7       } else {
 8         return ElevatorState.FLOORING;
 9       }
10     }
11     return original();
12   }
13
14   public boolean toggleService() {
15     elevator.setService(!elevator.isInService());
16     return elevator.isInService();
17   }
18 }
```

to refine the class `SimulationUnit` so that it is possible to toggle whether the elevator is in service. For the user interface, we have to also change the graphical unit represented by the class `MainWindow` which introduces a new `Service` button.

As our goal is to show the functionalities of *FeatureIDE*, we do not depict the source code for the UI classes. To update the classes anyhow, we already provide the class fragments in the example. As described in Instruction 14.5, we only need to copy the provided file into the feature module. After copying the file, the project might have errors in the class `MainWindow` as we need to couple the class with the `SimulationUnit`, which we will discuss next.

Instruction 14.5 (Adapting the User Interface for `Service`)

1. Copy the file `MainWindow.java` of the folder `guiVersions / Service`
2. Add the file to the `features` folder in the module `Service`.

Note that the class needs to be in the same package as the `MainWindow` *class in the* `Elevator` *module.*

To couple the `SimulationUnit` with the `MainWindow`, we have to change the constructor call to `MainWindow` and create a new method to switch the service mode. Thus, we first need to create a refining class `SimulationUnit` for the feature `Service`. The method `main` in the class `SimulationUnit` of the feature module `Elevator` creates an instance of the class `MainWindow` using the empty

Listing 14.4 Class fragment `SimulationUnit` of the feature modules `Service` and `Elevator`

```
1  public class SimulationUnit {                    feature module Elevator
2    public static void main(String[] args) {
3      SimulationUnit sim = new SimulationUnit();
4      simulationWindow = getMainWindow(sim);
5      sim.start(5);
6    }
7
8    private static MainWindow getMainWindow(SimulationUnit
         sim) {
9      return new MainWindow();
10   }
11
12   // further source code
13 }
```

```
14 public class SimulationUnit {                    feature module Service
15   private static MainWindow getMainWindow(SimulationUnit
         sim) {
16     return new MainWindow(sim);
17   }
18
19   public boolean toggleService() {
20     return controller.toggleService();
21   }
22 }
```

constructor. However, the constructor of `MainWindow` requires the `SimulationUnit` as a parameter to allow access to the service toggle functionality. The constructor is currently called in the method `main`. As feature-oriented programming does not allow fine-grained modifications as preprocessors can, we either need to replace the complete method or refine an additional method that only calls the constructor. In the following, we describe the latter.

In Listing 14.4, we present the necessary changes of the class `Simulation Unit`. In the upper listing, we present the changes of the feature module `Elevator`. To refine the constructor call later, we create a new method, `createMainWindow`, that initializes the `MainWindow` (cf. Lines 8–10). This allows us to create a corresponding method in the feature module `Service` and to override the initialization of the `MainWindow` instance (cf. Lines 15–17). However, for the instantiation of the class `MainWindow` in the feature module `Service`, we also need the instance of the created `SimulationUnit` from the main method. For this reason, the method has the `SimulationUnit` as a parameter.

Until now, the new graphical unit creates the service button, but the toggle functionality is missing. Therefore, we create the method `toggleService` in the feature module `Service` (cf. Lines 19–21). The method is already referenced by the service button in the class `MainWindow`.

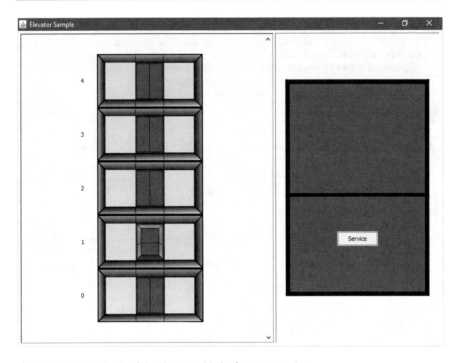

Fig. 14.5 Graphical unit of the elevator with the feature `Service`

Using the final version of our product line, we can select and generate a product with the feature `Service`. We refer the reader to Sect. 3.7 on Page 27 to get detailed information about the product generation and execution mechanism of *FeatureIDE*. In Fig. 14.5, we present the graphical representation of a product with the feature `Service`. Here, we can see the toggle button named *Service* that is available in the cabin of the elevator. If the button is used to switch into the service behavior, the elevator moves to the ground floor and stays there. If we press the button again, the elevator switches to the sabbath behavior.

14.3   Adding Feature "FIFO" to the Elevator Product Line

In this section, we describe how to add a further feature that allows an additional control logic of the elevator. In contrast to the feature `Service`, the feature `FIFO` will be an alternative to the already existing sabbath mode. For the feature `FIFO`, we have to integrate several changes to the elevator implementation. In detail, it is necessary to add a call button to each floor and a call button for each floor inside of the elevator's cabin. Based on these buttons, a user can call the elevator to a specific floor to directly move the elevator to this floor. If several floor requests exist, the feature `FIFO` ensures that the requests are handled in the order in which

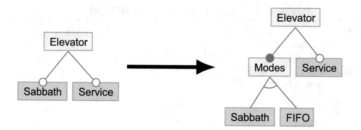

Fig. 14.6 Feature-model changes for the extended version with the feature FIFO

they occurred. As the feature FIFO is an alternative feature to the feature Sabbath, it is also possible to combine it with the feature Service.

As a first step to integrate the feature FIFO, we have to add the feature to the feature model. In detail, we add a mandatory abstract feature, Mode, between the features Sabbath and Elevator using *Create feature above* on the feature Sabbath. Afterward, we can add the feature FIFO below of the feature Mode. As FIFO is an alternative feature to the already existing feature Sabbath, we change the relation to be alternative (cf. Chap. 5 on Page 43). In Fig. 14.6, we present the intended result of our changes to the feature model. As a result of these feature-model changes, the new feature module is automatically created in the folder features.

At this point, we initialized the feature module FIFO and we can start to add the implementation artifacts. To add the new behavior, we need to handle button requests from each floor and, thus, we have to create a new class Request. Furthermore, it is necessary to inform the control unit about a request so that it is possible to handle them. For this purpose, we create the interface ITriggerListener and adapt the class ControlUnit accordingly. Additionally, we need to change the class SimulationUnit and the interface ITickListener to inform the graphical unit about a finished request. In the following, we introduce all changes in detail.

Class Request   To represent requests from button calls, we need to create a new class Request in the module FIFO. The class will simply store the requested floor. To create the new class, we again use Instruction 14.4 to add a new source file for the class Request in the controller package (i.e., the same package as ControlUnit). In Listing 14.5, we present the source code of the class. We create the field floor in which we store the floor that is requested (cf. Line 2). Furthermore, we create a constructor so that the floor information will be initialized for each instance of this class (cf. Line 8). To access the floor information from outside, we create the method getFloor to read the floor information (cf. Line 4). Finally, we implement the equals method which is used later so that there are no two requests to the same floor.

Listing 14.5 Class fragment Request of the feature module FIFO

```
1  public class Request {                        feature module FIFO
2    private int floor;
3
4    public int getFloor() {
5      return floor;
6    }
7
8    public Request(int floor) {
9      this.floor = floor;
10   }
11
12   public boolean equals(Object other) {
13     return ((Request)other).floor == floor;
14   }
15 }
```

Listing 14.6 Class fragment ITriggerListener of the feature module FIFO

```
1  public interface ITriggerListener {           feature module FIFO
2    void trigger(Request request);
3  }
```

Listing 14.7 Class fragment ITickListener of the feature module FIFO

```
1  public interface ITickListener {              feature module FIFO
2    void onRequestFinished(Elevator elevator, Request
          request);
3  }
```

Interface ITriggerListener As a next step, we create a new interface, ITriggerListener. Using Instruction 14.4, we add the new source file to the feature module of the feature FIFO. Check the box *interface* to create an interface. The wizard will create an interface called ITriggerListener in the controller package. The final interface is depicted in Listing 14.6. Here, we create a method that informs the class implementing this interface, about a floor request (cf. Line 2).

Interface ITickListener To inform the graphical unit about a finished request, it is also necessary to create a refinement of the interface ITickListener. Again, we use Instruction 14.4 and create the corresponding interface in the controller package. We depict the final version of the ITickListener in Listing 14.7. In detail, we add a new method, onRequestFinished, that can be used by a specific listener to get the information about a finished request (cf. Line 2).

Class ControlUnit To integrate the main behavior of the feature FIFO, we also need to refine the class ControlUnit. Again, we create a new source file using Instruction 14.4. In Listing 14.8, we present an overview of this class. As a first step, we add the interface `ITriggerListener` to this class (cf. Line 3). As a result, it is also necessary to add the method `trigger` as it is part of the interface `ITriggerListener` (cf. Line 6). To store the request, we add a queue called `requests` to the class (cf. Line 4). Using this queue, we store the incoming requests when the `trigger` method is called. To avoid storing requests twice, we check whether the same request is already stored in the queue before adding the new request.

After storing the requests in a queue, we can access and use them for the scheduling algorithm of `FIFO`. Therefore, we refine the method `calculateNextState` in which the requests are handled in the desired order (cf. Line 12). The `FIFO` algorithm works as follows. If the requested floor is not reached yet, then the elevator moves toward this floor, returning either `MOVING_UP` or `MOVING_DOWN`. If the floor is reached, the request is removed from the queue and the implementations of `ITickListener` are informed using the new method `requestFinished` (cf. Line 29).

Finally, the buttons of the UI need to know whether the elevator is already in the requested floor. This will avoid that this request is added to the queue. Thus, we add the new method `getCurrentFloor` which returns the current floor of the elevator (cf. Line 35).

Listing 14.8 Class fragment `ControlUnit` of the feature module `FIFO`

```
1  import java.util.LinkedList;                    feature module FIFO
2  import java.util.Queue;
3  public class ControlUnit implements ITriggerListener {
4    private Queue<Request> requests = new
          LinkedList<Request>();
5
6    public void trigger(Request request) {
7      if (!requests.contains(request)) {
8        requests.offer(request);
9      }
10   }
11
12   private ElevatorState calculateNextState() {
13     final int currentFloor = elevator.getCurrentFloor();
14     if (!requests.isEmpty()) {
15       Request nextRequest = requests.peek();
16       int floor = nextRequest.getFloor();
17       if (floor > currentFloor) {
18         return ElevatorState.MOVING_UP;
19       } else if (floor < currentFloor) {
20         return ElevatorState.MOVING_DOWN;
21       } else {
22         requestFinished(requests.poll());
23         return ElevatorState.FLOORING;
24       }
25     }
26     return original();
```

```
27    }
28
29    private void requestFinished(Request request) {
30      for (ITickListener listener : this.tickListener) {
31        listener.onRequestFinished(elevator, request);
32      }
33    }
34
35    public int getCurrentFloor() {
36      return elevator.getCurrentFloor();
37    }
38 }
```

Class SimulationUnit To start an elevator simulation with the behavior FIFO, it is also necessary to create a refinement for the class SimulationUnit in the feature module FIFO. Using Instruction 14.4, we create the corresponding source file. Listing 14.9 depicts all necessary implementations. As the listener for the console implements the interface ITickListener, we also need to add the method onRequestFinished for the feature FIFO. However, as we cannot make changes to anonymous classes, we first need to extract the class to an inner class ConsoleListener (cf. Line 17) in the feature module Elevator. We can now create a new instance of this listener and add it to the controller (cf. Line 10). As the listener is now extracted, we can refine it in the module FIFO. Therefore, we add the refinement for the inner class ConsoleListener and add the missing method onRequestFinished (cf. Line 27).

As for the feature Service, the graphical component MainWindow needs access to the instance of the class SimulationUnit to trigger the requests. For this purpose, we also override the method createMainWindow and initialize the MainWindow (cf. Line 31).

Next, we need to forward the requests of the MainWindow to the controller so that the graphical unit can actually perform a floor request. We create a new method, floorReqest, which forwards the incoming requests of the graphical unit to the controller using trigger.

Finally, we add the method getCurrentFloor which allows the buttons to check for the current floor. With that, the implementation of the SimulationUnit for the feature FIFO is finished.

Similar to the previous descriptions, we avoid describing changes to the graphical units. To complete the source code with the feature FIFO, we again provide the source code for the classes MainWindow.java and FloorComposite.java. To include the refinements of the two classes, follow Instruction 14.6. The two files will automatically refine the UI elements to add the buttons required for FIFO.

Listing 14.9 Class fragment `SimulationUnit` of the feature module `FIFO` and changes to the class fragment in the module `Elevator`

```
 1  public class SimulationUnit {                      feature module Elevator
 2
 3    // further source code
 4
 5    public void start(int maxFloor) {
 6      Elevator elevator = new Elevator(maxFloor);
 7      controller = new ControlUnit(elevator);
 8
 9      Thread controllerThread = new Thread(controller);
10      controller.addTickListener(new ConsoleListener());
11      controller.addTickListener(simulationWindow);
12
13      simulationWindow.initialize(elevator.getMaxFloor());
14      controllerThread.start();
15    }
16
17    private static class ConsoleListener implements
            ITickListener {
18      public void onTick(Elevator elevator) {
19      System.out.printf(String.format(
20        "%s - %s -- Current Floor %d \n",
21          new SimpleDateFormat("HH:mm:ss").format(new
                Date()),
22          elevator.getCurrentState(),
                elevator.getCurrentFloor()));
23      }
24    }
25  }
```

```
26  public class SimulationUnit {                      feature module FIFO
27    private static class ConsoleListener {
28      public void onRequestFinished(Elevator e, Request r)
            {}
29    }
30
31    private static MainWindow getMainWindow(SimulationUnit
          sim) {
32      return new MainWindow(sim);
33    }
34
35    public void floorRequest(Request floorRequest) {
36      controller.trigger(floorRequest);
37    }
38
39    public int getCurrentFloor() {
40      return controller.getCurrentFloor();
41    }
42  }
```

Instruction 14.6 (Adapting the User Interface for FIFO)

1. Copy the files MainWindow.java and FloorComposite.java of
   the folder guiVersions / FIFO
2. Add the file to the features folder in the module Service.

*Note that the classes need to be in the same package as the MainWindow and
FloorComposite classes in the Elevator module.*

In Fig. 14.7, we present the product in which the feature FIFO is selected and
the feature Service is deselected. The graphical unit presents for each floor a
button that triggers the floor request. Similarly, a button for each floor exists in
the elevator cabin. Based on this, we can control the behavior of the elevator using
the implementation of FIFO.

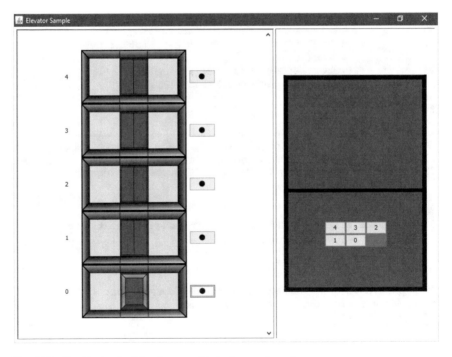

Fig. 14.7 Graphical unit of the elevator with the feature Service

14.4 Summary and Further Reading

Developing product lines using feature-oriented programming is tedious without specialized tool support. We showed how *FeatureIDE* helps developers use feature-oriented programming using our running example of an elevator (cf. Chap. 4 on Page 31). With the automated integration of composition tools into *Eclipse*, they can be easily used. Feature dependencies can be designed using feature models (cf. Chap. 5 on Page 43), and products can be configured using the configuration editor (cf. Chap. 6 on Page 63). The actual generation of the products is hidden from the user due to an automated mechanism.

In the following chapters for feature-oriented programming, we use the extended running example to illustrate further specialized tool support in *FeatureIDE*. In Chap. 15 on Page 173, we show how *FeatureIDE* helps to deal with software variability, how to trace features, and how to get an overview on the variability. When implementing feature-oriented programs, failures due to variability may happen. How *FeatureIDE* helps to ensure good code quality for feature-oriented programming is explained in Chap. 16 on Page 183.

Feature Traceability for Feature-Oriented Programming

15

Feature traceability refers to the ability to locate features in software artifacts. Traceability helps developers to identify relevant artifacts during development and maintenance. While we discussed feature traceability for feature modeling and configurations in Chap. 7 on Page 73 and for conditional compilation in Chap. 11 on Page 123, this chapter is devoted to feature-oriented programming. In particular, we will focus on feature traceability for feature modules as domain artifacts.

In contrast to conditional compilation, feature-oriented programming already simplifies feature traceability. The reason is that each concrete feature defined in a feature model is implemented in a separate feature module. Hence, feature-oriented programming establishes a one-to-one mapping between features and artifacts, whereas conditional compilation comes with a many-to-many mapping. While all artifacts belonging to a feature are contained in a single feature module, the inherent complexity of variable software poses challenges for developers. In particular, the interaction of a feature module with other feature modules can easily lead to unwanted feature interactions (Apel et al. 2013c). Thus, developers need support to understand which other feature modules are also relevant for their intended changes. In addition, debugging feature-oriented programs is typically challenging, as during the composition of feature modules the mapping disappears.

FeatureIDE provides a means to navigate within the implementation of individual features, to identify interacting feature modules, and to locate features in generated source code. In Sect. 15.1, we show how colors in the project explorer can help to identify feature modules and features in generated code. Once the developer has identified relevant files, the colors indicate which lines belong to a feature as explained in Sect. 15.2. During development, the *FeatureIDE* outline discussed in Sect. 15.3 helps developers to identify other features directly interacting with the particular file. Finally, in Sect. 15.4, we illustrate how the collaboration diagram can be used to keep track of the mapping between feature modules and files, such as Java classes.

© Springer International Publishing AG 2017
J. Meinicke et al., *Mastering Software Variability with FeatureIDE*,
DOI 10.1007/978-3-319-61443-4_15

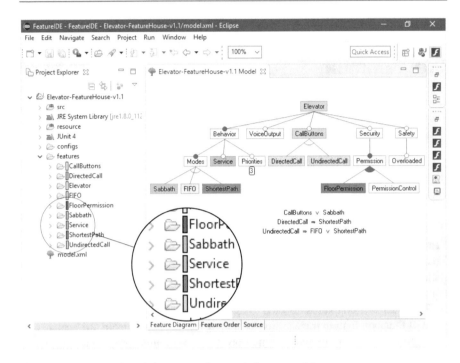

Fig. 15.1 *Project Explorer* helps to trace features in feature modules

15.1   Tracing Features in Project Explorer

Industrial product lines often contain hundreds or thousands of features. However, not all of them are relevant during software evolution. With *FeatureIDE*, developers can select a subset of all features to be traced in domain artifacts. Those relevant features can then be assigned to colors as discussed in Sect. 7.1. For the elevator product line, we assigned each concrete feature to a different color. Please follow Instruction 15.1 to open an example project in *FeatureIDE*. Figure 15.1 shows how *feature modules* can easily be found in the *Project Explorer*, due to the colored boxes in front of feature names.

Instruction 15.1 (Import the FeatureHouse-v1.1 Example)

1. Open the example wizard by any of the following options:
   - Press *New* → *Example* in the context menu of the Project/Package Explorer

(continued)

Instruction 15.1 (continued)
- Press *New → Examples → FeatureIDE → FeatureIDE Examples* in the upper-left menu toolbar of *Eclipse*
- Press *File → New → Example* in the menu bar of *Eclipse*
2. Select *FeatureIDE Examples*
3. Press *Next*
4. Select *Book Example* tab
5. Select the project *Part IV → Chapter 15 → Elevator-FeatureHouse-v1.1*
6. Press *Finish*

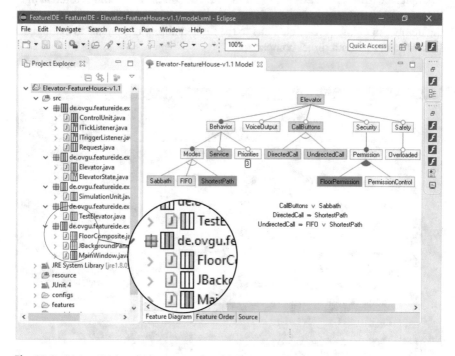

Fig. 15.2 *Project Explorer* helps to trace features in generated code

Even though feature modules establish a one-to-one mapping from features to feature modules, the borders of features disappear during composition. This is problematic, as debugging particular variants requires to work with the generated source code to a certain extent. For example, assume a class is refined by ten features, and then there is a class in generated products containing fragments of up to ten feature modules. *FeatureIDE* supports developers in identifying classes influenced by certain features. In Fig. 15.2, the project explorer illustrates which packages and classes of the currently generated product contain which features. For instance, we can see that the last package contains artifacts from the feature CallButtons. In particular, the feature influences all classes in that package except JBackgroundPanel.

The feature traceability for generated products is especially useful to understand the architecture of a particular product. Developers immediately get an overview on how and which features are distributed over the hierarchical structure into packages and classes. According to our experience, the majority of features are crosscutting to packages and classes. Hence, this quite simple illustration can save much time during development and help to locate features in generated artifacts.

The visualization scales also to large feature models with thousands of features, as developers can assign multiple features of interest to the same color. In the example, the features DirectedCall and UndirectedCall are both colored in light blue. In fact, an arbitrary number of features can be assigned to the same color. Only the number of colors is restricted due to the limited ability of humans to distinguish further colors without direct comparison.

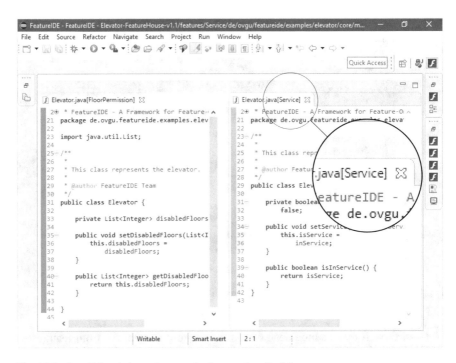

Fig. 15.3 *Java Editor* helps to keep track of currently edited features

15.2   Tracing Features in Java Editor

The identification of relevant classes and packages is not enough for maintenance. In particular, developers need to understand which parts in those files are mapped to which features. In principle, this is easy for feature modules, as each feature module is assigned to a single feature only. However, in our experience, developers can easily get confused between files of different feature modules. One cause is that files with the same name typically exist in several feature modules. To avoid confusion, *FeatureIDE* highlights the respective feature with colored annotations at the left of the editor as shown in Fig. 15.3. Furthermore, feature names are displayed in brackets in the editor title.

Tracing features in generated artifacts is even more challenging, because a single file often contains code of several features. Given that developers identified relevant classes using the project explorer, *FeatureIDE* helps to distinguish features within a class by means of background colors as shown in Fig. 15.4. As classes typically do not fit completely onto the screen, small colored markers indicate relevant features next to the scrollbar.

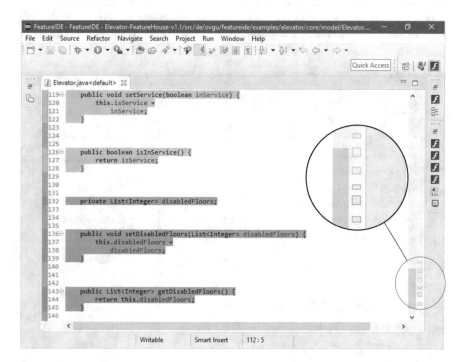

Fig. 15.4 *Java Editor* helps to trace features in generated code

15.3   Tracing Features in FeatureIDE Outline

A useful tool when editing source code is the *Eclipse* outline. For a Java file, it lists fields, methods, and subclasses including their visibility and signatures in a tree structure. The standard *Eclipse* outline can be used the same way for feature modules. In Fig. 15.5, we opened the class `Request` from the feature `FloorPermission`, and the *Eclipse* outline is located on the right side. This view establishes an overview on the file and can be used to navigate to the respective source code. In the example, we selected the method `getPrice` to highlight its declaration in the editor.

The *Eclipse* outline shows only members of the currently edited file, which is, according to our experience, often insufficient for feature-oriented programming. If classes are split over several feature modules, developers need to know which member is declared in which feature module. With *FeatureIDE*, we provide a special outline for feature modules giving an overview on all members of a class, even if distributed over several feature modules. In Fig. 15.5, the *FeatureIDE* outline is shown left of the *Eclipse* outline. To distinguish which of the members are defined in the currently edited feature module, *FeatureIDE* displays members only defined in other feature modules with gray color. In addition, below each member, there is a list of all features defining the particular member. Again, features are colored to

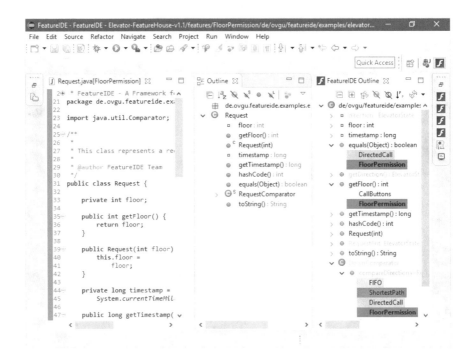

Fig. 15.5 FeatureIDE *Outline* helps to navigate between feature modules

ease the traceability of relevant features. The list is especially helpful to identify related feature modules and to navigate between them. In the top-right corner, there is a toolbar with buttons to collapse, filter, and sort the displayed members, similar to the toolbar in the *Eclipse* outline.

15.4 Tracing Features in Collaboration Diagram

Above, we discussed *FeatureIDE*'s extensions to project explorer and editors as well as the *FeatureIDE* outline. Each enables a particular view on the architecture of the feature-oriented program. To provide a more flexible view on the architecture, *FeatureIDE* adopts the notion of collaboration diagrams (Smaragdakis and Batory 1998, 2002).

A collaboration diagram is a table, in which columns represent software artifacts and rows represent feature modules (aka collaborations). In particular, each class or other software artifacts, such as images, result in a column. If a certain feature module contributes to that class, it is indicated by a table cell (aka role). Table cells typically indicate how the feature module contributes to that class (e.g., with which methods and fields). Follow Instruction 15.2 to create a collaboration diagram similar to the one shown in Fig. 15.6.

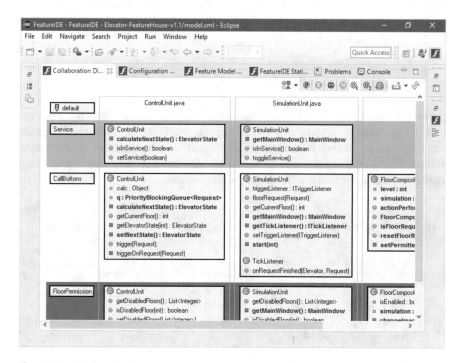

Fig. 15.6 *Collaboration Diagram* helps to understand the architecture of feature modules

The order of feature modules (i.e., rows) is equivalent to the feature order defined in the feature model editor (cf. Sect. 5.6 on Page 59). Thus, roles are introduced at the topmost role of a particular column and refined by roles below. Methods and classes with refinements are displayed in bold (i.e., methods refined in other features). If developers hover over a role, it shows a tooltip with detailed information about the number of fields, methods, and nested classes per role. Furthermore, the collaboration diagram can be used to quickly navigate between feature modules. By simply double-clicking on a certain member of a role, the editor will switch its content to the corresponding file and member. New roles can also directly be created and deleted within the collaboration diagram.

As collaboration diagrams illustrate the complete architecture of feature-oriented programs, they typically do not fit on the screen. There are numerous ways on how to cope with the size of the diagram and make it scale. Most notably, developers can apply a filter on those features being selected in the currently selected configuration. This is similar to the view on the architecture of generated products in the package explorer (cf. Sect. 15.1) unified with the *Eclipse* outline for each role (cf. Sect. 15.3).

A more flexible way to scale the diagram is to select a subset of features or subset of classes of interest. In Fig. 15.6, we used a filter on both three features and three classes. If only a certain class is selected, the collaboration diagram shows about the same data as the *FeatureIDE* outline for that particular file (cf. Sect. 15.3). In contrast, when selecting only a particular feature, a developer can get an overview on the contributions of that feature. If the diagram is still too large, there are more filters available to hide certain members within roles (e.g., all private fields).

15.5   Summary and Further Reading

Feature-oriented programming facilitates feature traceability by decomposing programs into feature modules. Nevertheless, the interplay between those feature modules can be complex and potentially result in errors during maintenance. *FeatureIDE* provides a number of views to help developers in navigating from artifacts to other relevant artifacts during development.

Instruction 15.2 (Open and Customize *FeatureIDE* Collaboration Diagram)

1. Open the collaboration diagram by any of the following options:
   - Press *FeatureIDE Collaboration Outline* in the lower part of *Eclipse* next to the other *FeatureIDE* views
   - Press *Window → Show View → FeatureIDE Collaboration Diagram* in the menu bar of *Eclipse*

(continued)

Instruction 15.2 (continued)

2. Open any file from the project, as the input of the view depends on the current editor
3. Select one or multiple Elements of the collaboration diagram
4. Change the displayed elements by any of the following options:
   - Check *Show unselected features* in the context menu of the selected elements to show all features
   - Uncheck *Show unselected features* in the context menu of the selected elements to show only features which are selected in the current configuration
5. Select one or multiple Elements of the collaboration diagram
6. Filter the displayed elements by any of the following options:
   - Check *Filter* in the context menu of the selected elements to show only the selected elements
   - Uncheck *Filter* in the context menu of any element of the view to show all elements again
7. Filter the displayed elements by type by:
   - Press on one of the filter buttons in the upper-right menu toolbar of the collaboration view

In Chap. 7 on Page 73, we discussed challenges to trace features in feature model and configurations. The traceability problems with conditional compilation discussed in Chap. 11 on Page 123 are rather orthogonal to those of feature-oriented programming, but each comes with limitations that *FeatureIDE* addresses by means of tool support. Feature traceability is important to ease product-line development and reduce the likelihood to introduce errors such as feature interactions. However, even with dedicated tool support, interactions may be introduced and the next chapter is devoted to their detection in feature-oriented programs.

It is known for more than four decades that modularity is a key for efficient development (Parnas 1972) and product lines (Parnas 1976). However, modularization techniques need to address the crosscutting nature of concerns (Tarr et al. 1999). While feature-oriented programming aims to simplify the mapping from features to code, feature traceability is still far from trivial. With *FeatureIDE*, we adopted the notion of collaboration diagrams (Smaragdakis and Batory 1998, 2002). Furthermore, *FeatureIDE* is inspired by several tools that we integrated into *Eclipse*, such as *AHEAD* (Batory 2003, 2006), *FeatureC++* (Apel et al. 2005), *FeatureHouse* (Apel et al. 2013b), and *Fuji* (Apel et al. 2012). A more extensive discussion of feature traceability is available elsewhere (Apel et al. 2013a). For further concepts to establish feature traceability in *FeatureIDE* with outlines and context assists, we refer to our prior work (Schröter et al. 2014).

Quality Assurance for Feature-Oriented Programming

16

Assuring good software quality is essential to effectively deploy reliable systems. The concept of a software product line already improves the quality of the products by reusing common artifacts. However, the variability of the software to implement reuse also comes with problems, such as bugs due to feature interactions, difficulties for code comprehension, and the sheer amount of products that can be derived.

In the previous chapter, you have learned how *FeatureIDE* helps with code comprehension in the context of variability in feature-oriented programming. Some of the presented views, such as the outline and the collaboration view, already help to understand the variability and to fix the faults. However, it is hard to detect variability bugs in the first place as they might only appear for certain configurations. *FeatureIDE* provides functionality that helps to prevent and identify such faults.

In this section, we show how *FeatureIDE* helps to check and maintain the *consistency* between features as defined in the feature model and their usage in feature modules. You will further learn how *FeatureIDE* supports the *systematic derivation* and *automated analysis* of products. Finally, we introduce several *statistics* and *metrics* provided by *FeatureIDE* that you can use to determine and improve the quality of the product line.

This chapter is designed as hands-on. All instructions of this chapter are based on the example *Elevator-FeatureHouse-v1.0*. Thus, to recreate the explanations, check out the example as described in Instruction 16.1.

There are several types of problem markers in *Eclipse*. To differentiate easier between different types, we suggest to group the problem markers by types in the *Problems view*. How to group the markers is explained in Instruction 16.2. After that, the problems view should show at least four types of problems: *Builder Problems* are problems generated by *FeatureIDE* on source files, *Configuration Problems* are markers on configuration files, *Feature Module Markers* are warnings regarding the folders of features, and *Java Problems* are warnings generated by the

© Springer International Publishing AG 2017
J. Meinicke et al., *Mastering Software Variability with FeatureIDE*,
DOI 10.1007/978-3-319-61443-4_16

Java compiler. In the following of this chapter, we show how to detect and resolve these problems with *FeatureIDE*.

Instruction 16.1 (Import the Elevator-FeatureHouse-v1.0 Example)

1. Open the example wizard by any of the following options:
   - Press *New* → *Example* in the context menu of the Project/Package Explorer
   - Press *New* → *Examples* → *FeatureIDE* → *FeatureIDE Examples* in the upper-left menu toolbar of *Eclipse*
   - Press *File* → *New* → *Example* in the menu bar of *Eclipse*
2. Select *FeatureIDE Examples*
3. Press *Next*
4. Select *Book Example* tab
5. Select the project *Part IV* → *Chapter 16* → *Elevator-FeatureHouse-v1.0*
6. Press *Finish*

Instruction 16.2 (Group Warnings by Their Type in the Problems View)

1. Open the problems view by any of the following options:
   - Press *Problems* in the lower part of *Eclipse* next to the *FeatureIDE* views
   - Press *Window* → *Show View* → *Problems* in the menu bar of *Eclipse*
2. Change the group option to type by:
   - Press *Group By* → *Type* in the context menu (small triangle) of the problems view

---

16.1   Consistency Checking for Feature Modules

To achieve separation of concerns, feature-oriented programming encapsulates features into separate modules. *FeatureIDE* helps to organize these modules by automatically creating folders for the concrete features defined in the feature model. Still there are inconsistencies that cannot be automatically resolved, namely, not

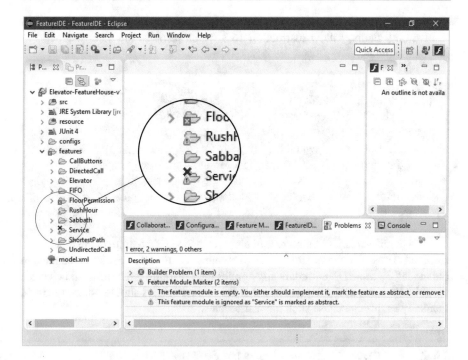

Fig. 16.1 Markers to show inconsistencies of modules.

implemented features and undefined features. *Not implemented features* are features that have no corresponding source files. These features are defined to be concrete though. Thus, the feature should either be implemented or defined abstract in the feature model. This implementation can never be selected and is thus dead. *Undefined features* are folders in the feature directory that have no corresponding feature in the feature model. If the folder does not contain any source files, the folder is automatically removed. For both defects, *FeatureIDE* creates error markers at the corresponding folder.

In Fig. 16.1, we exemplary show the marker types for the elevator product line. As shown, the feature modules for RushHour and Service have problem markers due to inconsistencies. The module RushHour is empty. However, the module has a corresponding concrete feature in the feature model. The folder will not be removed automatically, as either the feature should be set abstract or the module should be implemented. Note that empty folders that do not have a corresponding concrete feature will be removed automatically. The other module FloorPermission is implemented, but its feature is marked abstract in the model. Thus, the feature should be set to concrete. The same holds for modules that have implementations, but no corresponding feature in the model. In that case, a feature should be created, as the implementation cannot be contained in any configuration otherwise. To resolve both faults, follow Instruction 16.3 which resolves the inconsistencies in the feature model.

Instruction 16.3 (Resolve Inconsistencies with the Feature Model)
Perform the following operations on the feature diagram:

1. Resolve not implemented feature problem by:
   - Set the feature `RushHour` to be abstract (cf. Instruction 5.5)
2. Resolve implementation without concrete feature problem by:
   - Set the feature `Service` to be concrete (cf. Instruction 5.5)

Such inconsistencies of feature modules may happen if a feature in the model gets renamed. Thus, also the module needs to be renamed, too. If a feature is renamed in the model, *FeatureIDE* automatically applies the renaming refactoring and changes the folder's name accordingly. Note that the feature folders should not be renamed manually as this can cause such inconsistencies.

16.2   Product-Based Analyses for Feature Modules

In feature-oriented programming, most faults appear just after the actual product is generated. However, some faults can only be detected if a certain feature is selected or even only if a combination of multiple features is selected. Furthermore, the actual program is composed and compiled in a separate source folder. Thus, it can be hard to identify the actual module that contains the fault. In this section, we show how *FeatureIDE* helps detecting such faults automatically and how *FeatureIDE* propagates all analyses and their reports to the modules (i.e., to the actual sources of the fault).

Detecting Syntax Faults

The most basic faults when writing software are syntax faults. As the modules cannot be composed correctly due to these faults, we show an error marker at the module's file where the fault occurred. Consider the example in Fig. 16.2. As the class `ControlUnit` cannot be composed, it would be hard to detect the fault that a semicolon in Line 43 is missing. To detect syntax faults with *FeatureIDE*, it is *not* necessary that the corresponding feature is selected in the current configuration. To resolve the fault in the example, follow Instruction 16.4.

Fig. 16.2 Marker for syntax fault in feature module

Instruction 16.4 (Resolve the Syntax Fault in ControlUnit.java)
Perform the following operation in the class `ControlUnit` of the module
`FloorPermission`:

1. Add the missing semicolon in the `getDisabledFloors` method

Propagation of Compilation Problems

As discussed in Chap. 13 on Page 143, in feature-oriented programming, features
are implemented separately from the actual source folder. The underlying *Eclipse*
project and its compiler are only aware of the source folder containing the composed
source files. Thus, the warnings generated by the compiler and any other static
analysis are only shown at the composed files. As the features are implemented
separately, the warnings should be shown at the files in the feature modules.
FeatureIDE automatically *propagates* the errors from the source folder to the
corresponding location in the feature modules.

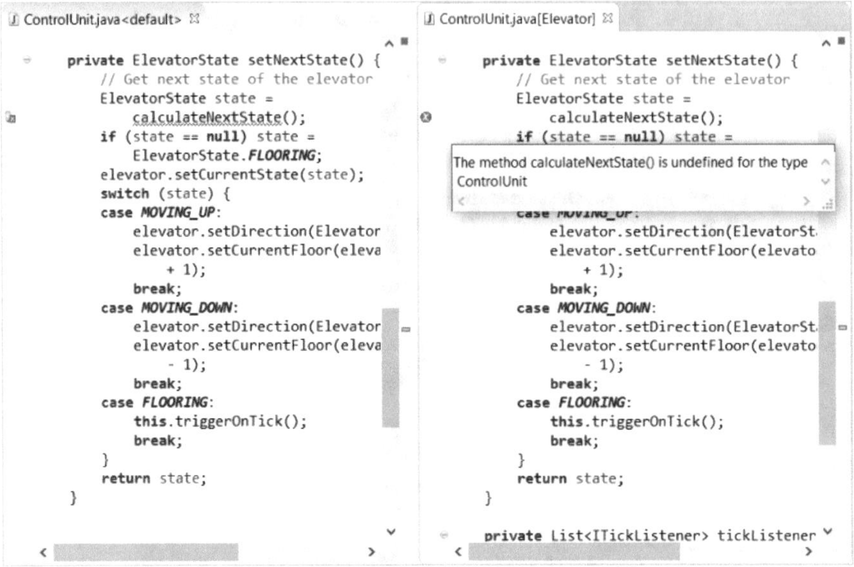

Fig. 16.3 Propagation of faults from source folder to feature module

In Fig. 16.3, we show the propagation of a compilation fault. To recreate the fault in the example, follow Instruction 16.5. In the example, the method `calculateNextState` is undefined. The file on the left is the composed file which is contained in the source folder. Thus, *Eclipse* finds this fault and reports it to the source file. *FeatureIDE* then propagates this fault back to the corresponding location in the feature modules. If there are multiple instances of the file in different modules, *FeatureIDE* also finds the correct feature module. In the right editor, the line in the module of `Elevator` causing the fault is marked with the marker for the fault. Note that this propagation from the source folder only applies to the current configuration as the actual source code needs to be generated and compiled.

Instruction 16.5 (Recreate the Example for Compiler Faults)
Perform the following operations on the current configuration:

1. Select the feature `FIFO`
2. Deselect the feature `CallButtons`

Automated Detection of Variability Faults

As the example shows, faults may only appear for a certain feature combination (e.g., FIFO and not CallButtons). This combination of feature selections is called a *feature interaction*. Detecting feature interactions manually is difficult as there are too many combinations of features that would need to be checked.

FeatureIDE provides support to *automatically derive* and analyze products to detect feature interaction faults (cf. Chap. 8 on Page 81). To analyze the generated products, *FeatureIDE* currently supports *static analysis* provided by the Java compiler and *testing* with *JUnit* (Al-Hajjaji et al. 2016b). When generating the products, the sources are automatically compiled. If the generated product contains a fault detected by the compiler, the fault is again propagated back to the corresponding feature module.

To automatically generate product, follow Instruction 16.6 and see Fig. 16.4. In Fig. 16.5, we show support for product-based analysis with automatically generated products. Some of the variants in the products folder have error markers (cf. Package Explorer). For example, the generated class of ControlUnit (shown in the lower editor) has an error marker because original cannot be found. As there are multiple products that contain this and other faults, we again propagate the marker back to the corresponding file in the feature modules (upper editor).

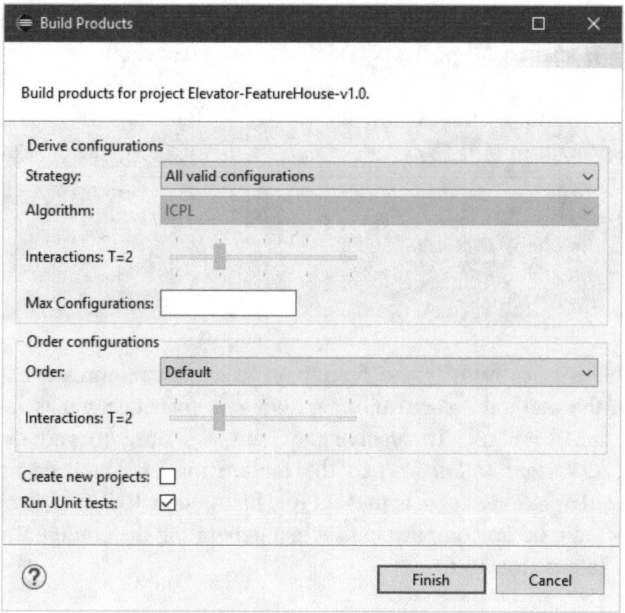

Fig. 16.4 Build your products by using the wizard provided by *FeatureIDE*

Fig. 16.5 Propagation of faults from products to the feature module

---

Instruction 16.6 (Automatically Derive Configurations)

1. Open the build products dialog by:
   • Press *FeatureIDE → Product Generator* in the context menu of the Project/Package Explorer
2. Select a generation strategy (e.g., *All valid configurations*)
3. Optionally check *Run JUnit tests*
4. Press *Finish*

The problem is caused by the feature `FIFO` which requires a call button to work. Thus, the method `calculateNextState` is missing as it is introduced in the feature `CallButtons`. To resolve the fault, we need to add the cross-tree constraint *CallButtons ∨ Sabbath* to the feature model which ensures that the method `calculateNextState` is present (cf. Instruction 16.7). After resolving the fault, there should be no compiler fault when generating the configuration again as explained in Instruction 16.6.

Instruction 16.7 (Resolve the Problem of Missing Cross-Tree Constraint)
Perform the following operation on the feature diagram:

1. Add the constraint *CallButtons* ∨ *Sabbath*

In *FeatureIDE*, we support several strategies to detect faults that are only contained in certain configurations, namely, *All Valid Configurations, All Current Configurations, T-Wise Configurations,* and *Random Configurations.* The strategy *All Valid Configurations* generates and analyzes all configurations represented by the feature model. As this strategy might not scale well for large configuration space, the strategy *T-wise* generates only as much configurations to find all interactions among T features. In the Build Products wizard, we allow to define different algorithms and the value for T (e.g., T equals two, to find interactions between two features). The strategy *All Current Configurations* takes the user-defined configurations contained in the folder `configs`. The last strategy *Random Configurations* generates configurations randomly. For all strategies, we further allow to specify how many configurations should be generated at most. This is especially necessary if the configuration space is large and the strategy *Random Configurations* or *All Valid Configurations* was chosen.

Automated Testing of Multiple Products

Beyond static analyses, *FeatureIDE* also supports automated testing of the generated products. To additionally test the generated programs, follow Instruction 16.8. After the products are generated and compiled, *FeatureIDE* executes all test cases of the products (i.e., public methods that are annotated with `@Test`). As test violations may only occur only in certain products, it is necessary to identify which configuration corresponds to which test executions. Thus, we modified the content of the JUnit view to additionally contain the information of the configuration the test was executed in.

Instruction 16.8 (Automatically Test Generated Products)

1. Open the build products dialog by:
   • Press *FeatureIDE* → *Product Generator* in the context menu of the Project/Package Explorer
2. Select a generation strategy (e.g., *All Valid Configurations*)
3. Check *Run JUnit tests*
4. Press *Finish*

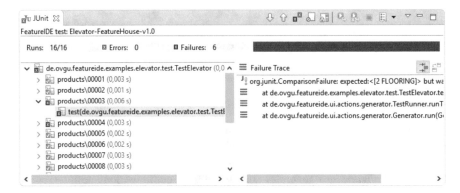

Fig. 16.6 Product-based testing for feature-oriented programming

Figure 16.6 shows an example test scenario for the elevator. In the left half of the JUnit view, each product has a separate entry for the test class. This helps to retrace the fault for the configuration that contains it. For example, the faulty configuration 00003 can be used as current configuration for debugging purposes. Note that testing of the current configuration can be done as usual as the underlying project is a standard *Eclipse* project. On the right side of the JUnit view, the failure trace for the fault is shown. Have a look at the class `TestElevator` in the module `Elevator` to see how to implement a JUnit test.

16.3   Code Metrics for Feature Modules

Code metrics help to understand the complexity of the program and to identify probably error-prone code. As feature-oriented programming is different from implementing a single program, we need specialized metrics to understand the implementation of the product line. In feature-oriented programming, we have several dimensions to analyze, namely, classes, features, roles, fields, and methods. In the statistics view, we show metrics for all these dimensions. The *FeatureIDE Statistics* view should be already open in *Eclipse* as it is part of the *FeatureIDE* perspective. However, if it is not open yet, follow Instruction 16.9.

Instruction 16.9 (Open the Statistics View)
Open the statistics view by any of the following options:

- Press *FeatureIDE Statistics* in the lower part of *Eclipse* next to the other *FeatureIDE* views
- Press *Window* → *Show View* → *FeatureIDE Statistics* in the menu bar of *Eclipse*

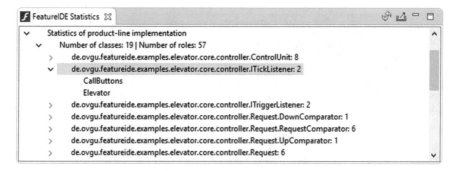

Fig. 16.7 Statistics on number of classes and roles

Classes that have many refinements are probably harder to understand than classes that are never refined. Thus, the first metric is about classes and how many features refine them. In Fig. 16.7, we show the statistics of the elevator product line for classes and roles. As shown, the statistics show that there are 19 classes of the elevator which are implemented with 57 roles. Each class has an own entry in the statistics view which indicates the number of roles that refine it. For example, the interface ITickListener is implemented by two features, namely, CallButtons and Elevator. The entries for the classes can be ordered alphabetically or by the number of refinements. To change the order, double-click on the entry starting with *Number of classes*.

The second metric is about how the classes are refined by the roles. Methods and files can be defined and refined in multiple features. We show how many method and field definitions there are and how often they get refined by features. This allows to easily detect methods and fields that are error prone.

In Fig. 16.8, we show the statistics on fields of the elevator example. As shown, the implementation consists of 51 unique fields and a total number of 65 fields. This statistic means that there are 51 fields with a unique definition. However, as fields can be defined, the total number of field definitions is 65. In the example, we also see that the field simulation is defined by four different features. This means there is one unique field called simulation, which is however implemented four times.

Additionally to fields, we also show the statistics on methods in Fig. 16.9. As shown, the implementation consists of 103 unique fields and a total number of 159 fields. The definition of unique methods is accordingly to the definition of unique fields. For methods, we can also see statistics on each method, for example, the method calculateNextState is defined by three features.

Finally, large features are probably more error prone than small features. The statistics view shows the lines of code per feature and by file extension. This helps to identify possibly too large features, which might need to be refactored or require more testing. In Fig. 16.10, we show the statistics on lines of code for the elevator. For example, we see that the scheduling features Sabbath, FIFO, and ShortestPath consist each of only 50, 43, and 19 lines of code, respectively.

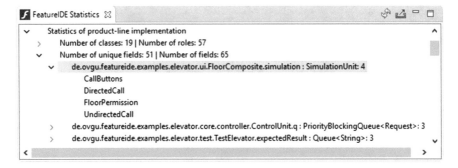

Fig. 16.8 Statistics on numbers of (unique) fields

Fig. 16.9 Statistics on numbers of (unique) methods

Fig. 16.10 Statistics on lines of code of the product line implementation

16.4 Summary and Further Reading

Feature-oriented programming allows to realize separation of concerns by implementing features in separate modules. This separation comes with challenges for software analyses as the source code in the modules is not the same as the source code that is used for compilation. *FeatureIDE* helps ensuring code quality of feature-oriented software product lines with several mechanisms. First, *FeatureIDE* ensures that the feature modules correspond to the features defined in the feature model. Second, as analyzing multiple products is time consuming, *FeatureIDE* provides automated generation and analyses of multiple configurations. To increase the detection rate, *FeatureIDE* allows to use T-wise configurations that cover all interactions among T features. Third, *FeatureIDE* integrates *Fuji* (Kolesnikov et al. 2013), a variability-aware type checker, that allows to efficiently type check all products at once. Finally, *FeatureIDE* allows to reason about the variability of the product line. With the statistics view, it is possible to see how variability is implemented and to find possibly error-prone code, for example, methods that have a high number of refinements.

In Chap. 8 on Page 81, we described how *FeatureIDE* supports domain analysis and ensures valid feature dependencies. In this section, we connected this analysis with the actual source code. Thus, *FeatureIDE* helps to ensure the code represents the previously designed variability model. In Chap. 15 on Page 173, we showed how *FeatureIDE* helps to understand the variations in the program. Both code comprehension and software analysis for preprocessors help to implement better software with variability and should be always used in concert.

Analyzing a sample of products is often not sufficient as interactions causing failures might be missed. Variability-aware analyses are proposed for efficient testing (Meinicke et al. 2016b), model checking (Thüm et al. 2014; Apel et al. 2013d), and formal verification (Thüm et al. 2014). The approaches are not integrated in *FeatureIDE*, but are supported with an automatically generated product simulator.

Part V

Further Tool Support in FeatureIDE

Tool Support Beyond Preprocessors and Feature Modules

17

In feature-oriented software product lines, products can be generated completely automatic for each valid configuration. In Parts III and IV, we already focused on two implementation techniques, namely, conditional compilation and feature-oriented programming, which enable such automatic generation. In this chapter, we give an overview on further implementation techniques that are supported within FeatureIDE.

Implementation techniques for feature-oriented product lines are typically distinguished into composition-based and annotation-based techniques (Apel et al. 2013a). Annotation-based techniques, such as conditional compilation, use annotations to remove certain artifacts or parts thereof. In contrast, with composition-based techniques, such as feature-oriented programming, a selection of partial artifacts is composed into the artifacts of a product. In this sense, conditional compilation and feature-oriented programming are representative techniques used in previous parts. Nevertheless, there is no consensus in research what is the best technique and, thus, other techniques have been integrated into *FeatureIDE* additionally.

In this chapter, we focus on runtime variability resolving variability decisions at runtime (cf. Sect. 17.1), black-box frameworks enabling compile-time variability in terms of plug-ins (cf. Sect. 17.2), and aspect-oriented programming weaving crosscutting concerns into a base application (cf. Sect. 17.3). Plug-ins and aspects are considered composition-based techniques (Apel et al. 2013a), whereas runtime variability is closer to conditional compilation. In the following, we illustrate how those techniques are supported within FeatureIDE.

© Springer International Publishing AG 2017

J. Meinicke et al., *Mastering Software Variability with FeatureIDE*,

DOI 10.1007/978-3-319-61443-4_17

17.1 Product-Line Implementation with Runtime Variability

With runtime variability, we refer to the ability of software to be customized with branching in the language of choice (e.g., Java or C). That is, parts of the source code are activated or deactivated based on a given configuration. Which source code is activated or deactivated is resolved at runtime. Hence, it is called *runtime variability*.

Instruction 17.1 (Open Example with Property Files)

1. Open the example wizard by any of the following options:
   - Press *New* → *Example* in the context menu of the Project/Package Explorer
   - Press *New* → *Examples* → *FeatureIDE* → *FeatureIDE Examples* in the upper-left menu toolbar of *Eclipse*
   - Press *File* → *New* → *Example* in the menu bar of *Eclipse*
2. Select *FeatureIDE Examples*
3. Press *Next*
4. Select *Book Example* tab
5. Select the project *Part V* → *Chapter 17* → *HelloWorld-RuntimeProperties*
6. Press *Finish*
7. Open the class `HelloWorld` to see how features are implemented
8. Open the class `PropertyManager` generated by *FeatureIDE* to inspect how feature values are accessed from Java source code
9. Open the file `runtime.properties` to see how feature values are stored
10. Open, change, and save the current configuration to understand when and how the file `runtime.properties` is updated
11. Run `HelloWorld`

Before a program with runtime variability can be started, we need to decide how to make the configuration accessible in the source code. That is, a mechanism is required such that the selection value of each feature can be evaluated in branching statements. FeatureIDE currently supports two strategies to propagate configuration decisions to runtime variability, namely, property files and global variables. With property files, whenever the configuration is updated, it is also stored in a property file. This property file is then loaded on the start-up of the program. With global variables, FeatureIDE creates a class with boolean constants representing the features of the product line. Whenever the configuration changes, those constants are assigned to true or false. During runtime, those constants can be evaluated by the program.

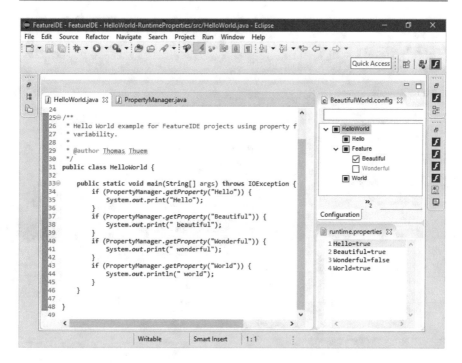

Fig. 17.1 HelloWorld example with runtime variability in terms of property files

In this chapter, we illustrate all implementation techniques using a smaller example than the elevator for brevity. In particular, we will use examples similar to the HelloWorld product line already used in Chap. 3 on Page 19. In those tiny examples, we can focus on the main differences of each technique rather than getting lost in details.

Follow Instruction 17.1 to understand how property files are used in *FeatureIDE* to implement product lines with runtime variability. In Fig. 17.1, we show some relevant parts of the example. The current configuration is not only stored in a config file but also in a property file called runtime.properties. The property file is updated once the current configuration is changed and saved. The product-line code refers to features by means of the automatically generated class PropertyManager, which reads feature values from the property file and gives an easy-to-use interface to access feature selection states.

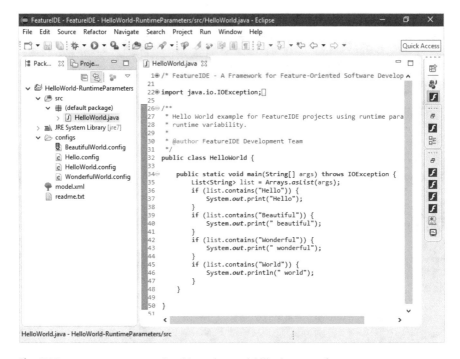

Fig. 17.2 `HelloWorld` example with runtime variability in terms of parameters

---

Instruction 17.2 (Open Example with Runtime Parameters)

1. Open the example wizard by any of the following options:
   - Press *New → Example* in the context menu of the Project/Package Explorer
   - Press *New → Examples → FeatureIDE → FeatureIDE Examples* in the upper-left menu toolbar of *Eclipse*
   - Press *File → New → Example* in the menu bar of *Eclipse*
2. Select *FeatureIDE Examples*
3. Press *Next*
4. Select *Book Example* tab
5. Select the project *Part V → Chapter 17 → HelloWorld-RuntimeParameters*
6. Press *Finish*
7. Open the readme.txt and follow instructions to set up the project
8. Open the class `HelloWorld` to see how features are implemented
9. Run `HelloWorld`
10. Run different configurations of the example by switching to another configuration

Similarly, runtime variability can be implemented with command-line parameters (for short runtime parameters) instead of property files. Follow Instruction 17.2 to understand how runtime variability with parameters is supported in *FeatureIDE*. In Fig. 17.2, we show how the parameters of the main method can be used to implement runtime variability. In the example, we simply check whether certain feature names have been passed as a parameter to the main method or not. *FeatureIDE* makes sure that the parameters passed to the main method are those features being selected in the current configuration.

Runtime variability is not to confuse with dynamic software product lines (Hallsteinsen et al. 2008), in which the configuration can be switched even during runtime. Here, we only illustrate what is also known as load-time variability: a configuration is already fixed before loading the program and then never changed during execution. Dynamic product lines additionally need a mechanism to translate the current program state of one configuration safely into another configuration, which is so far not addressed by FeatureIDE.

17.2   Product-Line Implementation with Black-Box Frameworks

A further common way to implement variability is *black-box frameworks*. Similar to feature-oriented programming, the implementation is modularized according to features. In contrast to feature-oriented programming, in which all classes and methods can be refined, all future extensions have to be anticipated and enabled by means of extension points [cf. preplanning problem (Apel et al. 2013a)]. An extension point provides one or several interfaces, which can be implemented by extensions. Besides the framework itself, all source code is modularized into plug-ins. Each plug-in implements a number of extensions and may itself provide extension points to other plug-ins.

Eclipse itself is considered a black-box framework implemented based on OSGi (Gruber et al. 2005). Each plug-in is developed in a special kind of Java project. All extensions and extension points of a plug-in are specified in XML, which enables *Eclipse* to load plug-ins only once their source code is accessed by the framework or other plug-ins. However, *Eclipse* does neither provide a mechanism to specify valid configurations with a feature model nor does it allow to check whether certain configurations are valid. In particular, we cannot easily switch between numerous configurations within *Eclipse*. Rather, we have to manually install and uninstall features. In the *Eclipse* world, a feature is basically a set of plug-ins and provides a unit being used for installation.

FeatureIDE aims to close this gap by combining black-box frameworks with feature modeling. Feature models and configurations are created and maintained as discussed before. During the creation of a *FeatureIDE* project, we have to select *Framework* as composer. The created *FeatureIDE* project is supposed to contain all artifacts (i.e., source code) of the framework itself. For each feature, developers have to create a separate Java project, which is then being compiled as a jar file and only loaded during the start-up of the framework, if the according feature is

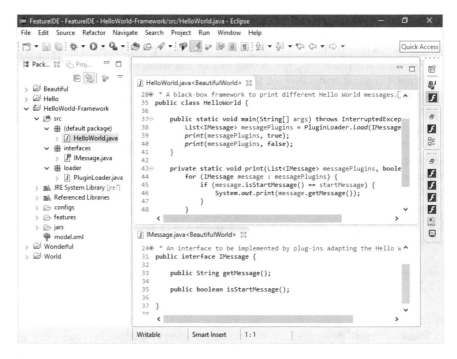

Fig. 17.3 HelloWorld example implemented as black-box framework

selected in the current configuration. *FeatureIDE* provides a simple plug-in loader implementation, which is automatically added to the project on creation.

Follow Instruction 17.3 to understand how *FeatureIDE* supports black-box frameworks with plug-ins. In Fig. 17.3, we show the source code of the class HelloWorld being the framework and its interface IMessage. The latter is a standard Java interface, which can be implemented by plug-ins to add part of the HelloWorld message. The class HelloWorld retrieves a list of all plug-ins from the plug-in loader and iterates over them to print a message by each of them.

In contrast to feature-oriented programming, the order in which plug-ins are loaded is typically not specified using a total order and rather depends on the particular plug-in loader. In contrast to conditional compilation and runtime variability, the order of features matters for frameworks. *FeatureIDE*'s plug-in loader loads plug-ins in alphabetical order. Hence, the HelloWorld example is slightly more complex due to the fact that the order of plug-ins loaded simply depends on their name. To print the word Hello before the word beautiful (against alphabetical order), we introduced the method isStartMessage to print the word Hello before all other plug-ins. A more general solution could be to assign plug-ins priorities (i.e., integer values) and load or process them according to their priorities. In our example, two different priorities were simply enough (i.e., start message or not).

Instruction 17.3 (Open Example with Black-Box Frameworks)

1. Open the example wizard by any of the following options:
   - Press *New → Example* in the context menu of the Project/Package Explorer
   - Press *New → Examples → FeatureIDE → FeatureIDE Examples* in the upper-left menu toolbar of *Eclipse*
   - Press *File → New → Example* in the menu bar of *Eclipse*
2. Select *FeatureIDE Examples*
3. Press *Next*
4. Select *Book Example* tab
5. Select the project *Part V → Chapter 17 → HelloWorld-Framework*
6. Press *Finish*
7. Open the classes `HelloWorld` and `IMessage` to see how the framework itself is implemented
8. Open the class `Hello` and the file `info.xml` in the project Hello to see how plug-ins are implemented
9. Run `HelloWorld`
10. Inspect how *FeatureIDE* sets the classpath based on the current configuration by:
    - Press *Run As. . . → Run Configurations. . . → Java Application → HelloWorld → Classpath* in the upper menu toolbar of *Eclipse*
    - Press *Run As → Run Configurations. . . → Java Application → HelloWorld → Classpath* in the context menu of the Project/Package Explorer
    - Press *Run (Ctrl + F11) → Run Configurations. . . → Java Application → HelloWorld → Classpath* in the menu bar of *Eclipse*
11. Open the class `PluginLoader` generated by *FeatureIDE* to inspect how plug-ins are loaded

In Fig. 17.4, we show all artifacts necessary to implement the plug-in `Hello`. The Java code consists of a single class implementing the interface `IMessage` in a straightforward manner. However, *FeatureIDE*'s plug-in loader relies on the fact that plug-ins make their extensions to given interfaces explicit in a simple XML file. The file `info.xml` contains the knowledge needed to know when loading all classes for a particular interface. In our example, the plug-in extends only the interface with the full qualified name `interfaces.IMessage` by means of the class named `Hello`. Given that the according feature is selected, the plug-in loader will load the class `Hello` if the framework asks for classes implementing the interface `IMessage` (cf. first line of the main method in Fig. 17.3).

In the context of software product lines, it is not intended to always load all plug-ins. To only load plug-ins for features selected in the current config-

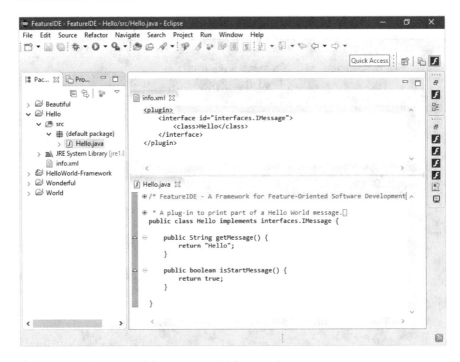

Fig. 17.4 Plug-in `Hello` of the `HelloWorld` framework

uration, *FeatureIDE* modifies the classpath of the Java project representing the framework. In Fig. 17.5, we show how the classpath looks if all features except the feature `Wonderful` are selected. *FeatureIDE* creates a jar for each plug-in and adds only those jars to the classpath, for which the according feature is selected in the current configuration. On each change of a configuration, the classpath is updated. Similarly, on each change of a plug-in, the respective jar is updated.

Readers might wonder why this implementation technique is called black-box framework. In black-box frameworks, the framework itself and each plug-in can compiled separately (Apel et al. 2013a). In our example, each plug-in is even a separate Java project that can be compiled without having the source code of any other part. Plug-ins, however, need at least the class files of the framework for compilation. Hence, the source code of plug-ins does not need to be available for the framework and vice versa. In contrast, in white-box frameworks, any extension needs access to the source code of the framework and cannot be compiled separately (Apel et al. 2013a).

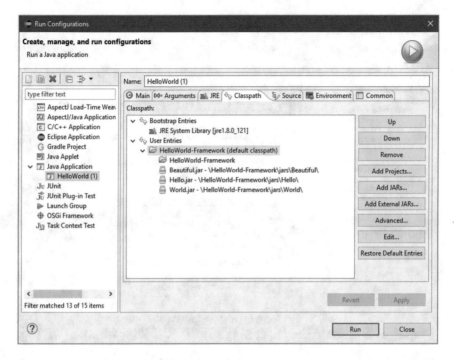

Fig. 17.5 *FeatureIDE* automatically includes and excludes plug-in jars into the framework's classpath depending on the current configuration

17.3 Product-Line Implementation with Aspect-Oriented Programming

Aspect-oriented programming is a further technique, which can be employed to implement product lines (Apel et al. 2013a). However, the initial intention was not to be used for product lines, but rather to decompose an application into its concerns or to change an existing application without modifying its source code (Kiczales et al. 1997). In particular, we have a base application implemented in an object-oriented language (e.g., Java), and then aspects are implemented in an aspect-oriented extension of that language (e.g., AspectJ).

In contrast to conditional compilation and runtime variability, the goal is to modularize source code with respect to features. In this respect, aspect-oriented programming is similar to feature-oriented programming and black-box frameworks. The main difference to frameworks is that extensions do not have to be anticipated in advance [cf. preplanning problem (Apel et al. 2013a)]. In contrast to feature-oriented programming, aspect-oriented languages typically have a complex language to make any possible change to an existing application without changing its source code.

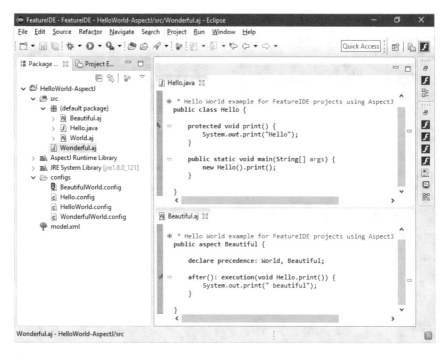

Fig. 17.6 `HelloWorld` example implemented using aspect-oriented programming with AspectJ

Follow Instruction 17.4 to understand how *FeatureIDE* extends the AspectJ Development Tools with support for product lines. In Fig. 17.6, we show the class `Hello` and an aspect called `Beautiful`. In this example, the base application merely consists of the class `Hello`, which essentially prints `Hello` to the command line. Aspects are defined similarly to classes but are indicated by the keyword `aspect` instead of `class`. The aspect `Beautiful` alters the base application in the following way; after every execution of the method `print` in the class `Hello`, the word `beautiful` is printed to command line. The according three lines include a piece of advice (i.e., the code to execute additionally) and a pointcut (i.e., a predicate identifying when to execute this additional code). In essence, advice is similar to method refinement in feature-oriented programming, but AspectJ allows more sophisticated ways to change the control flow of a given Java Application. The aspects `World` and `Wonderful`, however, do not need more language constructs than aspect `Beautiful`.

A further language construct that is required for our HelloWorld example is related to the ordering of aspects. Similar to feature modules and plug-ins, the order in which aspects are composed can influence the result. In contrast to feature modules and plug-ins, AspectJ provides a dedicated language construct to define a partial order on aspects. The keyword `declare precedence` is followed by a list of aspects, whereas aspects are woven into the application from right to left.

In our example, it is sufficient to specify only the order of two pairs, namely, that Wonderful comes before World and that Beautiful comes before World. The order of Beautiful and Wonderful is simply irrelevant, as they can never be selected together due to the constraints in the feature model.

Due to the large number of language constructs of AspectJ, this section can only give a brief introduction and cannot provide a full overview of all language features of AspectJ. Similarly, the tool support provided by the AspectJ Development Tools is not provided in detail here. We refer interested readers to dedicated literature at the end of the chapter.

Instruction 17.4 (Open Example with Aspect-Oriented Programming)

1. Open the example wizard by any of the following options:
   - Press *New → Example* in the context menu of the Project/Package Explorer
   - Press *New → Examples → FeatureIDE → FeatureIDE Examples* in the upper-left menu toolbar of *Eclipse*
   - Press *File → New → Example* in the menu bar of *Eclipse*
2. Select *FeatureIDE Examples*
3. Press *Next*
4. Select *Book Example* tab
5. Select the project *Part V → Chapter 17 → HelloWorld-AspectJ*
6. Press *Finish*
7. Open the class Hello to see the base application, which essentially prints Hello
8. Open the aspects Beautiful, Wonderful, and World to inspect how aspects modify the base application
9. Run Hello
10. Select another configuration as current configuration and see in package explorer how aspects are added and removed from the classpath
11. Remove or change a line in the aspect Beautiful or the aspect Wonderful starting with declare precedence and investigate the effect by running the example under different configurations

---

As a side remark, the AspectJ Development Tools seem not to be actively developed anymore. In particular, there was not any stable release until April 2017 for *Eclipse* 4.4 or newer versions. In other words, the latest stable version has been released in 2013. Hence, AspectJ can be used with *Eclipse* 4.4 or newer versions only using a development build of the AspectJ Development Tools, which, according to our experience, we cannot recommend for productive development. If there are no further stable releases, we sadly recommend to use *Eclipse* 4.3 or older versions.

17.4   Summary and Further Reading

In this chapter, we discussed further techniques to implement feature-oriented software product lines. In particular, we focused on runtime variability, frameworks, and aspect-oriented programming. While frameworks and aspect-oriented programming like most techniques in this book enable compile-time variability, with runtime variability, the source code of every product is essentially the same. Runtime variability uses branching depending on feature selections to implement differing behavior. *FeatureIDE* provides two mechanisms for runtime variability, namely, property files and command-line parameters. Besides conditional compilation and feature-oriented programming, *FeatureIDE* supports black-box frameworks with plug-ins and aspect-oriented programming with AspectJ for compile-time variability. For plug-ins and aspects, variability is achieved by modifying the classpath to add or remove certain plug-ins or aspects according to the current configuration. The main difference of both techniques is that frameworks require to make extension points explicit in terms of interfaces, whereas each aspect can modify arbitrary positions in the control flow by means of pointcuts.

Parts III and IV extensively focused on *FeatureIDE*'s tool support for conditional compilation and feature-oriented programming. This chapter was devoted to other implementation techniques for which tool support exists in a similar fashion, although not all functionalities are implemented for all implementation techniques yet. In Chap. 19 on Page 227, we give an overview on all implementation techniques and to which extent they are supported in *FeatureIDE*. Whereas this chapter focuses on some implementation techniques that have been neglected in previous parts, the next chapter is devoted to further development tasks that *FeatureIDE* supports, such as refactoring or specification.

A more extensive discussion of those implementation techniques and their advantages and disadvantages can be found elsewhere (Apel et al. 2013a). For aspect-oriented programming, we also refer to the original work proposing it (Kiczales et al. 1997) and a language description of AspectJ (Kiczales et al. 2001).

Tool Support for Product-Line Maintenance 18

Software product lines are typically instances of long-living software. One reason is that a product line must be maintained as long as any of its products needs maintenance. Another reason is that the goal of product lines is to foresee future evolution and plan for it in advance. Hence, product lines are typically maintained for years, and this maintenance is more challenging than that of single systems. First, product lines are typically developed by larger development teams. Second, there are more artifacts to be maintained than for a single product of the product line. Consequently, code quality and code documentation are crucial for product-line maintenance.

Tasks required to maintain product lines have already been touched in previous parts of the book. In Part II, we presented how to evolve feature models and configurations. In Parts III and IV, we focused on the evolution of product lines implemented with preprocessors and feature modules. Also related is that we discussed how to trace the features of a product line, which is a typical task during maintenance. Furthermore, as each change can influence the quality of products, quality assurance techniques are related, too. In this chapter, we focus on techniques that help developers to understand the product-line code more easily. For brevity, we focus on feature-oriented programming only, which is the best supported technique in *FeatureIDE* with respect to maintenance at the moment. Support for other implementation techniques is available or planned for future releases.

During maintenance, it might turn out that changes to the internal structure of the product line can improve its readability. In Sect. 18.1, we discuss how refactorings are used within *FeatureIDE* to improve the structure of feature modules. *FeatureIDE* supports developers in maintaining source-code documentation for informal specification and even formal specifications in terms of method contracts as presented in Sects. 18.2 and 18.3, respectively.

© Springer International Publishing AG 2017
J. Meinicke et al., *Mastering Software Variability with FeatureIDE*,
DOI 10.1007/978-3-319-61443-4_18

18.1   Refactoring of Product Lines

Refactoring is a mechanism to restructure the source code while preserving its external behavior (Fowler 2000; Murphy-Hill et al. 2012). The goal of refactoring source code is to improve the program's properties, such as reusability, readability, and maintainability. Modern IDEs usually provide automated refactorings that ensure correct application.

In object-oriented programming, common refactorings are renaming and pull-up. The *Rename* refactoring changes the name of an element, such as a method, a field, and a local variable. *Pull-Up* moves an element to a shared class in the inheritance hierarchy. Even though these refactorings appear to be straightforward, automated mechanisms need to ensure that the modifications do not change the behavior of the system. For example, the *Rename* refactoring needs to check whether there is already another element with the same name, and whether this causes a conflict, such as a renamed variable which shadows a field (cf. Fig. 18.1).

Existing refactorings of object-oriented programming cannot be applied directly to SPLs as they are oblivious to variability. Thus, applying a refactoring to a single product might break the behavior of others. To support refactorings for SPLs, *variant-preserving refactorings* are needed (Schulze et al. 2012; Fenske et al. 2017; Apel et al. 2013a). Such refactorings are aware of variability, and thus can preserve the behavior of all products and do not break valid products from the product line. In *FeatureIDE*, we work on the rename and the pull-up refactoring for feature-oriented programming. These refactorings are still work in progress, but they will be available in future releases.

Rename Refactoring for Feature-Oriented Programming

To correctly rename all occurrences of code elements, especially fields, classes, and methods, which can spread across multiple feature modules, the automated refactoring needs to check all usages of this element across all feature modules. We exemplify the renaming refactoring using the features shown in Fig. 18.2. The feature model consists of two concrete features, A and B. In Listing 18.1, we depict the source code for the two features. The classes Foo and Bar are spread across the two features. All these class elements use the shared method called method.

```
1 int value = 0;              int value = 0;
2 int method(int a) {         int method(int value) {
3   return value;               return value;
4 }                           }
```

Fig. 18.1 Shadowing of a field after incorrect rename refactoring of the parameter's name from "a" to "value"

In a *Rename* refactoring, we want to change the name of method to myMethod. Thus, we need to change the method usages in all class fragments of the two feature modules. The resulting source code is shown in Listing 18.2. Instead of calling method, always the new method myMethod is used. The refactoring does not change the behavior of the program variants and also does not affect the variability of the product line.

The rename refactoring for classes and fields works accordingly. However, each refactoring needs to apply different checks for correctness, such as shadowing of fields when renaming local variables.

Fig. 18.2 Feature model for renaming example in Listings 18.1 and 18.2

Listing 18.1 Example of renaming a method *before* the refactoring

```
1  class Foo {                                    feature module A
2     void method() {
3        ...
4     }
5  }

6  class Foo {                                    feature module B
7     void method() {
8        original();
9        ...
10    }
11 }

12 class Bar {                                    feature module B
13    Foo foo = new Foo();
14    void test() {
15       foo.method()
16    }
17 }
```

Listing 18.2 Example of renaming a method *after* the refactoring

```
1  class Foo {                                    feature module A
2     void myMethod() {
3        ...
4     }
5  }
```

```
 6 class Foo {                                    feature module B
 7   void myMethod() {
 8     original();
 9     ...
10   }
11 }
```

```
12 class Bar {                                    feature module B
13   void test() {
14     Foo.myMethod()
15   }
16 }
```

Pull-Up Refactoring for Feature-Oriented Programming

If two classes inherit from the same super class and define the same method, then the method can be moved to the super class without changing the external behavior. The same holds for methods, fields, and classes in separate feature modules. For example, if the same method is redundantly defined in two feature modules, then the method can also be moved to a common feature instead. These refactorings are called *pull-up* or *pull-up to common feature*, respectively (Fenske et al. 2017).

In the example of Listing 18.3, the method commonMethod is defined redundantly. In the example, we do not show the actual source code of the method. However, note that the methods need to be exact clones of each other to be refactored into a common feature module. Assuming that the methods are functionally equivalent, we want to pull up the method to the feature Common, which is implied by the features A and B. If there were no such a relation among these features, we could also create a new feature, which is implied if either of the two features gets selected using cross-tree constraints.

In our example, the feature Common is marked as abstract. Thus, the refactoring first needs to change the feature to be concrete (cf. the feature model on the right in Fig. 18.3). However, it does not affect the actual products that will be generated, and thus is still variant preserving.

Fig. 18.3 Feature models for pull-up to common feature example in Listing 18.3 (*left*) and Listing 18.4 (*right*)

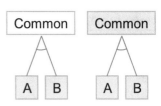

Listing 18.3 Example of pull-up to common feature *before* the refactoring

```
1  class Foo {                                          feature module A
2    int x = 10;
3    void commonMethod() {
4      ...
5    }
6  }
```

```
7  class Foo {                                          feature module B
8    int x = 0;
9    void commonMethod() {
10     ...
11   }
12 }
```

Listing 18.4 Example of pull-up to common feature *after* the refactoring

```
1  class Foo {                                          feature module Common
2    void commonMethod() {
3      ...
4    }
5  }
```

```
6  class Foo {                                          feature module A
7    int x = 10;
8  }
```

```
9  class Foo {                                          feature module B
10   int x = 0;
11 }
```

When applying the refactoring to the actual source code, the refactoring engine first needs to check whether the methods are actual code clones. Then it needs to see whether there are any further conflicts (e.g., there exists already a method with the same signature in the common feature). If all checks are successful, the redundant methods get removed and a single definition is added to the common feature as shown in Listing 18.4. All other elements stay unaffected by the refactoring.

With the two refactorings, *Rename* and *Pull-Up to common feature*, it is possible to restructure the code, reduce the number of code clones, and thus increase the maintainability of the product line. For further information on the refactorings and how it can be used to reduce code clones, we refer to our paper (Fenske et al. 2017)

18.2   Source-Code Documentation with Javadoc

One important aspect for software maintenance is source-code documentation, such as *Javadoc* for products based on Java. If a developer is not familiar with a specific product, this kind of documentation can help to get an impression of the source code and to ease its comprehension. Accordingly, source-code documentation is also essential for the development and maintenance of product lines themselves. Therefore, *FeatureIDE* provides a mechanism to define and generate source-code documentation for product lines that are tailored to the needs of a developer.

Using the example of the elevator product line that is based on feature-oriented programming, we introduce the tool support provided by *FeatureIDE*.

In Listing 18.5, we depict an excerpt of the class ControlUnit for a simple elevator product. For the documentation of the class and its members, special comments are used to describe the source code and to allow the generation of the final documentation with the tool *Javadoc*.[1] In detail, a comment for the tool *Javadoc* is always surrounded with /** */ (cf. Lines 1–5) and contains a description (cf. Line 1) and multiple block tags beginning with the character @ (cf. Line 2). For instance, the class ControlUnit provides a general description and two tags that define the source-code authors and one tag that gives information about the version (cf. Lines 2–4). Depending on the source-code element, several other tags are possible. Regarding constructors or methods, we can also use the tag @param (cf. Line 8) or @return (cf. Line 19) to give information about the parameter or the returned value of the method. Additionally, we also use the tag @see to inform the developer about other parts of the documentation with additional information (cf. Line 13, Line 20). Based on these comments, we can use the tool *Javadoc* to generate a documentation represented in the hypertext markup language (HTML). In Fig. 18.4, we present the output for the constructor of the class ControlUnit.

Listing 18.5 The documentation of a single elevator product using Javadoc

```
 1  /**This class controls the elevator.
 2   * @author FeatureIDE Team - Author 1
 3   * @author FeatureIDE Team - Author 2
 4   * @version 1.0
 5   */
 6  public class ControlUnit implements Runnable {
 7    /**Constructs a ControlUnit for an elevator.
 8     * @param elevator for which the control unit needs to
           defined
 9     */
10    public ControlUnit(Elevator elevator) { /* */ }
11
12    /**Executes a step of the elevator.
13     * @see Runnable#run()
14     */
15    public void run() { /* */ }
16
17    /**Determines the next step of the elevator that
18     * is executed in the run method.
19     * @return the next state of the elevator
20     * @see ControlUnit#run()
21     */
22    private ElevatorState calculateNextState() {
23      return ElevatorState.FLOORING; }
```

---

[1] For more information on *Javadoc* see http://www.oracle.com/technetwork/java/javase/documentation/index-jsp-135444.html.

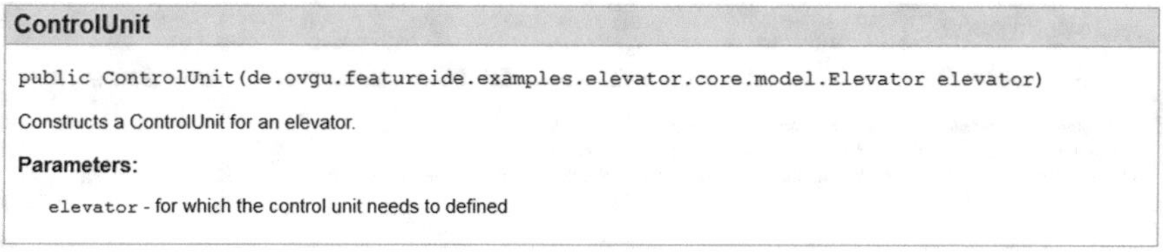

ControlUnit

```
public ControlUnit(de.ovgu.featureide.examples.elevator.core.model.Elevator elevator)
```

Constructs a ControlUnit for an elevator.

Parameters:

   `elevator` - for which the control unit needs to defined

Fig. 18.4 Output of the tool *Javadoc* for the constructor

Compared to the documentation of single products, the documentation of product lines comes with additional requirements. In detail, the granularity and kind of information given in a documentation depend on the specific application scenario. For instance, a source-code documentation is needed for a specific product but also for the maintenance of the whole product line. Both scenarios require a different representation, structure, and level of detail of the documentation output. For this purpose, *FeatureIDE* supports an advanced documentation concept for product lines that allows us to generate tailored documentations. In the following, we introduce all available documentation types that *FeatureIDE* supports. Afterward, we give a brief overview of the implemented concept and how to generate the documentation for a specific application scenario.

Documentation Types for Product Lines

Depending on the application scenario of a product-line documentation, the granularity and kind of information that are represented in a documentation differ. In the following, we present a brief overview of four documentation types for product lines described as *product documentation, meta documentation* (also called SPL documentation), *context-interface documentation* (also called context documentation), and *feature documentation* (Krieter et al. 2015).[2] To illustrate the differences between each documentation type, we use the elevator product line of our hands-on chapter that contains the concrete features `Elevator`, `Sabbath`, `FIFO`, and `Service`.

The first documentation type that *FeatureIDE* supports is the product documentation. This kind of documentation includes all information that correspond to a specific product. As a consequence, the documentation includes general information as well as information that are specific to involved features of this product. For instance, if a documentation for the product with the features `Elevator`, `FIFO`, and `Service` is needed, the documentation does not contain information about the feature `Sabbath`. In Fig. 18.5, we present the documentation of the method `calculateNextState` for the purpose of illustration. The first line of the description introduces a general information, whereas the following lines introduce

---

[2]For more information about the main idea behind each documentation, we refer the reader to the corresponding paper of Krieter et al. (2015).

calculateNextState

```
private de.ovgu.featureide.examples.elevator.core.model.ElevatorState calculateNextState()
```

Determines the next step of the elevator that is executed in the run method.
Ensures that the elevator determines the next state according to the behavior FIFO.
If the service button is presssed, the method ensures that the elevator determines the next state according to the service mode.

Returns:

the next state of the elevator
`ElevatorState.FLOORING`, `ElevatorState.MOVING_UP`, or `ElevatorState.MOVING_DOWN` according to the current step of the mode FIFO
`ElevatorState.FLOORING` or `ElevatorState.MOVING_DOWN` in service mode.

See Also:

`run()`

Fig. 18.5 Product documentation for the method `calculateNextState` according to a product with the features `Elevator`, `FIFO`, and `Service`

calculateNextState

```
private de.ovgu.featureide.examples.elevator.core.model.ElevatorState calculateNextState()
```

Determines the next step of the elevator that is executed in the run method.

Returns:

the next state of the elevator

See Also:

`run()`

Fig. 18.6 Meta documentation for the method `calculateNextState` of the elevator product line with the features `Elevator`, `FIFO`, and `Service`

specific information if the behavior of a specific feature is involved. Similarly, the information about the return value is structured.

The second documentation type is the meta documentation. This type can be used to get a first overview of the functionality of a complete product line without too much details about a specific behavior of single features. For this purpose, the documentation contains all defined general information about members of the product line. For instance, considering the elevator product line, the documentation includes the general information of all classes and its members. In Fig. 18.6, we present the output for the method documentation `calculateNextState`. This documentation only contains a general description of the method and its return value.

The third documentation type is the context documentation. This documentation was designed for feature-context interfaces, which only present classes and its members that are accessible from the current implementation context (Schröter et al. 2014). For instance, if a developer implements or maintains the feature `FIFO`, this interface presents all classes and members that are usable (i.e., the class or member is accessible) in the feature module `FIFO`. As some members only exist in the optional feature `Service`, a feature-context interface for the feature `FIFO` does not contain these members as it is not guaranteed to access them in all products in which the feature `FIFO` is involved. However, as also optional features can affect the behavior of a class or its members, the corresponding context documentation

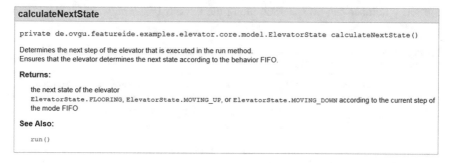

calculateNextState

```
private de.ovgu.featureide.examples.elevator.core.model.ElevatorState calculateNextState()
```

Determines the next step of the elevator that is executed in the run method.
[FIFO] Ensures that the elevator determines the next state according to the behavior FIFO.
[Service] If the service button is presssed, the method ensures that the elevator determines the next state according to the service mode.

Returns:

the next state of the elevator
[FIFO] `ElevatorState.FLOORING`, `ElevatorState.MOVING_UP`, or `ElevatorState.MOVING_DOWN` according to the current step of the mode FIFO
[Service] `ElevatorState.FLOORING` or `ElevatorState.MOVING_DOWN` in service mode.

See Also:

`run()`

Fig. 18.7 Context documentation for the method `calculateNextState` to support the maintenance of the feature `FIFO` according to the product line with the features `Elevator`, `FIFO`, and `Service`

calculateNextState

```
private de.ovgu.featureide.examples.elevator.core.model.ElevatorState calculateNextState()
```

Determines the next step of the elevator that is executed in the run method.
Ensures that the elevator determines the next state according to the behavior FIFO.

Returns:

the next state of the elevator
`ElevatorState.FLOORING`, `ElevatorState.MOVING_UP`, or `ElevatorState.MOVING_DOWN` according to the current step of the mode FIFO

See Also:

`run()`

Fig. 18.8 Feature documentation for the method `calculateNextState` according to the feature `FIFO` of the elevator product line

presents all possible feature information. For instance, in Fig. 18.7, we present the documentation for the method `calculateNextState` for the feature-context interface `FIFO`. In this case, the documentation includes the general information of the method as well as the specific documentation for the features `FIFO` and `Service`.

The fourth documentation type is the feature documentation. This documentation presents detailed information about a specific feature with its classes and members. This is helpful if a developer wants to extract the functionality and to reuse it in another implementation scenario. For this purpose, the documentation includes the general information as well as the specific information of the selected feature. In Fig. 18.8, we present the feature documentation of the method `calculateNextState` for the feature `FIFO`. Here, the general and feature-specific information of the method is represented.

Documentation Support in FeatureIDE

To support the different documentation types, *FeatureIDE* implements the documentation concept of Krieter et al. (2015) and allows to generate all described documentation types. To illustrate the mechanisms, we use the elevator product line and add documentation comments to the source code. Afterward, we introduce how to generate the documentation with *FeatureIDE*.

To generate a tailored documentation for the different documentation types, the documentation comments are divided in feature-specific and feature-independent (i.e., general) documentation information (Krieter et al. 2015). For this purpose, two keywords were introduced that must be added to the beginning of a *Javadoc* comment. The keyword *general* is used to mark feature-independent information. Feature-specific information is marked with the keyword *feature*. Therefore, in order to specify feature-independent and feature-specific information in one feature module, multiple *Javadoc* comments must be used (cf. Listing 18.6). Feature-independent information for a particular source-code element should only be specified in one feature module. By contrast, feature-specific information should be provided by each feature module that introduces or refines a source-code element. In order to properly merge feature-specific information from different feature modules, a priority number can be specified along the keyword *feature*, which is then used for conflict resolution.

Listing 18.6 Documentation of the class fragment `ControlUnit` for the feature modules `Elevator`, `FIFO` and `Service`

```
 1  public class ControlUnit {                          feature module Elevator
 2    /**{@general}
 3     * Determines the next step of the elevator that is
           executed
 4     * in the run method.
 5     * @return the next state of the elevator
 6     * @see ControlUnit#run()
 7     */
 8    /**{@feature 0}
 9     * Ensures that the elevator remains in the current
           floor.
10     * @return {@link ElevatorState#FLOORING}
11     */
12    private ElevatorState calculateNextState() { /* */ }
13  }
```

```
14  public class ControlUnit {                              feature module FIFO
15    /**{@feature 1}
16     * Ensures that the elevator determines the next state
17     * according to the behavior FIFO.
18     * @return {@link ElevatorState#FLOORING},
19     * {@link ElevatorState#MOVING_UP},
20     * or {@link ElevatorState#MOVING_DOWN} according to the
21     * current step of the mode FIFO
22     */
23    private ElevatorState calculateNextState() { /* */ }
24  }
```

```
25  public class ControlUnit {                          feature module Service
26    /**{@feature 1}
27     * If the service button is pressed, the method
28          ensures that
29     * the elevator determines
30     * the next state according to the service mode.
31     * @return {@link ElevatorState#FLOORING},
32     * or {@link ElevatorState#MOVING_DOWN} in
33     * service mode.
34     */
35    private ElevatorState calculateNextState() { /* */ }
36  }
```

In Listing 18.6, we present a small excerpt of the product-line documentation for the features `Elevator`, `FIFO`, and `Service`. The feature `Elevator` introduces multiple comments, a general and a feature-specific comment with priority 0 (cf. Lines 2–7, Lines 8–11). Even if it is not important for the final result in which feature the general documentation is integrated, we consider the root feature `Elevator` as optimal location for this kind of information. In addition, the method of the feature `Elevator` also contains feature-specific information with the priority 0 (cf. Lines 8–11). The priority ensures that a more important feature documentation can overwrite it. For instance, the features `FIFO` and `Service` also contain feature-specific information but with a higher priority (cf. Lines 15–22, Lines 26–34). As a result, the feature-specific information of the feature `Elevator` is not included in any valid product as each product contains a feature-specific information with a higher priority.

Based on the introduced concept and annotations, we can use *FeatureIDE* to generate the specific documentation types presented in the beginning of this section. Therefore, we use the explanations of Instruction 18.1. According to the selected documentation type, *FeatureIDE* creates a new directory in which the final documentation is located. The name of the directory depends on the documentation. Thus, in the directory `Docu_Variant`, the documentation for the product of the current configuration is located. The directory `Docu_SPL` represents the product-line documentation, and the `Docu_Context_<Feature>` and `Docu_Feature_<Feature>` directories contain the feature and context documentation of the specific feature.

Instruction 18.1 (Create Javadoc for a Documentation Type)

1. Open the documentation wizard by:
   - Press *FeatureIDE → Documentation → Create <type> documentation (Javadoc)* in the context menu of a project in the Project/Package Explorer

(continued)

Instruction 18.1 (continued)
2. Follow the instructions of the wizard
3. Press *Finish*

18.3   Formal Specification with Method Contracts

Informal specification of source code is essential to document the intentions of developers, especially for interfaces and central parts of a software. However, natural language specifications may contain ambiguities and cannot automatically be employed for quality assurance.

In contrast, the idea of formal specifications is to have a mathematically rigorous specification in a machine-readable form. *FeatureIDE* provides tool support for formal specifications in the form of method contracts. For a given method, a method contract is defined in a formal language similar to predicate logic (Meyer 1988; Beckert et al. 2007). In essence, a method contract consists of a predicate called *precondition*, which describes what the method expects from callers, and a predicate called *postcondition*, which specifies what callers can rely on after the method call. Method contracts avoid ambiguities and have numerous application scenarios including source-code documentation, runtime assertion checking, test-case generation, and formal verification (Hatcliff et al. 2012).

FeatureIDE supports method contracts in the Java Modeling Language (JML) (Thüm 2015). In JML, method contracts are specified in special comments, similar to *Javadoc* comments (Beckert et al. 2007). To distinguish JML specifications from *Javadoc*, JML's comments start with the character @. As JML is only designed to specify Java programs, *FeatureIDE* provides a feature-oriented extension to also specify feature-oriented method refinements. That is, feature modules can refine not only the implementation but also the specification of methods and classes.

Instruction 18.2 (Open Example with Method Contracts)

1. Open the example wizard by any of the following options:
   - Press *New → Example* in the context menu of the Project/Package Explorer
   - Press *New → Examples → FeatureIDE → FeatureIDE Examples* in the upper-left menu toolbar of *Eclipse*
   - Press *File → New → Example* in the menu bar of *Eclipse*
2. Select *FeatureIDE Examples*
3. Press *Next*

(continued)

Instruction 18.2 (continued)
4. Select *Book Example* tab
5. Select the project *Part V → Chapter 18 → HelloWorld-FH-JML*
6. Press *Finish*
7. Open the class `HelloWorld` in the feature module `Hello` to see how method contracts are specified in JML
8. Inspect other feature modules to understand how *FeatureIDE*'s extension of JML allows to refine contracts in a similar fashion as method implementations
9. Open the generated class `HelloWorld` to see how feature-oriented method contracts are composed
10. Change the current configuration to see its influence on contract compositions
11. Try to spot which feature module does not conform to its formal specification

Listing 18.7 `HelloWorld` example formally specified with method contracts in a feature-oriented extension of JML

```
1  public class HelloWorld {                              feature module Hello
2    /*@
3    @ requires message != null:
4    @ ensures \result.contains ("Hello");
5    @*/
6    protected String print(String message) {
7      return message.concat("Hello");
8    }
9
10   public static void main(String[] args) {
11     System.out.println(new HelloWorld().print(""));
12   }
13 }
```

```
14 public class HelloWorld {                              feature module World
15   /*@
16   @ requires \original;
17   @ ensures \original && \result.contains ("world");
18   @*/
19   protected String print(String message) {
20     return message.concat(" world");
21   }
22 }
```

Follow Instruction 18.2 to understand how *FeatureIDE* composes method contracts defined in a feature-oriented extension of JML. In Listing 18.7, we show the class `HelloWorld` specified in JML. The precondition starts with `requires` and indicates that the message passed to the method `print` must not be `null`. If `null` is passed to the method, it would result in a `NullPointerException`. Hence, the

Listing 18.8 Generated JML specification for the HelloWorld example

```
 1  public class HelloWorld {
 2    /*@
 3     @ requires message != null:
 4     @ ensures \result.contains("Hello");
 5     @*/
 6    private String print__wrappee__Hello(String message) {
 7      return message.concat("Hello");
 8    }
 9
10    /*@
11     @ requires message != null;
12     @ ensures \result.contains("Hello") &&
13     @                    \result.contains("world");
14     @*/
15    protected String print(String message) {
16      return print__wrappee__Hello(message).concat("
         world");
17    }
18
19    public static void main(String[] args) {
20      System.out.println(new HelloWorld().print(""));
21    }
22  }
```

precondition makes the developer's intention explicit what the method expects from callers. In return, the method's postcondition starting with ensures specifies what the caller can rely on; the caller of print can expect that the word Hello is contained in the result of the method print.

As the implementation of the method print is refined by other features, we may also want to refine its JML specification accordingly. In *FeatureIDE*, we can simply provide a new method contract next to a refinement, which replaces the existing method contract. For the feature module World, we specify that the method's output also contains the word world. To avoid cloning the rest of the precondition and postcondition, *FeatureIDE*'s feature-oriented extension of JML provides the keyword original as known from the implementation. The keyword refers to the previous precondition if called within a precondition and to the previous postcondition if called from a postcondition. Hence, depending on the feature selection, the keyword original may refer to a different postcondition.

In order to use any existing JML tools, feature-oriented JML specifications need to be composed given a selection of features. The reason is the keyword original and that feature modules are typically not valid Java programs themselves. In Listing 18.8, we show the result of composing the feature modules Hello and World. Method contract from the feature Hello is simply copied to the renamed print method. For the method contract of the feature World, the keyword original is replaced by precondition and postcondition of the feature Hello. The result of composition is a Java program with a JML specification, which can then be used for documentation purposes, to generate runtime assertions or test cases, and even for formal verification.

18.4   Summary and Further Reading

Maintenance of product lines is challenging and requires proper tool support. In this chapter, we used feature-oriented programming to explain *FeatureIDE*'s support for refactoring as well as informal and formal specification of source code. Refactorings available for single systems (e.g., for Java source code) can typically not be applied as is, as they do not cope with variability. Even if they can be applied, their application can result in compile errors or even errors at runtime. Similarly, techniques to document or specify source code need to be extended to cope with variability. In particular, we discussed new keywords for *Javadoc* comments and JML specifications. Those keywords control how comments and specifications are composed for a given configuration.

FeatureIDE's functionality discussed in this chapter is orthogonal to the product-line implementation technique. That is, refactorings, documentation, and specification are required not only for feature-oriented programming but also for other implementation techniques, such as conditional compilation (cf. Part III), runtime variability (cf. Sect. 17.1), frameworks (cf. Sect. 17.2), and aspect-oriented programming (cf. Sect. 17.3). Nevertheless, we focused on feature-oriented programming only, and the next chapter gives an overview on what the current *FeatureIDE* version supports and what is planned for future releases.

Refactoring of software product lines is an active research area (Laguna and Crespo 2013; Apel et al. 2013a; Fenske et al. 2014). In this chapter, we focused on variant-preserving refactoring (Schulze et al. 2012), which refers to operations to improve the structure of an existing product line. Variant-preserving refactoring is not to confuse with variant-preserving migration used to migrate from clone-and-own to a product-line architecture, and different from variant-preserving mapping which translates a product line from one implementation technique to another (Fenske et al. 2014). Nevertheless, *FeatureIDE*'s variant-preserving refactorings can also be employed for variant-preserving migration (Fenske et al. 2017). *FeatureIDE*'s support for *Javadoc* comments and JML specification within feature modules is explained elsewhere in more detail (Krieter et al. 2015; Thüm 2015).

Overview on FeatureIDE

19

The goal of this chapter is to give an overview on *FeatureIDE*'s functionality. While previous parts and chapters focused on particular aspects of the tool support only, we aim to present the big picture in the following. That is, we present the goal of particular views and editors as well as how they differ when using other implementation techniques as composers. In addition, we discuss what tool support is already available in the current release, in experimental versions, or planned for future releases.

We give an overview on implementation techniques, tools, and languages supported in *FeatureIDE* in Sect. 19.1. In Sect. 19.2, we discuss editors and views related to feature modeling. Tool support configurations are presented in Sect. 19.3. In Sect. 19.4, we explain differences in the project structure for different implementation techniques and how features are traced in code. Finally, in Sect. 19.5, we summarize tool support with source-code editors and further views on code.

19.1 Overview on Implementation Techniques

In the course of this book, we typically discussed *FeatureIDE*'s functionality with respect to a given implementation technique, such as conditional compilation of feature-oriented programming. In Table 19.1, we give an overview on techniques being discussed in previous chapters. For each technique, we also list all tools and languages currently available in *FeatureIDE* as well as the chapters focusing on them, respectively.

In experimental versions of *FeatureIDE*, there is support for further tools and languages. First, delta-oriented programming with *DeltaJ* (Schaefer et al. 2010) has been integrated into *FeatureIDE* but is currently only available for older *Eclipse* versions. However, it is planned to integrate a newer version of *DeltaJ* (Koscielny et al. 2014) in the near future. Second, feature-oriented programming for C code is supported with *FeatureC* (Benduhn et al. 2016) and planned

© Springer International Publishing AG 2017
J. Meinicke et al., *Mastering Software Variability with FeatureIDE*,
DOI 10.1007/978-3-319-61443-4_19

Table 19.1 An overview on implementation techniques, languages, and tools supported in *FeatureIDE* for composition

Implementation technique	Tools and languages	Chapters and sections
Conditional compilation	Munge	Section 9.2
	Antenna	Section 9.3, Chaps. 10–12
	C Preprocessor/Colligens	cf. Medeiros et al. (2013)
Feature-oriented programming	FeatureHouse	Chapter 3, Sect. 13.2, Chaps. 14–16, 18
	AHEAD	Section 13.3
	FeatureC++	Section 13.4
	FeatureC	cf. Benduhn et al. (2016)
Runtime variability	Properties and parameters	Section 17.1
Black-box frameworks	PluginLoader	Section 17.2
Aspect-oriented programming	AspectJ	Section 17.3
Delta-oriented programming	DeltaJ	cf. Thüm et al. (2014), Schaefer et al. (2010), Koscielny et al. (2014)
	DeltaEcore	cf. Seidl et al. (2014)

for a future release of *FeatureIDE*. Finally, with *Colligens* and *DeltaEcore*, others have extended *FeatureIDE* with support for *conditional compilation* with the C preprocessor (Medeiros et al. 2013) (*CPP*) and *delta-oriented modeling* based on Ecore meta modeling (Seidl et al. 2014).

19.2   Editors and Views for Feature Models

Feature models constitute the most essential document of a software product line. In *FeatureIDE*, there are several editors and views for feature modeling, which are largely independent of the languages and tools used for domain implementation. One difference is that each tool typically comes with its own restrictions on feature names, for which violations are reported by *FeatureIDE*. Another difference is that a feature order can only be specified for feature-oriented programming. Follow Instruction 19.1 to try out differences of the *Feature Model Editor* for different composers.

In Fig. 19.1, we show the three tabs of the Feature Model Editor in the top row. As only one tab can be opened at the same time, we opened identical feature models of three HelloWorld examples. The first tab of the editor allows to view and edit feature models graphically in terms of feature diagrams. That is, users can specify features and their valid combinations of features. In the feature diagram, colors can be assigned to features to trace them in other views and artifacts. In the second tab, a total order of features can be specified for *AHEAD*, *FeatureHouse*, and *FeatureC++* projects. Finally, the third tab can be used to alter a textual representation of the feature model in XML.

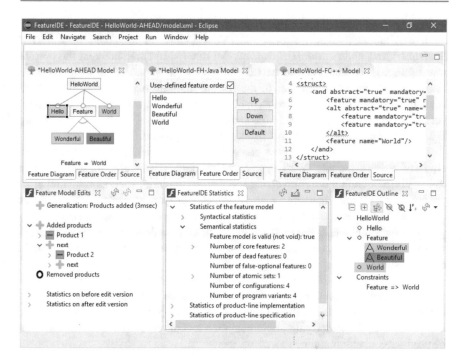

Fig. 19.1 Feature Model Editor, Feature Model Edit View, *FeatureIDE* Statistics View, and *FeatureIDE* Outline support different tasks in feature modeling

---

Instruction 19.1 (Import HelloWorld Examples)

1. Open the example wizard by any of the following options:
   - Press *New → Example* in the context menu of the Project/Package Explorer
   - Press *New → Examples → FeatureIDE → FeatureIDE Examples* in the upper-left menu toolbar of *Eclipse*
   - Press *File → New → Example* in the menu bar of *Eclipse*
2. Select *FeatureIDE Examples*
3. Press *Next*
4. Select *Book Example* tab
5. Select all or some projects in *Part V → Chapter 19*
6. Press *Finish*
7. Open files from those projects to inspect how the development of feature models, configurations, and code is supported

Besides the Feature Model Editor, *FeatureIDE* provides three views for feature modeling, namely, *Feature Model Edit* View (Thüm et al. 2009), *FeatureIDE Statistics* View, and *FeatureIDE Outline*. All three views are shown at the bottom row of Fig. 19.1. The Feature Model Edit View is supposed to help users in analyzing the impact of changes to the feature diagram (i.e., whether the change is a refactoring). The view compares the last saved version with the currently edited version of the feature diagram. In the example, we changed the type of the feature Hello from mandatory to optional resulting in new products.

The *FeatureIDE* Statistics View computes the syntactical and semantical properties of feature models. With syntactical properties, we refer to statistics that can easily be computed by traversing the feature diagram, such as the number of concrete and abstract features. With semantical properties, we refer to analyses that translate the feature diagram to a propositional formula and use a satisfiability solver to reason about it. For instance, it can determine dead features (i.e., features which cannot be selected due to cross-tree constraints) or the number of valid configurations.

Finally, the *FeatureIDE* Outline provides the feature model as a tree structure. Most operations available in the feature diagram, such as feature creation or coloring, can also be accessed in the outline. All these views provide their functionality independent of the underlying implementation technique. In particular, it can even be used without any mapping to a composer.

19.3   Editors and Views for Configurations

Once features and their valid combinations are specified in a feature model, users can create and edit configurations. Configurations are used as input for the generation of products. Hence, it is necessary that they are valid according to the feature model. *FeatureIDE* provides a *Configuration Editor* and several views to support the user in creating valid configurations.

In Fig. 19.2, we give an overview on all views and editors relevant for product configuration. Similar to the Feature Model Editor, the Configuration Editor provides three tabs for configuration activities, shown in the right top corner of Fig. 19.2. The first tab contains an editor, which allows to select features, but only if their selection does not violate the constraints of the feature model. It is possible to search for features and there is guidance for turning invalid into valid configurations. The editor in the second tab is similar, but also enables the explicit deselection of features, which may require less decisions during configuration. Finally, the third tab is a textual representation of a configuration, which contains all selected, concrete features.

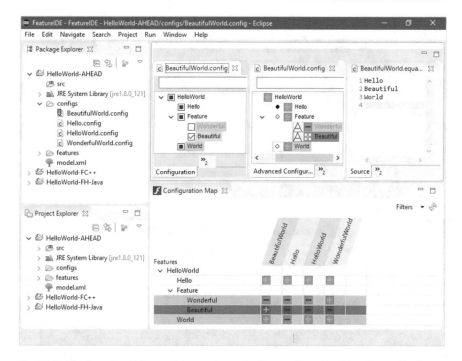

Fig. 19.2 Configuration Editor enables to view and edit a configuration file, whereas Configuration Map gives an overview on differences of all configurations

In the bottom right of Fig. 19.2, we show the *Configuration Map*. It is merely a table in which there are a row for each feature and a column for each user-defined configuration. Configuration maps are useful to compare multiple configurations. As the feature model may contain hundreds or thousands of features, there are several options to fold based on the hierarchy and to filter features based on their selection status. In most views and editors, features can be traced with colors. The views to the left are discussed in the next section.

19.4 Package Explorer and Project Explorer

At first sight, *Package Explorer* and *Project Explorer* shown in the left of Fig. 19.2 seem to provide quite similar functionality. Both provide an overview on the structure of a *FeatureIDE* project and access to feature models, configurations, and source files. However, each comes with unique features that are useful for development. The Package Explorer comes with dedicated menu entries to create new files in *FeatureIDE* projects, if the *FeatureIDE* perspective is selected (cf. Instruction 3.1 on Page 20). The Project Explorer enables feature traceability by means of colors assigned to features (cf. Chaps. 7, 11, and 15).

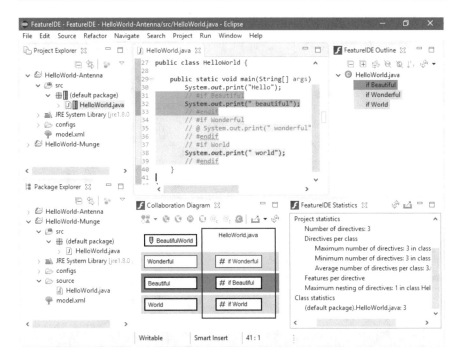

Fig. 19.3 Package Explorer, Project Explorer, Java Editor, *FeatureIDE* Outline, Collaboration Diagram, and *FeatureIDE* Statistics View support conditional compilation

In Fig. 19.3, we illustrate that Project Explorer supports feature traceability. The colors can be used to identify whether features assigned to colors are contained in certain source files. Hence, we can easily locate all artifacts for certain features.

While feature-oriented programming eases feature traceability as each feature is implemented in a separate feature module, the colors are nevertheless used to identify the folders as shown in Fig. 19.4. To support developers in debugging, *FeatureIDE* provides color bars also for generated code in a similar fashion as for conditional compilation.

19.5   Editors and Views for Source Code

Besides Package Explorer and Project Explorer, there are further editors and views in *FeatureIDE* for source code. However, their content largely differs depending on the implementation technique. In Fig. 19.3, we show the *Java Editor* and several views for conditional compilation. In the Java editor, color bars to the left, to the right, and as a *background color* are used to help developers with feature location. A difference of preprocessors is whether they modify the files they process by commenting out lines not selected or whether they produce a separate file. The

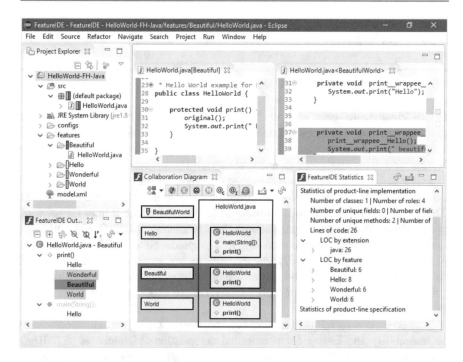

Fig. 19.4 Project Explorer, Java Editor, *FeatureIDE* Outline, Collaboration Diagram, and *FeatureIDE* Statistics View support feature-oriented programming

example code shown is a file modified by Antenna, whereas the Package Explorer shows an input and an output file with the same name for our *Munge* example.

As opposed to a typical Outline for Java source code, the *FeatureIDE Outline* gives an overview on features referenced in the current file and allows to jump to these locations. The *Collaboration Diagram* is a table mapping files to features, which contains the complete architecture of the product line. Finally, the *FeatureIDE Statistics* view enables developers to access simple metrics about the feature-to-code mapping and may also be used to identify locations in the source code which could be simplified by means of refactorings.

In contrast, we show *FeatureIDE*'s views for feature-oriented programming in Fig. 19.4. How code is annotated with colors depends on whether it is source code or generated code. Source code only has a marker to the left showing the color of the feature. In generated code, there is similar highlighting as for conditional compilation. For feature modules, the *FeatureIDE* Outline shows all members of a class (e.g., the main method), even if not defined within the currently opened file (i.e., HelloWorld.java of feature Beautiful). The Collaboration Diagram is similar to a UML class diagram, except that classes are split over feature modules. As for conditional compilation, the Collaboration Diagram shows the entire architecture or can be filtered to relevant parts. Finally, the Statistics View computes metrics, such as the lines of code for each feature and the number of methods and fields.

19.6   Summary and Further Reading

In this chapter, we gave an overview on *FeatureIDE* main functionality, while previous parts of the book presented *FeatureIDE* in more detail. *FeatureIDE* supports several implementation techniques for software product lines, including feature modeling, configuration, and several views to a product line's source code.

Initial ideas for an integrated development environment for features and a first prototype have been presented at an *Eclipse* workshop in 2005 (Leich et al. 2005). This prototype was continuously improved to be used in our lecture on software product lines. We decided to present our efforts to integrate *AHEAD*, *FeatureHouse*, and *FeatureC++* with feature modeling in a graphical editor at ICSE'09 (Kästner et al. 2009; Thüm et al. 2009). As students in our lecture were also supposed to use conditional compilation, aspect-oriented programming, and delta-oriented programming as well, we extended *FeatureIDE* for those purposes (Thüm et al. 2014).

Numerous new functionalities have been presented at different conferences, such as traceability and testing for conditional compilation (Meinicke et al. 2016a), sampling algorithms for quality assurance (Al-Hajjaji et al. 2016a,b), explanations for anomalies and implicit dependencies in feature models (Kowal et al. 2016; Ananieva et al. 2016), and scalable product configuration (Pereira et al. 2016). Parts of this book are based on a tutorial held at SPLC'16 in Beijing, China (Thüm et al. 2016). For more detailed discussions of software product lines, feature modeling, and implementation techniques, we refer interested readers to dedicated books (Apel et al. 2013a; Czarnecki and Eisenecker 2000).

References

AL-HAJJAJI, M., KRIETER, S., THÜM, T., LOCHAU, M., AND SAAKE, G. 2016a. IncLing: Efficient Product-line Testing Using Incremental Pairwise Sampling. In *Proc. Int'l Conf. Generative Programming: Concepts & Experiences (GPCE)*. ACM, New York, NY, USA, 144–155.

AL-HAJJAJI, M., MEINICKE, J., KRIETER, S., SCHRÖTER, R., THÜM, T., LEICH, T., AND SAAKE, G. 2016b. Tool Demo: Testing Configurable Systems with FeatureIDE. In *Proc. Int'l Conf. Generative Programming: Concepts & Experiences (GPCE)*. ACM, New York, NY, USA, 173–177.

AL-HAJJAJI, M., THÜM, T., LOCHAU, M., MEINICKE, J., AND SAAKE, G. 2016c. Effective Product-Line Testing Using Similarity-Based Product Prioritization. *Software and System Modeling (SoSym)*.

ANANIEVA, S., KOWAL, M., THÜM, T., AND SCHAEFER, I. 2016. Implicit Constraints in Partial Feature Models. In *Proc. Int'l Workshop Feature-Oriented Software Development (FOSD)*. ACM, New York, NY, USA, 18–27.

ANTKIEWICZ, M., JI, W., BERGER, T., CZARNECKI, K., SCHMORLEIZ, T., LÄMMEL, R., STĂNCIULESCU, S., WĄSOWSKI, A., AND SCHAEFER, I. 2014. Flexible Product Line Engineering with a Virtual Platform. In *Proc. Int'l Conf. Software Engineering (ICSE)*. ACM, New York, NY, USA, 532–535.

APEL, S., BATORY, D., KÄSTNER, C., AND SAAKE, G. 2013a. *Feature-Oriented Software Product Lines: Concepts and Implementation*. Springer, Berlin, Heidelberg.

APEL, S., KÄSTNER, C., AND LENGAUER, C. 2009. FeatureHouse: Language-Independent, Automated Software Composition. In *Proc. Int'l Conf. Software Engineering (ICSE)*. IEEE, Washington, DC, USA, 221–231.

APEL, S., KÄSTNER, C., AND LENGAUER, C. 2013b. Language-Independent and Automated Software Composition: The FeatureHouse Experience. *IEEE Trans. Software Engineering (TSE) 39*, 1, 63–79.

APEL, S., KOLESNIKOV, S., LIEBIG, J., KÄSTNER, C., KUHLEMANN, M., AND LEICH, T. 2012. Access Control in Feature-Oriented Programming. *Science of Computer Programming (SCP) 77*, 3, 174–187.

APEL, S., LEICH, T., ROSENMÜLLER, M., AND SAAKE, G. 2005. Feature C++: On the Symbiosis of Feature-Oriented and Aspect-Oriented Programming. In *Proc. Int'l Conf. Generative Programming and Component Engineering (GPCE)*. Springer, Berlin, Heidelberg, 125–140.

APEL, S., VON RHEIN, A., THÜM, T., AND KÄSTNER, C. 2013c. Feature-Interaction Detection Based on Feature-Based Specifications. *Computer Networks 57*, 12, 2399–2409.

APEL, S., VON RHEIN, A., WENDLER, P., GRÖSSLINGER, A., AND BEYER, D. 2013d. Strategies for Product-Line Verification: Case Studies and Experiments. In *Proc. Int'l Conf. Software Engineering (ICSE)*. IEEE, Piscataway, NJ, USA, 482–491.

BATORY, D. 2003. A Tutorial on Feature-Oriented Programming and Product Lines. In *Proc. Int'l Conf. Software Engineering (ICSE)*. IEEE, Washington, DC, USA, 753–754.

BATORY, D. 2005. Feature Models, Grammars, and Propositional Formulas. In *Proc. Int'l Software Product Line Conf. (SPLC)*. Springer, Berlin, Heidelberg, 7–20.

BATORY, D. 2006. A Tutorial on Feature Oriented Programming and the AHEAD Tool Suite. In *Proc. Generative and Transformational Techniques in Software Engineering*. Springer, Berlin, Heidelberg, 3–35.

BECKERT, B., HÄHNLE, R., AND SCHMITT, P. 2007. *Verification of Object-Oriented Software: The KeY Approach*. Springer, Berlin, Heidelberg.

BENAVIDES, D., SEGURA, S., AND RUIZ-CORTÉS, A. 2010. Automated Analysis of Feature Models 20 Years Later: A Literature Review. *Information Systems 35*, 6, 615–708.

BENDUHN, F., SCHRÖTER, R., KENNER, A., KRUCZEK, C., , LEICH, T., AND SAAKE, G. 2016. Migration from Annotation-Based to Composition-Based Product Lines: Towards a Tool-Driven Process. In *Proc. Conf. Advances and Trends in Software Engineering (SOFTENG)*. IARIA, 102–109.

BERGER, T., RUBLACK, R., NAIR, D., ATLEE, J. M., BECKER, M., CZARNECKI, K., AND WĄSOWSKI, A. 2013. A Survey of Variability Modeling in Industrial Practice. In *Proc. Int'l Workshop Variability Modelling of Software-Intensive Systems (VaMoS)*. ACM, New York, NY, USA, 7:1–7:8.

CHVATAL, V. 1979. A Greedy Heuristic for the Set-Covering Problem. *Mathematics of operations research 4*, 3, 233–235.

CZARNECKI, K. AND EISENECKER, U. 2000. *Generative Programming: Methods, Tools, and Applications*. ACM/Addison-Wesley, New York, NY, USA.

CZARNECKI, K., HELSEN, S., AND EISENECKER, U. 2005. Staged Configuration through Specialization and Multi-Level Configuration of Feature Models. *Software Process: Improvement and Practice 10*, 2, 143–169.

DUBINSKY, Y., RUBIN, J., BERGER, T., DUSZYNSKI, S., BECKER, M., AND CZARNECKI, K. 2013. An Exploratory Study of Cloning in Industrial Software Product Lines. In *Proc. Europ. Conf. Software Maintenance and Reengineering (CSMR)*. IEEE, Washington, DC, USA, 25–34.

FEIGENSPAN, J., KÄSTNER, C., APEL, S., LIEBIG, J., SCHULZE, M., DACHSELT, R., PAPENDIECK, M., LEICH, T., AND SAAKE, G. 2013. Do Background Colors Improve Program Comprehension in the #Ifdef Hell? *Empirical Software Engineering (EMSE) 18*, 4, 699–745.

FEIGENSPAN, J., SCHULZE, M., PAPENDIECK, M., KÄSTNER, C., DACHSELT, R., KÖPPEN, V., AND FRISCH, M. 2011. Using Background Colors to Support Program Comprehension in Software Product Lines. In *Proc. Int'l Conf. Evaluation Assessment in Software Engineering (EASE)*. 66–75.

FENSKE, W., MEINICKE, J., SCHULZE, S., SCHULZE, S., AND SAAKE, G. 2017. Variant-Preserving Refactorings for Migrating Cloned Products to a Product Line. In *Proc. Int'l Conf. Software Analysis, Evolution and Reengineering (SANER)*. IEEE, Piscataway, NJ, USA, 316–326.

FENSKE, W., THÜM, T., AND SAAKE, G. 2014. A Taxonomy of Software Product Line Reengineering. In *Proc. Int'l Workshop Variability Modelling of Software-Intensive Systems (VaMoS)*. ACM, New York, NY, USA, 4:1–4:8.

FOWLER, M. 2000. *Refactoring: Improving the Design of Existing Code*. Addison-Wesley.

GARVIN, B. J., COHEN, M. B., AND DWYER, M. B. 2011. Evaluating Improvements to a Meta-Heuristic Search for Constrained Interaction Testing. *Empirical Software Engineering (EMSE) 16*, 1, 61–102.

GRUBER, O., HARGRAVE, B. J., MCAFFER, J., RAPICAULT, P., AND WATSON, T. 2005. The Eclipse 3.0 Platform: Adopting OSGi Technology. *IBM Syst. J. 44*, 2, 289–299.

HALLSTEINSEN, S., HINCHEY, M., PARK, S., AND SCHMID, K. 2008. Dynamic Software Product Lines. *IEEE Computer 41*, 4, 93–95.

HATCLIFF, J., LEAVENS, G. T., LEINO, K. R. M., MÜLLER, P., AND PARKINSON, M. 2012. Behavioral Interface Specification Languages. *ACM Computing Surveys 44,* 3, 16:1–16:58.

JOHANSEN, M. F., HAUGEN, Ø., AND FLEUREY, F. 2011. Properties of Realistic Feature Models Make Combinatorial Testing of Product Lines Feasible. In *Proc. Int'l Conf. Model Driven Engineering Languages and Systems (MODELS)*. Springer, Berlin, Heidelberg, 638–652.

KANG, K. C., COHEN, S. G., HESS, J. A., NOVAK, W. E., AND PETERSON, A. S. 1990. Feature-Oriented Domain Analysis (FODA) Feasibility Study. Tech. Rep. CMU/SEI-90-TR-21, Software Engineering Institute.

KÄSTNER, C. AND APEL, S. 2009. Virtual Separation of Concerns – A Second Chance for Preprocessors. *J. Object Technology (JOT) 8,* 6, 59–78.

KÄSTNER, C., APEL, S., AND KUHLEMANN, M. 2008. Granularity in Software Product Lines. In *Proc. Int'l Conf. Software Engineering (ICSE)*. ACM, New York, NY, USA, 311–320.

KÄSTNER, C., GIARRUSSO, P. G., RENDEL, T., ERDWEG, S., OSTERMANN, K., AND BERGER, T. 2011. Variability-Aware Parsing in the Presence of Lexical Macros and Conditional Compilation. In *Proc. Conf. Object-Oriented Programming, Systems, Languages and Applications (OOPSLA)*. ACM, New York, NY, USA, 805–824.

KÄSTNER, C., THÜM, T., SAAKE, G., FEIGENSPAN, J., LEICH, T., WIELGORZ, F., AND APEL, S. 2009. FeatureIDE: A Tool Framework for Feature-Oriented Software Development. In *Proc. Int'l Conf. Software Engineering (ICSE)*. IEEE, Washington, DC, USA, 611–614. Formal demonstration paper.

KICZALES, G., HILSDALE, E., HUGUNIN, J., KERSTEN, M., PALM, J., AND GRISWOLD, W. G. 2001. An Overview of AspectJ. In *Proc. Europ. Conf. Object-Oriented Programming (ECOOP)*. Springer, London, UK, 327–354.

KICZALES, G., LAMPING, J., MENDHEKAR, A., MAEDA, C., LOPES, C., LOINGTIER, J.-M., AND IRWIN, J. 1997. Aspect-Oriented Programming. In *Proc. Europ. Conf. Object-Oriented Programming (ECOOP)*. Springer, Berlin, Heidelberg, 220–242.

KOLESNIKOV, S., VON RHEIN, A., HUNSEN, C., AND APEL, S. 2013. A Comparison of Product-Based, Feature-Based, and Family-Based Type Checking. In *Proc. Int'l Conf. Generative Programming: Concepts & Experiences (GPCE)*. ACM, New York, NY, USA, 115–124.

KOSCIELNY, J., HOLTHUSEN, S., SCHAEFER, I., SCHULZE, S., BETTINI, L., AND DAMIANI, F. 2014. DeltaJ 1.5: Delta-Oriented Programming for Java 1.5. In *Proc. Int'l Conf. Principles and Practices of Programming on the Java Platform: Virtual Machines, Languages, and Tools (PPPJ)*. ACM, New York, NY, USA, 63–74.

KOWAL, M., ANANIEVA, S., AND THÜM, T. 2016. Explaining Anomalies in Feature Models. In *Proc. Int'l Conf. Generative Programming: Concepts & Experiences (GPCE)*. ACM, New York, NY, USA, 132–143.

KRIETER, S., SCHRÖTER, R., FENSKE, W., AND SAAKE, G. 2015. Use-Case-Specific Source-Code Documentation for Feature-Oriented Programming. In *Proc. Int'l Workshop Variability Modelling of Software-Intensive Systems (VaMoS)*. ACM, New York, NY, USA, 27:27–27:34.

KRUEGER, C. W. 2002. Variation Management for Software Production Lines. In *Proc. Int'l Software Product Line Conf. (SPLC)*. Springer, Berlin, Heidelberg, 37–48.

LAGUNA, M. A. AND CRESPO, Y. 2013. A Systematic Mapping Study on Software Product Line Evolution: From Legacy System Reengineering to Product Line Refactoring. *Science of Computer Programming (SCP) 78,* 8, 1010–1034.

LE, D., WALKINGSHAW, E., AND ERWIG, M. 2011. #ifdef Confirmed Harmful: Promoting Understandable Software Variation. In *Proc. Int'l Symposium Visual Languages and Human-Centric Computing (VL/HCC)*. IEEE, Washington, DC, USA, 143–150.

LEICH, T., APEL, S., MARNITZ, L., AND SAAKE, G. 2005. Tool Support for Feature-Oriented Software Development - FeatureIDE: An Eclipse-Based Approach. In *Proc. Workshop Eclipse Technology eXchange (ETX)*. ACM, New York, NY, USA, 55–59.

LIEBIG, J., APEL, S., LENGAUER, C., KÄSTNER, C., AND SCHULZE, M. 2010. An Analysis of the Variability in Forty Preprocessor-Based Software Product Lines. In *Proc. Int'l Conf. Software Engineering (ICSE)*. IEEE, Washington, DC, USA, 105–114.

LOHMANN, D., SCHELER, F., TARTLER, R., SPINCZYK, O., AND SCHRÖDER-PREIKSCHAT, W. 2006. A Quantitative Analysis of Aspects in the eCos Kernel. *40*, 4, 191–204.

MCILROY, M. D. 1968. Mass Produced Software Components. In *Proc. NATO Conf. Software Engineering*. Springer, 138–155.

MEDEIROS, F., LIMA, T., DALTON, F., RIBEIRO, M., GHEYI, R., AND FONSECA, B. 2013. Colligens: A Tool to Support the Development of Preprocessor-Based Software Product Lines in C. In *Proc. Brazilian Conf. Software: Theory and Practice (CBSoft)*. CBSOFT.

MEINICKE, J., THÜM, T., SCHRÖTER, R., KRIETER, S., BENDUHN, F., SAAKE, G., AND LEICH, T. 2016a. FeatureIDE: Taming the Preprocessor Wilderness. In *Proc. Int'l Conf. Software Engineering (ICSE)*. ACM, New York, NY, USA, 629–632.

MEINICKE, J., WONG, C.-P., KÄSTNER, C., THÜM, T., AND SAAKE, G. 2016b. On Essential Configuration Complexity: Measuring Interactions In Highly-Configurable Systems. In *Proc. Int'l Conf. Automated Software Engineering (ASE)*. ACM, New York, NY, USA, 483–494.

MELO, J., BRABRAND, C., AND WĄSOWSKI, A. 2016. How Does the Degree of Variability Affect Bug Finding? In *Proc. Int'l Conf. Software Engineering (ICSE)*. ACM, New York, NY, USA, 679–690.

MENDONCA, M. AND COWAN, D. 2010. Decision-Making Coordination and Efficient Reasoning Techniques for Feature-Based Configuration. *Science of Computer Programming (SCP) 75*, 5, 311–332.

MEYER, B. 1988. *Object-Oriented Software Construction* 1st Ed. Prentice-Hall, Inc., Upper Saddle River, NJ, USA.

MISRA, J. 2004. Private correspondence.

MURPHY-HILL, E., PARNIN, C., AND BLACK, A. P. 2012. How we refactor, and how we know it. *IEEE Trans. Software Engineering (TSE) 38*, 1, 5–18.

PARNAS, D. L. 1972. On the Criteria to be used in Decomposing Systems into Modules. *Comm. ACM 15*, 12, 1053–1058.

PARNAS, D. L. 1976. On the Design and Development of Program Families. *IEEE Trans. Software Engineering (TSE) SE-2*, 1, 1–9.

PEREIRA, J. A., KRIETER, S., MEINICKE, J., SCHRÖTER, R., SAAKE, G., AND LEICH, T. 2016. FeatureIDE: Scalable Product Configuration of Variable Systems. In *Proc. Int'l Conf. Software Reuse (ICSR)*. Springer, Berlin, Heidelberg, 397–401.

PREHOFER, C. 1997. Feature-Oriented Programming: A Fresh Look at Objects. In *Proc. Europ. Conf. Object-Oriented Programming (ECOOP)*. Springer, Berlin, Heidelberg, 419–443.

QUEIROZ, R., PASSOS, L., VALENTE, M. T., HUNSEN, C., APEL, S., AND CZARNECKI, K. 2017. The Shape of Feature Code: An Analysis of Twenty C-Preprocessor-Based Systems. *Software and System Modeling (SoSym)*.

RODRIGUES, I., RIBEIRO, M., MEDEIROS, F., BORBA, P., FONSECA, B., AND GHEYI, R. 2016. Assessing Fine-Grained Feature Dependencies. *J. Information and Software Technology (IST) 78*, C, 27–52.

RUBIN, J. AND CHECHIK, M. 2013. A Framework for Managing Cloned Product Variants. In *Proc. Int'l Conf. Software Engineering (ICSE)*. IEEE, Piscataway, NJ, USA, 1233–1236.

RUBIN, J., CZARNECKI, K., AND CHECHIK, M. 2013. Managing Cloned Variants: A Framework and Experience. In *Proc. Int'l Software Product Line Conf. (SPLC)*. ACM, New York, NY, USA, 101–110.

SCHAEFER, I., BETTINI, L., BONO, V., DAMIANI, F., AND TANZARELLA, N. 2010. Delta-Oriented Programming of Software Product Lines. In *Proc. Int'l Software Product Line Conf. (SPLC)*. Springer, Berlin, Heidelberg, 77–91.

SCHOBBENS, P.-Y., HEYMANS, P., TRIGAUX, J.-C., AND BONTEMPS, Y. 2007. Generic Semantics of Feature Diagrams. *Computer Networks 51*, 2, 456–479.

SCHRÖTER, R., KRIETER, S., THÜM, T., BENDUHN, F., AND SAAKE, G. 2016. Feature-Model Interfaces: The Highway to Compositional Analyses of Highly-Configurable Systems. In *Proc. Int'l Conf. Software Engineering (ICSE)*. ACM, New York, NY, USA, 667–678.

SCHRÖTER, R., SIEGMUND, N., THÜM, T., AND SAAKE, G. 2014. Feature-Context Interfaces: Tailored Programming Interfaces for Software Product Lines. In *Proc. Int'l Software Product Line Conf. (SPLC)*. ACM, New York, NY, USA, 102–111.

SCHULZE, S., THÜM, T., KUHLEMANN, M., AND SAAKE, G. 2012. Variant-Preserving Refactoring in Feature-Oriented Software Product Lines. In *Proc. Int'l Workshop Variability Modelling of Software-Intensive Systems (VaMoS)*. ACM, New York, NY, USA, 73–81.

SEIDL, C., SCHAEFER, I., AND ASSMANN, U. 2014. DeltaEcore - A Model-Based Delta Language Generation Framework. In *Proc. Modellierung*. Gesellschaft für Informatik, Bonn, Germany, 81–96.

SMARAGDAKIS, Y. AND BATORY, D. 1998. Implementing Layered Designs with Mixin Layers. In *Proc. Europ. Conf. Object-Oriented Programming (ECOOP)*. Springer, 550–570.

SMARAGDAKIS, Y. AND BATORY, D. 2002. Mixin Layers: An Object-Oriented Implementation Technique for Refinements and Collaboration-Based Designs. *Trans. Software Engineering and Methodology (TOSEM) 11*, 2, 215–255.

SPENCER, H. AND COLLYER, G. 1992. #ifdef Considered Harmful, or Portability Experience With C News. In *USENIX*. USENIX Association, 185–197.

TARR, P., OSSHER, H., HARRISON, W., AND SUTTON, JR., S. M. 1999. N Degrees of Separation: Multi-Dimensional Separation of Concerns. In *Proc. Int'l Conf. Software Engineering (ICSE)*. ACM, New York, NY, USA, 107–119.

THÜM, T. 2015. Product-Line Specification and Verification with Feature-Oriented Contracts. Ph.D. thesis, University of Magdeburg, Germany.

THÜM, T., BATORY, D., AND KÄSTNER, C. 2009. Reasoning about Edits to Feature Models. In *Proc. Int'l Conf. Software Engineering (ICSE)*. IEEE, Washington, DC, USA, 254–264.

THÜM, T., KÄSTNER, C., BENDUHN, F., MEINICKE, J., SAAKE, G., AND LEICH, T. 2014. FeatureIDE: An Extensible Framework for Feature-Oriented Software Development. *Science of Computer Programming (SCP) 79*, 0, 70–85.

THÜM, T., KÄSTNER, C., ERDWEG, S., AND SIEGMUND, N. 2011. Abstract Features in Feature Modeling. In *Proc. Int'l Software Product Line Conf. (SPLC)*. IEEE, Washington, DC, USA, 191–200.

THÜM, T., LEICH, T., AND KRIETER, S. 2016. Clean Your Variable Code with FeatureIDE. In *Proc. Int'l Software Product Line Conf. (SPLC)*. ACM, New York, NY, USA, 308–308.

THÜM, T., MEINICKE, J., BENDUHN, F., HENTSCHEL, M., VON RHEIN, A., AND SAAKE, G. 2014. Potential Synergies of Theorem Proving and Model Checking for Software Product Lines. In *Proc. Int'l Software Product Line Conf. (SPLC)*. ACM, New York, NY, USA, 177–186.

THÜM, T., RIBEIRO, M., SCHRÖTER, R., SIEGMUND, J., AND DALTON, F. 2016. Product-Line Maintenance with Emergent Contract Interfaces. In *Proc. Int'l Software Product Line Conf. (SPLC)*. ACM, New York, NY, USA, 134–143.

TRINIDAD, P. AND RUIZ-CORTÉS, A. 2009. Abductive Reasoning and Automated Analysis of Feature Models: How are They Connected? In *Proc. Int'l Workshop Variability Modelling of Software-Intensive Systems (VaMoS)*. Universität Duisburg-Essen, Essen, Germany, 145–153.

WHITE, J., SCHMIDT, D. C., BENAVIDES, D., TRINIDAD, P., AND RUIZ-CORTÉS, A. 2008. Automated Diagnosis of Product-Line Configuration Errors in Feature Models. In *Proc. Int'l Software Product Line Conf. (SPLC)*. IEEE, Washington, DC, USA, 225–234.

WIKIPEDIA. 2017. System generation (os).

ZHANG, W., ZHAO, H., AND MEI, H. 2004. A Propositional Logic-Based Method for Verification of Feature Models. *Formal Methods and Software Engineering*, 115–130.

Index

© Springer International Publishing AG 2017
J. Meinicke et al., *Mastering Software Variability with FeatureIDE*,
DOI 10.1007/978-3-319-61443-4

Printed in the United States
By Bookmasters